Morphological Theory and the Morphology of English

Edinburgh Textbooks on the English Language – Advanced

General Editor
Heinz Giegerich, Professor of English Linguistics, University of Edinburgh

Editorial Board
Laurie Bauer (University of Wellington)
Olga Fischer (University of Amsterdam)
Rochelle Lieber (University of New Hampshire)
Norman Macleod (University of Edinburgh)
Donka Minkova (UCLA)
Edgar W. Schneider (University of Regensburg)
Katie Wales (University of Leeds)
Anthony Warner (University of York)

TITLES IN THE SERIES INCLUDE:

Corpus Linguistics and the Description of English
Hans Lindquist

A Historical Phonology of English
Donka Minkova

A Historical Morphology of English
Dieter Kastovsky

Grammaticalization and the History of English
Manfred Krug and Hubert Cuyckens

A Historical Syntax of English
Bettelou Los

English Historical Sociolinguistics
Robert McColl Millar

A Historical Semantics of English
Christian Kay and Kathryn Allan

Construction Grammar and its Application to English
Martin Hilpert

Morphological Theory and the Morphology of English
Jan Don

Visit the Edinburgh Textbooks in the English Language website at www.
euppublishing.com/series/ETOTELAdvanced

Morphological Theory and the Morphology of English

Jan Don

EDINBURGH
University Press

Edinburgh University Press Ltd
The Tun, Holyrood Road,
12 (2f) Jackson's Entry,
Edinburgh EH8 8PJ
www.euppublishing.com

Typeset in 10.5/12 Janson by
Servis Filmsetting Ltd, Stockport, Cheshire,
and printed and bound in Great Britain by
CPI Group (UK) Ltd, Croydon CR0 4YY

A CIP record for this book is available from the British Library

ISBN 978 0 7486 4513 8 (hardback)
ISBN 978 0 7486 4512 1 (paperback)
ISBN 978 0 7486 4514 5 (webready PDF)
ISBN 978 0 7486 7838 9 (epub)

Contents

List of figures

Preface

The main goal of this book is to bring advanced students in linguistics with a basic knowledge of morphology to such a level that they can fruitfully read the current morphological literature on English. The focus of the book is on understanding theories and theoretical discussions within generative approaches to the morphology of English that have been important in shaping this field of linguistics since the late 1970s; a field that, judging from a growing number of publications and specialized journals, is becoming a more and more central topic of linguistic theorizing.

Every chapter has a particular morphological approach or theory as its main focus, and in explaining this approach or theory the empirical material that forms its basis is introduced at the same time. In choosing this way of introducing morphological theories I hope to have achieved in each chapter a certain level of theoretical depth that the student will need in order to be able to read new theoretical contributions on his or her own. This theoretical depth comes at the cost of breadth in coverage of the field. The field, because of its growing importance, has attracted more and more linguists, and as a consequence, there is a growing number of theories and theoretical approaches. This book only contains some of – what I see as – the more central approaches to the study of morphology of English.

At the end of each chapter some suggestions are made as to the further study of the topic and issues being introduced. These should be taken for what they are, i.e. *suggestions*, rather than my choice of a core or "must-read" list. Other criteria have played a role in their selection, such as their accessibility and the extent to which this literature is related to the issues being discussed in the main text. It may contain a further exploration along the same lines as those explored in the main text, or it may propose a different or even opposite view on the topical issues.

I would like to thank Heinz Giegerich for asking me to write this book. I do hope the result is not too far from what he expected it to be. I would also like to thank Paula Fenger and an anonymous reviewer for valuable comments and suggestions on an earlier version. Silke Hamann is gratefully acknowledged for advice on the proper phonetic transcription of some of the examples. Finally, I would like to thank Fiona Sewell for her meticulous reading of the manuscript and the many improvements she has made.

1 Knowledge of words

1.1 Introduction: Simplex words

What do we know if we say that we know a word? Probably, the first answer that comes to mind is that one knows what the word means. If one knows the word *equal* one knows it means something like 'same in size, amount, number, degree, value'. Of course, apart from the meaning, one also knows how to pronounce the word; for example, that *equal* starts with a vowel and that this vowel receives main stress. It may very well be that not everyone is able to describe this knowledge in these terms, but since native speakers of English pronounce the word *equal* as they do, they must know these things. Maybe the word reminds people of the famous Orwell quotation 'All animals are equal, but some animals are more equal than others.' So that can also be assigned to their knowledge of this word. Furthermore, one knows that the word is an adjective. This latter statement may come as a surprise and you may respond by saying 'that's just because I'm a linguist'. That may be true to the extent that as a linguist you consciously know that *equal* is an adjective, but again all native speakers of English (and quite a few are not linguists) somehow 'know' this, since they know that one can use the word in the syntactic context shown in (1).

(1)   All candidates had an equal opportunity.

So, while native speakers may not be able to classify *equal* as an adjective consciously, at the same time they won't make any mistakes in its syntactic usage. This shows that they somehow unconsciously 'know' the word-class to which *equal* belongs.

To make matters a bit more complicated, it turns out that native speakers may also use *equal* as a noun as in (2), or as a verb as in (3).

(2)   Finally, he met his equal.

(3)   The boy equalled his father both in strength and in ability.

1

Note that this nominal and verbal use of *equal* comes with a somewhat different meaning from that of the adjective, although both meanings of the noun and the verb have a clear relation to the meaning of the adjective. On top of this, native speakers know (in the same sense that they know that *equal* is an adjective) that *equality* is related to *equal*, as are *equalise* and *equally*. They also know that the stress in *equal* is on the first vowel (as noted above) but that it is on the second syllable in *equality*, and so on.

This brief inquiry into the knowledge native speakers have of the word *equal* is far from complete. However, it goes to show that *knowing a word* involves different types of knowledge. First, we should make a distinction between grammatical knowledge of words and what has been called encyclopedic knowledge of words. **Grammatical knowledge** of words, to which we will turn in more detail in a moment, is shared by the speakers of the same speech community and is invariable over the population. It is also rigid and formal in nature. In contrast, **encyclopedic knowledge** of a word may differ from person to person; it depends on someone's knowledge of the world. For example, if you are an ornithologist the word *robin* may be associated with a wealth of information involving the song, the type of nests these birds build, the difference between the mainland European bird and the British variant, the size of the eggs, etc., whereas a layperson may only have a vague image of a small bird with a red chest.

However, whether one is an ornithologist or not, the grammatical knowledge of the word will be shared by speakers of the same speech community. Above we mentioned that the word *equal* will remind at least some speakers of English of Orwell's quotation; this is a typical example of encyclopedic knowledge. Another example is that we know *equal* often occurs in combination with the noun *rights*, forming a more or less fixed expression. In many cases such combinations of words form idiomatic expressions, such as *full moon, blue film* or *dark horse*. The meaning of the combined words cannot be straightforwardly derived from the semantics of the parts, i.e. the semantics is partly or fully non-compositional. A *blue film* is of course not literally blue but at least it still refers to a special type of film. The phrase *dark horse* does not even need to refer to a horse.

On the basis of the little inquiry above, we can distinguish between at least four types of grammatical knowledge that speakers have of the words of their language. First, it includes phonological knowledge; knowledge that concerns the sound-form of the word, such as the number of syllables, the order of phonemes in these syllables, the location of stress, etc. The phonology of the word *equal* is normally represented in IPA symbols between square brackets, as in (4):

(4)   ['iːkwəl]

Second, language users know the meaning of words, normally referred to as their semantics. It can be extremely difficult to describe the subtleties of word meaning. Moreover, it is not immediately clear in what terms this description should be given. It would not do to use words, since it would be circular to represent the meaning of words in words. We cannot use the same language as our metalanguage. Some linguists have developed a theory of the type of representation that we use to encode meaning (e.g. Jackendoff 1990). We will get to this in somewhat more detail in Chapter 4. Until then I will simply circumvent this problem by writing down the words in capitals, or we will use paraphrases (using English words) between quotation marks. So, EQUAL represents the meaning of *equal*.

Third, speakers have syntactic knowledge of words. In the example above this takes the form of the word-class to which the word belongs. The main word-classes, often called lexical classes, are adjective, noun and verb, which will be indicated by a capital letter A, N or V respectively in subscript: [equal]$_A$. So a full representation of the word *equal* might then look as follows:

(5)   Phonology: ['iːkwəl]
      Semantics: EQUAL
      Syntax: [equal]$_A$

We assume that representations as in (5) are stored in the mental **lexicon** of speakers. The mental lexicon can be seen as the storehouse of the words of the language. There is an obvious need for such a storehouse since the form of words, their existence and meaning are not at all predictable. To illustrate, compare for a moment the word *equal* to the phrase *kiss a girl*. Once you know that the words *kiss* and *girl* exist, and you know the rules for building English phrases, i.e. you have some syntactic knowledge of English, you will be able to construct the phrase *kiss a girl* and derive its meaning. Form and meaning are fully predictable. Not so for words: it is not true that once we know that *e* and *qual* are viable syllables of English, the word *equal* could be derived with the meaning it has. *Equal* is an unanalysable whole with respect to its form and semantics, even though its sound-form can be analysed in smaller units (such as syllables and phonemes). Put differently, there is nothing banana-like in the word *banana*. The same fruit could just as well have been named *apple*. There are some notable exceptions to this broad generalisation concerning the form of words. Many languages including English have what is called onomatopoeia. This consists of words like *cuckoo* and *curlew* that do have an intrinsic relation between form and meaning. Both the cuckoo and the curlew are birds that have a 'song' or 'call' which is reflected in the pronunciation of their name. Despite these and several other exceptions,[1] as a rule there is no intrinsic relation in natural language between the form and meaning of words.

Furthermore, apart from this arbitrary relation between form and meaning, the mere existence of the word *equal* also needs to be listed somehow since it cannot be derived from anything else. The fact that the word *equal* exists but the word *elik* does not cannot be derived from more general properties of the grammar of English. The non-existence of *elik* is called an **accidental gap**; it could have been a word of English, it just happens that this is not the case. The fact that *equal* is a word of English is just as accidental.[2]

These properties of words, i.e. their existence and the arbitrary relation between form and meaning, necessitate a lexicon in which words and their meaning are stored. The representations in (5) are an approximation, or a hypothesis if you like, of the way this knowledge might be represented in the lexicon.

Fourth, knowing a word also involves morphological knowledge. Take again, for example, the word *equal*. As we have seen, this is a simplex word: it is an unanalysable whole. This is part of the morphological information speakers have about this word. Furthermore, speakers of English know that by adding the suffix *-ity* it can be turned into a noun. They also know that the word can be turned into a verb by adding the affix *-ise* and that it can be turned into a different verb, *to equal*, without making any changes to its phonology. Speakers know that there is no comparative form *#equaller*, but that in order to express this meaning, one needs to revert to the phrasal expression *more equal*. Generally, morphological knowledge encompasses information about the structure of words.

So the study of morphology is the study of word-structure. It asks questions such as 'How are complex words constructed? What types of complex words are there? What is the relation between these complex words? What is the meaning of these complex words in relation to their bases? What is the relation between the phonology of these complex words and their bases?'

Summarising so far, if we know a word, we know its (sound-)form, its meaning and the way it can function in syntax (coded as its word-class), and we may know several fixed combinations in which the word may occur. Let us now turn to what may be considered the heart of morphology, i.e. complex words.

1.2 Complex words

Not all words are as simple as the word *equal*. Some words are more complex than others in the sense that they consist of different parts that somehow contribute to the meaning of the whole. For example, the word *equality* can be analysed as in (6).

(6)   equal   +   ity

Knowing a word also involves knowledge of its relation to other words. Speakers have intuitions about the relation between *equal* and *equality*, i.e. they have knowledge of word-structure, in the sense that they know that *equality* is related to, or more specifically 'based on', *equal*. Since it is our goal to account for the knowledge that speakers have of words, we also need to make explicit this relation between *equal* and *equality*. Before we go into the details of how we may represent this, it is important to compare the analysis in (6) of the word *equality* and a different analysis of the same word in (7):

(7)   i.'kwɒ.lɪ.ti

In (7) an analysis is given in terms of the syllables that make up the word *equality*, where dots represent syllable boundaries. The difference between the units in (6), called morphemes, is that each of them somehow contributes to the meaning of the word as a whole, while there is no sense in assigning meaning to the syllables in (7). Every syllable in (7) may be part of another English word with a completely unrelated meaning (e.g. *e-mail*, *quality*, *literal*, *tiara*) whereas the morpheme *equal* is associated with a constant meaning that shows up in every word that has this same morpheme as part of its building blocks (e.g. *equalise*, *equality*, *equals*, *unequal*). The study of morphology is not concerned with the analysis of words in terms of syllables and sounds; that is part of phonology. The study of morphology concerns itself with the make-up of words in terms of morphemes, the building blocks from which we may derive the semantics, syntactic and phonological properties of complex words.

The pair *equal–equality* is a part of a pattern that also includes the examples in (8):

(8)   equal   equality
      agile   agility
      criminal   criminality
      fatal   fatality
      fragile   fragility
      personal   personality

public	publicity
readable	readability

A first quick look at this list will tell you that the words in the right-hand column are formed from those in the left-hand column by adding the morpheme *-ity* to their right. However, on closer inspection it turns out that the relation between the words in the right-hand column and those in the left-hand column is quite complex. For example, the phonology of the words in the left-hand column sometimes differs from the phonology of the corresponding part in the complex words in the right-hand column. Compare, for instance, the [aɪ]- sound in *agile* with the [ɪ]-sound in *agility*. In spelling they are the same, but the pronunciation clearly differs. Furthermore, there does not seem to be a transparent semantic relationship between the pairs of words. We will return to the complexities of this morphological pattern below, but in order to get an idea of the basic elements of a morphological pattern, we will first have a look at a somewhat simpler (i.e. more regular) one. Consider the related word-pairs in (9).

(9) | bitter | bitterness |
|--------|-----------|
| otiose | otioseness |
| oviparous | oviparousness |
| red | redness |
| selfish | selfishness |

Note that the words in the left-hand column are all adjectives, whereas the words in the right-hand column are all nouns. The words in the right-hand column share the ending *-ness* [nəs], while their related adjectives all lack this ending. Moreover, there are no other differences between the phonology of the words in the left-hand column and their corresponding parts in the right-hand column. That is, the pronunciation of the words in the right-hand column is fully predictable once we know how to pronounce the base-word and the affix. Also, the nouns in the right-hand column have a semantics that is more or less a constant function of the semantics of the adjective in the left-hand column. Very roughly, *redness* means 'the property of being red'; other *-ness* nouns may receive a similar description. So the pattern we observe can be informally described as follows: a noun ending in *-ness* has a related adjective with an identical phonology without *-ness*; the meaning of the noun in *-ness* can be described as 'the property of being A', where A stands for the meaning of the adjective. A slightly more formal notation of this pattern would be a rule such as the one in (10). Note that this rule applies in the opposite direction to the way we formulated the pattern. The rule produces the larger, complex words from smaller elements, whereas the informal formulation above of the pattern is analytic, breaking down the complex word into its constituting elements.

(10) $[X]_A \rightarrow [[X]ness]_N$

'PROPERTY OF BEING X'

Such rules, originally proposed by Aronoff (1976), not only account for the knowledge that speakers have of the relation between a complex word and its simpler base; they also account for the fact that speakers of a language have the ability to build new words from existing ones. This productive capacity follows certain rules, of which (10) is just an example.

Let us now introduce some basic terminology, some of which we have already used to describe the morphological patterns above. The rule in (10) is often referred to as a **word-formation rule** (hereafter: WFR). The element -*ness* is called an **affix**, more specifically a **suffix**. Suffixes occur at the right-hand of the base (in the case at hand: the adjective). Elements such as *un-* or *re-* that occur to the left of their base are called **prefixes**. Prefixes and suffixes are both different types of affixes. The adjective on the left-hand side of the arrow in (10) is called the **base**. It functions as the input of the rule. Because affixes cannot occur independently from their base, they are called bound affixes. So affixes are **bound morphemes**. **Free morphemes** do not need a base, but may occur on their own.

The WFR describes the phonological, syntactic and semantic characteristics of the complex word in relation to its base. The particular way this is done by the WFR will be further discussed in Section 1.4; there have been different theories about what would be the proper characterisation of the knowledge that speakers have of these relations between words, and the WFR will be a good starting point for this discussion. Before we go into this, we will first have a more detailed look into the morphological pattern exemplified by the data in (8). This will help us realise that not all word-formation is as transparent and straightforward as the rule in (10) suggests.

1.3 Phonological and semantic idiosyncrasies in word-formation

Consider again the examples in (8), here repeated for convenience as (11).

(11) equal   equality
     agile   agility

criminal	criminality
fatal	fatality
fragile	fragility
personal	personality
public	publicity
readable	readability

Just as in the pattern with the affix *-ness*, the words in the left-hand column are all adjectives, and the complex words in the right-hand column are all nouns. Judging from the semantics and phonology of the pair *agile–agility* the relation between base and complex form is exactly parallel to the morphological pattern with *-ness*. Therefore, it might seem that we could write a similar WFR to the one in (10):

(12) $[X]_A$ → $[[X] \text{ ity}]_N$

'PROPERTY OF BEING X'

However, if we check this rule against the pairs in (11) (and many other such pairs), it turns out that the rule faces some serious problems. First, the rule states that the noun can be derived from the adjective by simply adding the phonological string [ɪti] (spelled *-ity*). But in several examples other phonological changes occur in addition. The [aɪ] in *fragile* becomes [ɪ] in *fragility*. The [ə] in *personal* becomes [æ] in *personality*. This vowel-change goes hand in hand with a change in the location of main stress. In *'personal* main stress is on the first syllable, but it shifts to the syllable just before the suffix in *perso'nality*. Furthermore, the final [k] in *public* changes to [s] in *publicity*. Apparently, the phonology of the base may undergo some changes once the affix attaches. This points to a particular interaction between phonology and morphology to which we return in Chapter 2.

Second, focusing on the semantics of the derived words in (11) some unexpected differences may be observed. It would be quite odd to describe the semantics of *publicity* as 'the property of being public'. Similarly, the semantics of *personality* is not properly covered by the phrase 'the property of being personal'. The same remarks can be made for *criminality*, *fatality* and many more examples of this pattern. These words all have idiosyncratic meanings that cannot be (fully) predicted on the basis of the meaning of the base and a rule such as (12). These observations may cast doubt on the notion of such a rule. These doubts are further enhanced by the following observation:

(13) Adjective   *-ity*   *-ness*
      broad   -   broadness

human	humanity	humanness
open	-	openness
original	originality	originalness
thoughtful	-	thoughtfulness
polite	-	politeness
respectable	respectability	respectableness

We could have added many more forms to (13), but the essential pattern will not change: there are more words with *-ness* than there are with *-ity*. There are a lot of bases that cannot be suffixed with *-ity*, whereas basically all adjectives can be suffixed with *-ness*. We say that word-formation with *-ness* is **productive**. Word-formation with *-ity* is less so. The productivity of a morphological rule or pattern is then the extent to which we can make new forms with such a pattern or rule. The rule that derives forms in *-ity* is not unproductive, however. For example, it is productive after bases on *-able*. So it would be too simple to say that some rules of morphology are productive while others are unproductive. In some cases the morphological pattern is limited to only a handful of examples. In such cases, one may wonder whether we should speak of a rule at all.

Considering the fact that one cannot predict whether a particular form in *-ity* exists, given the limited productivity of the rule in (12), and also taking into account the irregularity of the resulting forms, it is clear that we need a storage device in our grammar to keep track of the irregularities and the existence of complex forms. The results of the application of rule (12) somehow need to be memorised. This property of (some) WFRs is highlighted by the term 'once-only rules', which is often used in connection with WFRs of this type. The idea expressed by this term is that these rules are used only once, after which the result, i.e. the complex word, is stored as a whole.

Although the rule in (12) clearly fails to predict correctly all properties of the complex words, or even their existence, at the same time it is undeniable that there is a pattern in the data with the suffix *-ity*. The data in (11) are far from random, and simply storing all the complex forms would deny this pattern and would unnecessarily complicate the grammar as a whole. For example, there are no exceptions to the observation that the complex words formed with *-ity* are nouns. Moreover, concerning the bases of these complex words, we also observe rule-like behaviour: all words in *-ity* have an adjective at their base. So, if we were to conclude on the basis of the observed irregularities that there could not be a rule such as (12), we would run the risk of throwing out the baby with the bathwater.

The following perspective may be helpful here. There is no need to consider (12) as a productive rule, in the sense that it builds new forms, but it can be considered an analytic rule that is used to analyse stored forms. The complex forms are stored in the lexicon with their irregularities and idiosyncrasies; the rule fills in those properties that are fully regular (such as their word-class, and many details of the phonology such as the stress-pattern). Rules of this type are called **lexical redundancy rules**: they generalise over stored forms and tease out those properties of complex forms that can be predicted.

In Jackendoff (1975), one of the earliest publications on the morphology of English in a generative framework, the idea of lexical redundancy rules is proposed. This idea is further developed in a dissertation by Bochner (1993). Bochner shows that redundancy rules may still have a function in a grammar that stores whole forms. In terms of the informational load that each word contributes to the lexicon, the amount added by a form that is fully in accordance with the rule is next to zero. Put differently, the information content of the lexicon hardly grows once we add a form that is in full conformity with a lexical redundancy rule. Viewed in this way the rule still has a clear function, since it will help us keep the lexicon manageable.

Another view, put forth by Halle (1973), is to think of the WFRs as fully productive; the fact that certain words do not exist or that certain phonological or semantic idiosyncrasies show up is then due to a special filter that filters out the non-existing forms and takes care of all idiosyncrasies. We will come back these views in Chapter 2.

Summarising so far, we note that there is a distinction between patterns of the *-ness* type that we could call productive, and patterns of the *-ity* type that are less productive, or maybe even unproductive. The fact that such patterns exist necessitates a storage device to keep track of irregularities and 'gaps'. WFRs, especially those that relate to unproductive patterns, may be viewed as lexical redundancy rules.

1.4 The building blocks of words

The notion of a WFR is a way of describing the capacity that speakers have to produce and analyse complex words in their language. As such it is a specific hypothesis about this capacity. We will now discuss several aspects of this hypothesis and point out some properties that have been at the centre of many morphological investigations of the past decades.

To facilitate the discussion, it is helpful to work from a concrete example, so we repeat WFR (10) here as (14), which will function as our prototypical WFR.

(14) $[X]_A \rightarrow [[X]ness]_N$

'PROPERTY OF BEING X'

The first property of this rule that we focus on is the status of the string -*ness*. The important thing to note is that -*ness* does not have morphemic status, since it is not assigned a meaning. The rule simply says that by adding this particular phonological string to the right of the base, a new word is formed. Part of the word-formation process is the instruction to add the string -*ness* to the right-hand side of the phonology of the base, but the string -*ness* is not a separate building block. It is not an object with a particular semantics or category, but just a part of a phonological operation that is part of the WFR. Therefore, -*ness* is not a morpheme in this theory. Since in this view of word-formation the WFR as a whole determines the properties of the complex word, it makes more sense to consider this WFR as a 'morpheme', rather than the affix.

This view of morphological rules crucially differs from a view that sees complex words as built up from smaller elements, objects if you like, with individual properties that together make a new whole. Recall our example of the phrase *kiss a girl* from above. The elements *a* and *girl* are viewed as different elements that taken together form a new structure, called a determiner phrase, or DP [*a girl*]. This crucially differs from the idea that there is a phrase-constructing operation that turns a noun into a DP through a rule that, apart from performing the relevant semantic operation, also adds a phonological string *a*. Rather, the phonology results from the concatenation of the phonological specifications (in the correct linear order) of the constructing elements. Similarly, the semantics results from the unification of the semantics of the affix and the semantics of the base. In this way, we compositionally derive the semantics of [*a girl*] from the semantics of the constituting elements.

Some morphologists (e.g. Lieber 1980, Selkirk 1982) have proposed that morphology essentially works the same way as the syntactic example. That is, complex words are built from smaller building blocks, i.e. morphemes that are taken from the lexicon. In this view, morphemes have properties such as a word-class, a phonological representation and a semantic specification. The structure of the word *politeness* can then be represented as in (15).

(15) $[[polite]_A [ness]_{N-1}]_N$

In this structure, -*ness* is not just a phonological string that happens to come with the WFR, but a constructing element in its own right, with a word-class and a semantic specification next to its phonology. In this view, morphology is piece-based: the hypothesis is that all word-formation comes about by bringing smaller elements together in a larger structure.

One of the reasons for the particular view that Aronoff (1976) put forward comes from the observation that word-formation may also happen without any phonological change. In (16) some examples of such an English word-formation process are given.

(16) bridge   to bridge
     hammer   to hammer
     nail   to nail
     plant   to plant
     tape   to tape

Clearly, there is a relation between these noun–verb pairs, and there is little or nothing that would make it different in principle from that between the pairs in (9). That is, apparently, these cases are instances of word-formation just as the affixation with -*ness* is. This type of word-formation is often referred to as **conversion**. Apparently, there are word-formation processes that have no concomitant phonological operation. How would we go about this in a 'syntactic' view of word-formation that sees it as resulting from building larger units from smaller elements? Put differently, how would we analyse the verbs in the right-hand column in (16) if we were to claim that all complex words can be analysed into smaller constituting elements? The answer that has been given in the literature (see e.g. Kiparsky 1982) is that there are what are called zero-affixes. These are elements on a par with any other affix, the only difference being that their phonology would be empty. The structure of the verb *to bridge* is then represented as in (17):

(17) $[[\text{bridge}]_N\ [\text{ø}]_{v-1}]_v$

We now understand why conversion is also often named **zero-derivation**. Aronoff (1976: 71) rejects this idea of zero-affixes, since there are several different word-formation processes in English that have no phonological correlate and we would thus need several zero-affixes to describe the morphology of English properly.

In a theory with WFRs, the phonological operation is merely one of the effects that the rule may (or, in the case of conversion, may not) have. So, in a theory that endorses WFRs, data such as (16) do not come as a surprise. Leaving out any particular semantic characterisation of the operation, WFR (18) accounts for the process.

(18) $[X]_N\ \rightarrow\ [[X]]_v$

Generalising, we could say that the hypothesis that word-formation is the result of WFRs claims that basically any phonological change to the base could be part of a WFR, including none. If, contrary to this, morphology is piece-based, in the sense that complex forms may only result from the composition of two or more elements, i.e. if morphology is only 'additive', then we would not expect any other phonological changes than the addition of phonological material. It will be clear that one of the issues at stake here is the proper analysis of conversion as exemplified by the data in (16).

We now turn to a second aspect of WFRs that has become an important topic of discussion in the theory of morphology. As is clear from the way WFRs are structured, a particular phonological operation always works in tandem with a semantic operation to form the WFR together. The one does not exist without the other. However, at least some morphologists (most forcefully Beard 1995) have claimed that this view is incorrect. They argue that the morphological operation (change in word-class, plus any semantic changes) should be separated from the phonological operation, which is seen as a mere 'realisation' of the morphological operation. This hypothesis is often referred to as the 'Separation Hypothesis'. An argument for this position is formed by data such as in (19):

(19) broad broaden cool to cool-ø electric electrify fertile fertilise
     deep deepen calm to calm-ø intense intensify general generalise
     wide widen warm to warm-ø solid solidify tranquil tranquillise

The verbs in (19) are all morphologically related to an adjectival base. However, there is no uniform phonological operation; in fact, there are four different ways in which the morphological operation is flagged. Some adjectives take the suffix *-en* (*broad*, etc.); others take *-ify* (*electric*, etc.); there is a third group taking *-ise* (*fertile*, etc.); and there is a group of adjectives that can be converted to verbs without any phonological realisation.

In a theory of morphology in which word-formation is accounted for by WFRs, the data in (19) would necessarily require four different WFRs. The concept of a WFR does not allow for the possibility of squeezing the different affixes in (19) into one and the same rule. However, four different rules would mean a loss of generalisation if no obvious differences exist between the verbs in (19) correlating with the different suffixes (or absence of marking). So, if there is no conspicuous way to assign different meanings to the different affixes involved, the conclusion seems to be that all the examples in (19) are the result of one and the same word-formation process. Consequently, for the theory of morphology this would mean that a single word-formation process could have more than one realisation. Plag (1999), however, argues that there is a semantic difference between the verbs in (19) exactly correlating with the different affixes.

'Separationist' theories of morphology analyse the data in (19) as resulting from one and the same morphological operation, having different 'spell-outs' depending on the base. The strict separation between affixes and morphological derivation also predicts that the same affix may be used to spell out different morphological derivations. Moreover, as Beard makes clear, 'separation' may also provide a natural explanation for the lack of phonological expression in the case of conversion (*to warm*, etc.). For if the process of the morphological derivation, i.e. the actual word-formation process, is strictly separated from the phonological 'realisation' of the process, we may expect word-formation processes without phonological realisation to occur.

A third aspect of the WFR in (14) that needs some discussion is the base. Aronoff (1976) claims that word-formation is word-based. That is, the input for WFRs is always an existing word. An alternative to this view would be to say that word-formation is morpheme-based. The reason that Aronoff takes the position that word-formation is word-based lies in the problems that Aronoff notes with respect to the notion of morpheme. Above we have discussed morphemes as the minimal units of meaning. If such a notion were valid, it would make sense to have a theory of word-formation that sees morphemes as the fundamental building blocks. However, Aronoff argues that such a notion is not valid. The arguments are presented below.

First, consider the word *cranberry*. We can easily identify the morpheme *berry*, which occurs with the same meaning in other words and also in isolation. However, there is no sense in which we can identify *cran* as a meaningful element that also occurs elsewhere in the language. It simply doesn't. The only environment in which we ever encounter this element is in the word *cranberry* (Aronoff 1976: 10). Therefore, it makes no sense to say that *cranberry* is built from *cran+berry*. We don't have independent evidence for the meaning or the existence of a morpheme *cran*. Similar problems of assigning a meaning to morphemes exist in cases such as *blueberry* or *blackberry*. Here, the elements *blue* and *black* do occur elsewhere but not with the same meaning. For example, not every black berry is a blackberry. So the meaning of the word *blackberry* cannot be compositionally derived from the meaning of the elements *black* and *berry*; it only makes sense to see the word as a whole as the location of the meaning, and there is no sensible way in which this meaning can be decomposed in smaller constituting elements.

However, one may argue that the criterion of compositionality is not the right criterion to decide the issue of whether morphemes can be assigned meaning. Consider a phrase such as *red wine.* Just as in the case of *blackberry*, not all red wine is actually red. Should we therefore conclude that *red* cannot be assigned a meaning? That seems at least a very counterintuitive conclusion. A more natural conclusion would be that different linguistic constructions, whether morphological or syntactic, may have idiosyncratic meanings.

A second argument comes from the data in (20) (from Aronoff 1976: 12):

(20)	X=*fer*	X=*mit*	X=*sume*	X=*ceive*	X=*duce*
	refer	remit	resume	receive	reduce
	defer	demit		deceive	deduce
	prefer		presume		
	infer				induce
	confer	commit	consume	conceive	conduce
	transfer	transmit			transduce
		submit	subsume		
		admit	assume		adduce
		permit		perceive	

The pattern in (20) consists of recurring stems in the columns combined with different prefixes in the different rows. Aronoff, seeking a constant meaning of the stems, observes (p. 12): 'There is no meaning which can be assigned to any of these stems and combined with the presumably constant meanings of the prefixes in a consistent way to produce meanings of all verbs in that stem.' For these reasons, Aronoff concludes that it does not make sense to define the notion of morpheme as the smallest meaningful element. Meaning only arises at the level of words. Therefore, Aronoff proposes a theory of word-formation in which words are derived from words. Note, however, this does not imply that Aronoff discards the notion of morpheme altogether. We will come back to this issue in the following section.

Summarising thus far, we have seen that there are at least three aspects of the theory of WFRs that have been challenged by different morphologists. First, some theories of morphology claim that morphology is piece-based, i.e. words can be analysed, just like sentences, into different building blocks. An extreme version of such a view would be that there is no separate morphological component of the grammar; word-formation is just a part of syntax. The theory of WFRs on the other hand claims that part of word-formation is a phonological operation

that may change the phonology of the base. This change is not necessarily 'additive', in the sense that an affix is attached; basically, any phonological change could be part of a WFR. Second, the theory of WFRs
claims that the phonological operation and the concomitant change in
word-formation necessarily operate in tandem. It predicts a one-to-one
correspondence between affixation and morphological derivation. This
claim is challenged by the Separation Hypothesis, which disconnects
affixation and derivation. The same derivation may be 'spelled out' by
different affixes, and the same affix may spell out different derivations.
Finally, we have seen that a definition of morpheme as the smallest
meaningful element runs into trouble. Therefore, some morphologists
have claimed that morphology should be word-based. However, as we
will see later in this book, this claim has also been disputed.

1.5 Allomorphy

Consider the following data, taken from Aronoff (1976: 100):

(21) Verb   *-ation*   *-(t)ion*   *-ition*

realise   realis*ation*   *realizion   *realition
educate   *educatation   educat*ion*   *educition
repeat   *repetation   *repetion   repetition
commune   *communation   commun*ion*   *communition
resume   *resumation   resump*tion*   *resumition
resolve   *resolvation   *resolv(t)ion   *resolvition

The verbs in the left-hand column all take different forms once they
are nominalised (turned into a noun). For all verbs only one form is the
correct one; that is, there is no verb having two different nominalisations. In a way this pattern is similar to the pattern formed by the data
in (19),where different word-formation operations can be applied to
form a verb from an adjective, but no adjective allows two different
ways to derive a verb. The situation is indeed similar: there seems to be
one and the same word-formation process (making nouns from verbs)
that is 'realised' by different affixes (or the lack thereof) depending on
the base. Semantically the different forms are identical, i.e. the different affixes are synonymous. Furthermore, the different realisations are
in complementary distribution. In such cases we speak of **allomorphy**.
Each morphological variant of the series *-ation*, *-(t)ion*, *-ition* is called an
allomorph.

For any linguist the synonymy and the complementary distribution
are strong indications that what superficially appear to be different

forms are somehow resulting from one and the same 'underlying' form. In a theory that adheres to WFRs this would mean that all the nouns in (21) result from the same WFR, which we could formulate as follows:

(22) $[X]_V$ → $[[X] \text{ ation}]_N$

After the WFR has applied, a set of allomorphy rules steps in that changes the form of the suffix -*ation*, according to the demands of the base. These allomorphy rules are idiosyncratic in the sense that they only apply in a particular morphological environment. Note that a case such as (19) cannot be treated in this particular way since the claim would be that the different allomorphs somehow could be phonologically related to one another, which would clearly be a bit of a stretch in that case.

However, in a theory of morphology that entertains the Separation Hypothesis, the analysis of (22) would not necessarily require a single underlying phonological form to express the same concept, namely that there is a single word-formation operation which is realised by the different allomorphs. In such a theory the WFR is separated from the phonological spell-out, and consequently, very different affixes that do not share the same underlying phonological form could spell out the same derivational rule.

The distribution of the different allomorphs in (21) is rather complex and we will not go into too much detail (see Aronoff 1976 for a detailed discussion). However, it will be useful to point out some crucial properties of the pattern. Very generally, the distribution of the allomorphs can be described as follows. The allomorph -*ation* is the 'general case'; if the conditions for the attachment of the other allomorphs are not applicable, then -*ation* will step in as a 'default'. The rules that account for the insertion of the other allomorphs are more specific and list specific contexts in which the allomorph in question should be inserted. The rules for the attachment of the different allomorphs are **ordered disjunctively**. This rule-ordering implies the following: we first try the most specific rule, and if it can be applied, the other rules will simply not apply. If the first, most specific rule is not applicable, the second rule of the set will be checked, and if it applies the remainder of the set of rules will be skipped. If that rule is also not applicable, the third rule comes into play, etc., until finally if all rules fail, the 'default' rule (the attachment of -*ation*) will step in, and mark only those forms that haven't received an affix by one of the earlier rules.

The case of allomorphy discussed above pertains to affixes: it is the affix that changes form according to the base to which it attaches.

Another type of allomorphy concerns the base itself, often referred to as **stem-allomorphy**. In such cases it is the base that takes a different shape in different morphological contexts. In (23) we have given some examples:

(23) resume   resump-tion   receive   recep-tion
      consume   consump-tion   conceive   concep-tion

      commit   comiss-ion   solve   solu-tion
      admit   admiss-ion   resolve   resolu-tion

In *resume* a [p] is inserted between the base and the affix. The same happens in *consume*, and in fact, it also happens in all verbs that share the part -*sume* (*presumption, assumption*). In the case of *receive* we see a different allomorphic change. The vowel changes, the [v] is deleted and a [p] is inserted. Exactly the same happens in *conceive*, and also in all other verbs sharing the element *ceive*. Similarly, in the forms with -*mit* and -*solve* specific changes occur. Again, we stress that these changes are idiosyncratic. They do not result from general phonological rules but are specific to the bases in question and result from their Romance origin. Now recall from Section 1.4 that we do not have a semantic reason to consider elements such as -*sume*, -*ceive*, -*mit*, etc. as separate morphemes. Here we see that despite the lack of semantic motivation, there is a formal reason to consider these elements as recognisable units within words. Since the phonological changes we witness are specific to the bases in question and do not follow from general rules, it must be the case that these units are separately stored together with their phonological particularities. So we can decide to see these elements as morphemes as soon as we acknowledge the fact that the notion of morpheme does not have a semantic definition, but only refers to recognisable units of word-formation that may have idiosyncratic properties (such as stem-allomorphy, explained above).

Morphologists often also encounter the mirror-image of allomorphy. Whereas in cases of allomorphy a set of different affixes share the same meaning, the mirror-image is a situation in which one and the same affix has different meanings. A famous, and much-discussed, example is the affix -*er*. In (24) we have given several morphologically complex words all involving this affix.

(24) a.   run   runn-er
           work   work-er

      b.   open   open-er
           zip   zipp-er

c. loan   loaner   (the car you get when yours is under repair)

d. screamer scream-er (as in: 'the comedian's act is a real screamer')

e. London   London-er
   Dublin   Dublin-er

f. foreign   foreign-er
   strange strang-er

g. happy   happi-er
   green   green-er

We observe that in the examples in (24) -*er* has very different functions, or very different meanings if you like. In (24a) it marks the Agent of the event expressed by the verb; in (24b) it marks an instrument; in (24c) it is the object- rather than the subject-role of the verb that is expressed by the -*er* noun; and in (24d) it is the causer being expressed by the -*er* derived noun. But still other meanings are possible: in (24e) it is an inhabitant, and the forms in (24f) are different again, since here the -*er* nouns are formed on the basis of adjectives rather than on verbs, as in (24a–d), or nouns, as in (24e). Finally, in (24g) we see that adjectives can also be derived with the same affix, -*er*.

How should we treat these different occurrences of the affix -*er*? Is it really the same affix that we see here in all these cases, or are some derived by another affix that just happens to have the same form? In principle, two analyses are possible. In one analysis one would say that the affix is **polyfunctional** or polysemous. This term is used in morphology to describe a situation in which a single affix expresses a range of meanings that all share some core element or part. In such an analysis it is the same affix that occurs in the forms that share this core meaning. Another possible analysis is to say that the affix is **homonymous**. Under such an analysis, it is claimed that there are two (or more) different affixes (e.g. -*er*$_1$ and -*er*$_2$) that are accidentally phonologically identical.

How can one decide whether we are dealing with an instance of poly-functionality, or whether an affix is simply homonymous with another affix? An obvious solution would be to look for differences in the morphological processes in which the affix occurs. For example, the fact that the categories of the bases in (24a–d) differ from those in (24e–g) might be taken as an indication that we are dealing with different morphological processes, and consequently, with different affixes. However, note that this is not a necessary consequence for all theories of morphology. For those theories that embrace the Separation Hypothesis, there is no reason to expect that an affix is different once it marks different morphological processes. Since in those theories morphological derivation is separated from the phonological realisation ('spell-out') of the derivation, one and the same affix may spell out completely different derivations. Therefore simply looking at the morphological processes which the affix may realise is not a helpful criterion.

A more promising possibility is to argue from allomorphic variation. The claim that affixes are homonymous implies that their phonological identity is a coincidence. How would such a coincidence come about? If two forms with different meanings end up having the same form, they have different historical origins. It is only in the course of history that their phonological forms have become identical. Consequently, homonymy implies historically different origins. If there are two historically different morphemes at the root of the homonymous form, then it should be expected that these different forms also have different allomorphs. It would be highly coincidental if not only did the two morphemes become phonologically identical during their historical development but also their allomorphs were identical.

From this it can be concluded that if two affixes have the same phonological form but have different allomorphs, we have a strong argument for their being homonymous rather than polyfunctional. So, for example, the fact that we have *in-lay* next to *il-legal* shows that we are dealing with two separate morphemes in this case. However, we cannot argue on the basis of the lack of allomorphic differences that two morphemes are in fact the same.

In other cases, different distributional properties of the phonologically identical affixes give away their homonymy. By looking at the distributional properties of *-er* we may separate the cases in (24g) from the others. The affix *-er* that we find in the comparative forms of English affixes is limited to stems that are essentially monosyllabic (in fact the restriction is a little more complicated, but that does not concern us here). As we can see from the other examples, (24a–f), we find that *-er* in those cases freely attaches to polyfunctional bases; therefore, we can safely conclude that we are dealing with a different affix, which happens to have the same phonological form.

A second criterion might be to look for synonyms. Affixes that share the same synonyms are synonymous themselves, whereas affixes having different synonyms cannot be synonymous themselves. So if *-er* can be replaced by the same synonym in some cases of (24) there is good reason to assume we are dealing with the same affix in these cases. Consider the affix *-ent/-ant* that we find in words such as *student, informant, president*, where the affix has the same function as *-er* has in words such as *runner* and *informer*. The same affix is also present in examples such as *agent*, *lubricant*, *coolant*, where it has the same function as *-er* in words such as *zipper* and *cooler*. On this basis we may conclude that at least in these functions *-er* and *-ent/-ant* are synonymous, and therefore that *-er* is the same affix in deriving subject nouns (such as *runner*) and instrument nouns (such as *zipper*) (see De Belder 2011).

1.6 Inflection

The examples of word-formation we have seen so far all build new words from other words. The newly derived word is semantically related to the word it is based on, but at the same time it is also clear that the new word has a different semantics. For example, *to hammer* refers to an action or motion, whereas the noun *hammer* refers to a particular object. Now consider the following examples:

(25) a.   I *walk* from Oban to Fort William.
      a'.   *I *walks* from Oban to Fort William.
      b.   He *walks* from Oban to Fort William.
      b'.   *He *walk* from Oban to Fort William.

In (25a) and (25b), we see two different words in italics. However, we may ask whether these are really different words. First of all, in the syntactic context of (25b), we wouldn't be allowed to insert the same word that we used in (25a), and vice versa (as can be seen from the ungrammaticality of the examples a' and b'). That is, the two forms are in complementary distribution. The syntactic context, the third person singular subject in this example, forces us to use the form *walks* in (25b), whereas the first person subject requires the form *walk* in (25a). For this reason it seems more appropriate to speak of two different word-forms: one used in the case of a third person singular subject, the other in all other subjects (considering the present tense forms only).

Second, there is no semantic difference between the forms in (25a) and (25b). The only difference lies in the different syntactic environments they require. For this reason, we often make a distinction between **word-formation** on the one hand, which refers to the formation of new words with a meaning different from their bases, and **inflection** on the other hand, which refers to the construction of different word-forms from a common base with the same semantics.

Again, we need a terminological aside to explain morphologists' usage of some notions. The notion **lexeme** is used to abstract away from the particular form (*walk*, *walks*, *walked*, *walking*) that it may take in a sentence. So, the lexeme WALK (we will use small capital letters to indicate lexemes) is realised as *walk* in (25a), and the same lexeme is realised as *walks* in (25b). We thus can say that word-formation builds new lexemes on the basis of already existing ones, whereas inflection is the realisation of a lexeme in a particular syntactic context.

Inflection in English is almost lacking as compared to many other languages. For example, English nouns have only a single form whereas in many languages nouns take different forms depending on the syntactic role they play in the sentence. So, for example, in Russian the noun *koška* 'cat' has five different forms, called cases, depending on the syntactic function it fulfils in the sentence.

(26) a. koška   (nominative; in subject position)
     b. koški   (genitive; 'of a cat')
     c. koške   (dative; 'to a cat', 'for a cat')
     d. košku   (accusative; in object position)
     e. koškoj   (agent of passive; 'by a cat')

Older stages of English did have different case-markings, but in the history of English they have been lost. A remnant of this former case system is the system of personal pronouns where we do find different forms, depending on the syntactic function of the pronoun. In the first and third persons of the English pronominal system we find two different forms. The 'nominative' form is only used when the pronoun is in subject position; the 'object' form is used in non-subject cases. Consider the schema in (27):

(27) Sing.   Nominative (subject)   Object
     1st person   I   me
     3rd person   he, she, it   him, her, it

     Plural
     1st person   we   us
     3rd person   they   them

We may now say that pairs such as *I* and *me*, *he* and *him*, etc. are different forms of the same lexeme. All word-forms together that a particular lexeme may take are called the **paradigm** of that lexeme. The paradigm of the 1st person pronoun in English is thus the set {I, me}.

In many languages not only nouns but also adjectives are inflected dependent upon certain properties of the nominal head (or of the subject in the case of a predicative use of the adjective) that it modifies, although in English there is only a single form of the adjective. For example, in French and other Romance languages, the adjective is inflected for gender and number. So the adjective will take a different form depending on the gender and number of the noun it modifies. In (28) we have given some examples from French:

(28) a. le   beau   garçon
          the.*masc.*   beautiful.*masc.*   boy

      b. la   belle   fille
          the.*fem.*   beautiful.*fem.*   girl

So, in French, the lexeme BEAU has at least two different word-forms *belle* [bɛl] and *beau* [bo], whose distribution is completely determined by the syntactic environment, i.e. by the noun that the adjective modifies.

The English verbal paradigm has at least five different slots. In (29) we have listed the paradigm for the lexeme HIDE.

(29) hide, hides, hid, hidden, hiding

Not in all verbs are these different slots filled with different forms. For example, in the verb *put*, the first, third and fourth slot are all filled with the form *put*.

Only five slots is a rather bleak figure in comparison to a language such as Turkish or Finnish where a verb may have thousands of different forms. Somehow the different forms in (29) are formally related; that is, we can derive the different forms in the paradigm from a single underlying form through rules of affixation in tandem with some rules of allomorphy. So, for example, the form *hides* is derived from *hide* through a simple affixation rule adding the third person affix -*s* to the verbal stem. The past tense form *hid* is the result of an allomorphy rule that changes the stem vowel from [aɪ] to [ɪ], whereas the participle *hidden* is the combined result of the same allomorphy rule and affixation of an -*en* suffix.

Suppose now that we had to make a similar list for the lexeme BE. This would take the following form:

(30) be, am, are, is, was, were, been, being

As we can see, there are eight different forms for this verb, and, more importantly, not all forms can be formally related to one another. It is easy to relate the form *be* to the form *been*, probably the same affix -*en* that is part of the participle *hidden* is attached to the stem *be*, but there is no way in which we could relate *be* to *am, are, is, was* or *were*. This is an example of **suppletion**. It refers to the situation in which one or more forms are part of a paradigm while they cannot be formally related to any of the other forms in the paradigm. Historically, these paradigms are the result of a merger of the paradigms of different lexemes. In the case of English lexeme BE, the paradigm is a merger of three historically different verbs. Old English *beon* had no past tense forms; they were provided by the verb *wesan*. But *beon* itself had two different sets of forms in the present: one made up from Germanic **es-/*s-* and **ar-* and the other from Germanic **beo-* (Hogg 1992). Since there is no formal relation in the case of suppletion, there is no other way than to assume that these forms are stored somehow with their inflectional properties (we will come back to a discussion of the proper treatment of inflection in Chapter 3).

Morphology is often seen as the study of word-formation and inflection. Word-formation involves the construction of new lexemes: the lexicon is extended as a consequence of word-formation. Contrary to this, inflection is the formation of new word-forms of the same lexeme. The choice of a particular word-form is determined by the syntax.

1.7 Compounds

Above, we have seen several examples of word-formation. So far all these cases are characterised by the fact that a bound morpheme (a prefix or a suffix) is attached to the base. Apart from affixation, there is another word-formation process that we encounter in English (as well as in many other languages). Let us first have a look at some examples:

(31)	black	board	blackboard
	chess	board	chessboard
	hover	craft	hovercraft
	landscape	architect	landscape-architect
	water	bottle	water-bottle
	water	mill	water-mill

In these examples, new lexemes are created by combining two free morphemes into what is called a compound word; this type of word-formation is known as **compounding**. The compounds in (31) are all nouns, but it is also possible to construct compound adjectives:

(32)	blue	green	blue-green
	sky	blue	sky-blue
	snow	white	snow-white

The constituting elements of these compounds do not contribute to the semantics of the compound as a whole in the same way. The right-hand element is the semantic head in the sense that a *coffee-machine* is a kind of machine, a *chessboard* is a kind of board, and *blue-green* is a particular type of *green*, etc. The semantic relation between the two elements of a compound can be manifold. In general, the non-head modifies the meaning of the head in some way. In *stone wall* the material is specified, in *water-bottle* it is a particular use ('a bottle for water'), in *water-mill* it is the source of energy, in *landscape-architect* it is the kind of objects that the architect designs, etc. Whatever the specific semantic relation between these elements, the head is modified in some way or another by the non-head.

It may be difficult to distinguish a compound, a word, from a phrase. If we compare the phrase *black bird* with the compound *blackbird*, a few criteria to separate the two may be discerned. First, the phonology of the phrase differs from the compound with respect to the location of main stress. The compound's stress is on the left-hand member (*bláck-bird*), the phrase has main stress on the right-hand member (*black bírd*). This criterion works quite well in nominal compounds. In adjectival compounds, however, stress may shift depending on the position of the compound adjective in the phrase. In a phrase such as a *sky-blue jacket* primary stress is on *sky*, whereas in *this jacket is sky-blue*, stress is on the right-hand element of the adjectival compound.

Second, since compounds are words, we expect them to be syntactic islands. That is, we do not expect that any part of the word can act as an antecedent for an anaphoric element in syntax. For example, a sentence such as (33) is odd (example from Bauer 2006: 721).

(33)   *I installed a combination$_i$ lock and now I can't remember it$_i$.

If *combination lock* were a phrase, the word *combination* should be a possible antecedent for *it* in (33). Apparently, *combination* is not a possible antecedent, which can be understood if we assume that *combination lock* is a compound. We will come back to the issue of words being syntactic islands in Chapter 2.

Third, from the examples above, one may conclude that the meaning of a compound is not fully transparent or at least has a certain specialisation. A *blackbird* is not simply any black bird, but a particular type of bird. However, that merely shows that the compound *blackbird* is **lexicalised**. That is, the compound as a whole has become a fixed entry in the English lexicon and as such has a special meaning. But being lexicalised is not the prerogative of compounds; phrases may also be lexicalised, as examples such as *red herring* and *dark horse* show. Therefore, the semantics will not be helpful in deciding whether a particular combination of words is a compound or a phrase.

In **endocentric compounds** there is always a single head. This head not only determines the meaning of the compound, as we have just seen, but also determines its word-class. So the compounds in (31) are all nominal compounds, since their head (the right-hand element) is a noun, whereas the compounds in (32) are adjectival, since they are headed by an adjective.

But endocentric compounds are not the only compounds around. In **exocentric compounds** there is no head. In (33) we have given some examples of exocentric compounds:

(34) loudmouth
      redhead
      paleface
      pickpocket

A *redhead* is not a particular type of head, but it is someone with a particular type of head (or better, hair). Exactly similar, a *loudmouth* is not a loud mouth but a person with a loud mouth. Exocentric compounds form a small class in comparison to endocentric compounds that can be productively formed in English.

Another type of compound that needs mentioning is that of verbal compounds or synthetic compounds. The property that separates these compounds from what are known as primary compounds (such as *blackbird*, *water-bottle* and *rainforest*) is that in synthetic compounds the right-hand element is always a deverbal noun or adjective, and the left-hand element is an argument of the verb from which the right-hand element is derived. A famous example of a synthetic compound is *truckdriver*, in which the noun *truck* is an argument (it is the object in a sentence *he drives a truck*) of the verb *drive*. We will discuss the proper analysis of such compounds in Chapter 4.

1.8 The limits of morphology

Not all new words result from WFRs. Consider, for example, the word *radar*. This is an acronym. Acronyms are formed on the basis of the initial letters of words that together form the name or description of the object or organisation that the word refers to. So the phrase **radio detection and ranging** is abbreviated to *radar*. Other examples include *NATO* (**North Atlantic Treaty Organization**), *CERN* and many more. Note that these acronyms are phonological words in the sense that they are not pronounced by spelling out the individual letters (as we would in *BMW*), but by making a single phonological word that has only one stressed syllable. In the case of *BMW*, we have in fact three phonological words, one for each individual letter, that together form a phrase.

In a sense, acronyms are a special case of a more general process known as clipping. Words such as *doc*(*tor*), *exam*(*ination*), *vet*(*erinarian*), *pub*(*lic house*), etc. are all examples of clipping in which the final part of the word is left out and the beginning is preserved; in others, such as (*para*)*chute* and (*tele*)*phone*, it is the first part that is deleted. Other variations do occur, such as *flu* (for *influenza*) and *pro-am* (*professional-amateur*). Apart from these clippings, there are other manipulations possible, such as blending. In the case of blending, two words are mixed into one by taking the first bit of one word and the second bit of the other. Examples include such words as *smog* (*smoke* + *fog*) and *brunch* (*breakfast* + *lunch*).

I do not consider these forms as instances of word-formation. This may strike you as rather odd, since there is no denying that the above-mentioned processes do form words. However, I think that there is a crucial difference between the processes discussed here, which are sometimes referred to as 'oddities' (cf. Aronoff 1976), and the regular processes of word-formation, such as affixation and compounding. The reason is that lexemes such as *radar*, *NATO* and *phone* result from a conscious and wilful act of creating a new word for a particular new concept. Word-formation as a linguistic process does not require special creative talents, nor does it come about as a result of a conscious process; rather, word-formation is an example of unconscious rule-following behaviour. We make new morphologically complex words on the fly, often even without realising that they are new. However, we cannot unconsciously form new words by clipping or blending. If somebody used *dent* for *dentist* or *surge* for *surgeon* they would not be understood, unless the context made any misunderstanding impossible. Then people's reactions would be a smile or a shrug, and if the form were particularly well chosen, people might start using it. But that would be an exception rather than a rule. On top of that, it is not so clear what the rules are in case of a clipping or blend. As we saw, clippings can result from deletion of just any part of the word, and there does not seem to be a clear pattern.

1.9 Preview

In this introduction, we have presented a few of the central ideas that have been put forward in the study of morphology over the last decades. These ideas will recur in the remainder of this book and will often shape the discussion of the empirical material. Briefly, some theories of morphology, called 'a-morphous', reject the idea that words are constructed from smaller pieces, i.e. from morphemes. These theories stress the fact that apart from adding a morpheme, other phonological changes may also be part of a word-formation operation. Other theories claim that morphology is, just like syntax, piece-based. On this view, words are constructed from smaller meaningful elements, called morphemes.

A second central dividing issue among theories of morphology is whether they view the phonological operation, or the attachment of an affix, as a crucial part of the word-formation operation, or whether word-formation and the phonological realisation are somehow separated.

In the second chapter of this book, we will go into lexical theories of word-formation. These theories basically claim that words are constructed in the lexicon before they are inserted in syntax. This implies that words are 'syntactic islands' in the sense that no syntactic rule can penetrate into the domain of a word. In a 'strong version' of the lexicalist hypothesis, inflection also originates in the lexicon. In this view, the different word-forms of a particular lexeme are all built 'before syntax'. However, as we have seen above, inflection is in large part determined by the syntactic environment. Consequently, given this lexicalist view of inflection, questions arise as to how syntax can determine what form should be produced in the lexicon. On the basis of such considerations, some researchers conclude that at least some of morphology (i.e. inflection) should be taken out of the lexicon and be part of syntax.

In the third chapter of this book, we will discuss inflection in more detail and see what type of arguments have been given for the lexicalist position and the position that inflection, and with it part of morphology, is post-syntactic. Here we will also discuss Anderson's 'a-morphous morphology', which analyses inflectional morphology as phonological operations that spell out certain features of constructs that have been built by syntax. Another version of this post-syntactic view of morphology is presented which entertains both a 'separationist' view on morphology and a piece-based view.

The idea that inflection is to a certain extent part of syntax may lead one to the view that all of morphology is partly (or even wholly) determined by syntax. In Chapter 4 we turn again to derivational morphology and see how nominalisations have played and still play an important role in theoretical morphology. We will distinguish between theories that consider morphology just a part of syntax and other theories that claim that morphology is a part of the grammar in its own right, with its own immanent principles. Here we will also go into the question of the extent to which morphology has a special relation with the lexicon. In this chapter we also introduce the notion of argument-structure and its related notions.

In Chapter 5 we look into verb-forming morphology. Here also the morphology-as-syntax perspective is present, as well as the view that morphology is a component on its own. The syntactic perspective analyses derived verbs in terms of underlying syntactic structures that encode the semantic relations between the base-noun or base-adjective and the derived verb. Any restrictions on the formation of derived verbs should follow from the syntactic theory. In the (lexical) morphological analyses, these relations are described by using what are called lexical conceptual structures. Restrictions on the formation of derived verbs follow from a theory on the composition of lexical conceptual structures.

Chapter 6 pays attention to a long and wide-ranging debate about the psychological reality of morphological rules. Interestingly, this debate centres on the rather narrow empirical domain of the English past tense formation. The central question in this debate is whether morphological rules (such as the rule that adds -*ed* to form the past tense) are just inventions of linguists to describe their data economically, or whether these rules correspond to a psychological reality.

Exercises

1. Give the lexical specification, just as in (5), of the words *ideal, work* and *remember.*

2. Analyse the following words in morphemes; determine the base, the affix, and the syntactic category of the base and the derivative. Use square brackets to present the result. For example, *agility* is represented as [[agile]$_A$ ity]$_N$. Make a note of any problems you encounter. *establishment, greenish, rain, undo, unrelated, illogicalness, industrialisation*

3. Consider the following complex words:

   (i)   undo   (ii) uncommon   (iii) unperson
         unfold   unimportant   unrest
         unlock   unnatural   untruth

   a) Formulate three different WFRs for the words in (i), (ii) and (iii).
   b) Can you make a single WFR for all three types of complex words? What problems do you encounter?
   c) Morphologists who endorse a 'separationist theory' of morphology would entertain a different analysis for the word-formations in (i), (ii) and (iii). How would they analyse the data in (i), (ii) and (iii), and how would that analysis constitute an argument for that position?

4. Consider again the data in (23). Try to come up with some more Latinate stems that show the same type of stem-allomorphy when affixed. (Tip: try your dictionary under *re-, con-,* etc.)

5. Given the list of verbs below (to which you can add as many as you like), would you consider the affix *-ise* homophonous (having two or even more different meanings), or would you call it polyfunctional? Give arguments that support your position.
   hospitalise, civilianise, jeopardise, localise, institutionalise, . . .

6. The form *walk* is used in many different cells of the English verbal paradigm (first, second and third person plural of the present indicative; first and second person of the singular present indicative; and as the infinitive form and the imperative form). The same holds for the form *walked*. List all the possibilities of this latter form.

Further reading

Bauer, Laurie (2001) *Morphological Productivity*, Cambridge: Cambridge University Press.

Beard, Robert (1990) 'The Nature and Origins of Derivational Polysemy', *Lingua* 81, pp. 101–40.

Lieber, Rochelle (2009) 'IE, Germanic: English', in Lieber, Rochelle and Pavol Štekauer (eds.), *The Oxford Handbook of Compounding*, Oxford: Oxford University Press.

Marchand, Hans (1969) *The Categories and Types of Present-Day English Word Formation: A Synchronic-Diachronic Approach*, 2nd edn, Munich: Beck.

Notes

1. Many exceptions are found in sign languages. Despite the abundance of iconic signs in these languages, this doesn't show that these languages differ fundamentally from spoken languages. It simply shows that the modality of gesturing lends itself better to iconicity than does speaking.

2. One may argue that there are good historical reasons for the existence of the word *equal* in the language, referring e.g. to the influence of French on English after 1066. However, such reasons are not (necessarily) part of the linguistic knowledge of the speaker/hearer. For the speaker/hearer it is an accidental fact that *equal* is a word of English and *mauvais* is not. Native speakers have to learn each and every simple word of the language and store it in their mental lexicons.

2 Word-formation in the lexicon

2.1 Introduction

Probably the most fundamental question concerning the study of morphology is the question of whether words exist. To the student beginning morphology, this may seem a rather odd question to ask, since words seem to be all around. Ask a layman what constitutes a language and the chances are good that he will reply in a way that makes crucial reference to words. So why would any linguist even begin to think of the possibility that words do not exist? Let us clarify the question first, sharpening our understanding of the notion 'word' at the same time.

A logical question to ask in the study of words is whether words consist of smaller elements that are somehow responsible for the properties of the words as a whole. In the preceding chapter, we have already seen that a phrase such as *kiss a girl* is built from a verb *kiss* and a smaller determiner phrase (or noun phrase) *a girl*. The meaning of the phrase as a whole as well as its phonology can be derived from these constituting elements. There is no need to claim that *kiss a girl* is represented somewhere in the grammar as such. It is just a phrase that can be built by applying particular rules for the construction of verb phrases from the elements available. In a similar vein, we may be inclined to split up a complex word such as *kissing* into two separate parts, *kiss* and -*ing*, and try to derive the meaning and the phonology from these smaller elements. Elements such as *kiss* cannot be further analysed and, therefore have to be listed with their meaning and phonology. There is simply no way in which we can derive their properties from any smaller elements. However, *kissing* is different in this respect; it might very well be possible to derive this word's properties from *kiss* and -*ing*. Just in the way that we derive the meaning of *kiss a girl* from the meaning of *kiss* and the meaning of *a girl*, we derive the meaning of *kissing* from the meaning of *kiss* and the meaning of -*ing*. Morphology conceived of in this way becomes a syntax of words. Taking this view to the extreme, we may say that words do not exist, in the same sense that phrases do not exist. Both phrases and words are just the result of a set of rules that build larger constructions from smaller elements. Since the early days of generative grammar, there have been linguists trying to show exactly this, that words are essentially the same as phrases.

The other view would be to say that words, unlike phrases, do have a special status in the grammar. That is, we need to recognise the existence of words, because they have properties that simply cannot be derived from their constituting elements. Of course, no one would deny the fact that it is useful to analyse *kissing* formally in two parts that both have properties that may help us understand the properties of the word *kissing*, but that does not necessarily imply that we do not also need to recognise the existence of the word *kissing*. Aronoff (2008) in this respect makes an insightful comparison between words and molecules. Molecules are built from atoms, but we cannot do chemistry without the acknowledgement of a molecular level at which properties arise that do not directly follow from the underlying atoms. Aronoff defends the view that words have 'molecular status'.

There are two further questions related to this issue. Once we acknowledge the existence of words in the above sense, that is as 'molecules', we need to answer the question where and how these words should be represented in the grammar. Many morphologists argue that words are stored in a lexicon, which also contains the building blocks such as *kiss* and -*ing*. This lexicon then is not only a mere warehouse of linguistic elements and their properties but also contains rules for the construction of complex words. Furthermore, as will become clear in the course of this chapter, people have argued that not only is morphology part of this lexicon, but the same lexicon also contains phonological rules. Others have claimed that there is no such lexicon and explicitly argue against lexical rules that build words. These morphologists argue that words result from the same machinery that is responsible for the construction of phrases. It will be clear that such a view also leads to a different position as to where and how words are stored.

The other related question is to what extent words are the only 'molecules'. Again, acknowledging the fact that words may have properties that do not arise from their constituting elements, it may in principle be possible that other constructions than words also have such idiosyncrasies, either phonologically, semantically or both. Take, for example, the idiom *kick the bucket*. A semanticist would have a hard time deriving the meaning DIE from the constituting elements in this case. On the other hand, it seems that by all (other) standards *kick the bucket* is a phrase. It conforms to exactly the same construction principles as *kiss the girl*. So, if non-compositionality arises not only in words but also in phrases, what do we conclude from that with respect to the status of words in the grammar?

These questions either explicitly or implicitly run through almost any contribution to the study of morphology. In this chapter we focus on lexicalist theories of morphology. They have been very influential and still determine for a large part our view of the study of word-formation. The basic assumption of these lexical models is that words are built and stored in the lexicon, which is considered a separate module of the grammar. We will come across detailed lexicalist proposals for English.

2.2 Pre-syntactic word-formation

Any student of word-formation will soon realise that complex words may have properties that cannot be predicted from their constituting elements. In the previous chapter we have already seen several examples of such idiosyncratic behaviour of complex words. To start with, many word-formation processes are not fully productive, which implies that we cannot predict whether a particular complex form exists. To give some oft-cited examples (from Halle 1973: 5): *derival, *confusal, *permittal are non-existing words, although the reason for their non-existence does not lie in the violation of a particular grammatical condition. Rather, these examples are accidental gaps; the relevant WFR is simply not (fully) productive. Some morphologists therefore make a distinction between **potential** (but non-existing) **words** and **existing words**. In order to make this distinction, the grammar needs a place where existing words can be listed, while the potential words have no permission to enter these premises.

Second, apart from accidental gaps, we also saw in the previous chapter that the semantics of complex words is not always predictable from the constituting elements. For example, words such as *personality, criminality* and *publicity* have idiosyncratic meanings. The word *recital* refers to a particular musical performance, which cannot be derived from the meaning of *recite* and the nominalisation process. Consequently, the idiosyncratic meanings somehow associated with these complex forms need to be listed or stored.

Third, complex words may also display idiosyncratic phonological behaviour. In words such as *sincerity, serenity* and *obscenity*, we see that the vowel in the third syllable from the right is shortened with respect to the stem vowel (*sincere, serene, obscene*). However, this does not happen in words such as *entirety, obesity,* and *nicety*. Why not? The answer may not be very satisfying since this seems to be just idiosyncratic behaviour that requires listing. Existence, idiosyncratic meaning and irregular phonology are all idiosyncratic properties of words that have led morphologists to the conclusion that words, even if they are complex, need to be listed in a lexicon.

It has been pointed out by morphologists and syntacticians alike that Chomsky's (1972) 'Remarks on Nominalization' is the starting point of the lexical view of morphology in generative grammar (e.g. Bauer 1983, Spencer 1991). In the syntactic theory proposed by Chomsky (1965) morphology was part of syntax. However, it soon became clear that this position was untenable. In 'Remarks on Nominalization' Chomsky tries to solve the following problem. The observation that we start from is that nouns and verbs have largely the same distribution. For example:

(1)   John refuses the offer

(2)   John's refusing the offer

(3)   John's refusal of the offer

In (1) the verb *refuse* comes with a subject and an object. Interestingly, and somewhat surprisingly, the nominalisations in (2) and (3) share this distribution with the verb: they may also take the same object, and what is called the prenominal possessive may be interpreted as a subject: in both (2) and (3) we may interpret *John* as the one who refuses. This distributional correlation may be taken as an indication that the nominalisations at some point in the derivation have really been verbs, or start out as verbs at some deeper level of representation. However, Chomsky argues against this transformational position for the nominalisation in (3), since the relation between the underlying verbal structure and the resulting nominalisation is to a large extent idiosyncratic. To illustrate, see the examples below (from Chomsky 1972: 15):

(4)   John's eagerness to please

(5)   John's refusal of the offer

(6)   John's criticism of the book

Chomsky notes with respect to the examples in (4)–(6) of what he calls 'derived nominals' in comparison to the 'gerunds' (such as (2)): 'Productivity is much more restricted, the semantic relations between the associated proposition and the derived nominal are quite varied and idiosyncratic, and the nominal has the internal structure of a noun phrase' (Chomsky 1972: 16). For these reasons Chomsky does not want to put the burden of explanation for these idiosyncrasies on the transformations, which would highly complicate this rule mechanism and the transformations would also have to be enriched in such a way that they could change the semantics. Instead, he takes a lexicalist position that is illustrated by the following citation: 'There are a few subregularities [in the relation between the derived nominal and the associated verb] that have frequently been noted but the range of variation and its rather accidental character are typical of lexical structure' (Chomsky 1972: 19).

Lexical structure can be idiosyncratic and not fully productive, in contrast to syntactic structure. Therefore, the derived nominals in (4), (5) and (6) do not result from an underlying verbal structure, but directly stem from the lexicon. Of course, that raises the question of how to explain the distributional correspondence observed in (1)–(2). If the verb and the 'derived nominal' have a different source, how is it that their distribution is so much alike? This is the central problem that Chomsky tries to solve in 'Remarks on Nominalization'. Chomsky proposes X-bar theory, assuming that the distribution of any major lexical category is always the same; any differences between nouns and verbs result from a difference in featural make-up: nouns share the features [+N, −V], whereas the features [−N, +V] characterise verbs. The idea is that an item such as *refuse* is part of the lexicon lacking any categorial features. This element has certain selectional restrictions (e.g. it takes animate subjects) and strict subcategorisation properties: it takes a noun phrase (NP) complement (*the offer, the bread*) or what is known as a reduced sentential complement (*to sleep, to go to bed*) which thus will appear whether the element shows up in nominal or verbal position. So *refusal* and *refuse* are the same lexical element; the only difference is that the first is the form that this element takes if it is inserted into a nominal head, whereas the second is the form the element takes when inserted into a verbal head. To cite Chomsky (1972: 21) again: 'Fairly idiosyncratic morphological rules will determine the phonological form of *refuse, destroy*, etc., when these items appear in the noun position.' Summing up, the transformational position is not the way to go since that would complicate the transformational component of the grammar too much. Alternatively, derived nominals are directly inserted from the lexicon into nominal syntactic position.

Halle (1973) is an early attempt to model the lexicon in such a way that it may account for these idiosyncratic properties of derived nominals and word-formation in general. In this paper, Halle proposes the model of the grammar in Figure 2.1.

In Halle's model the morphology consists in three separate components: the rules of word-formation, the filter and the dictionary. The rules of word-formation construct complex words on the basis of a list of morphemes. These words then go through the filter that is the

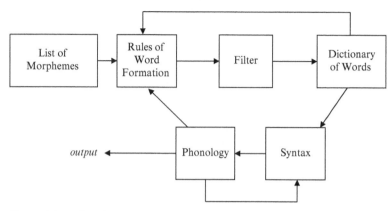

Figure 2.1 Halle's (1973) model of the lexicon, redrawn after Halle (1973: 8)

storehouse of all the idiosyncratic information pertaining to complex words. So, for example, the word *obesity* will be formed by a WFR that adds the morpheme *-ity* to the stem *obese*, both being in the list of morphemes. This form will go through the filter, where it will receive a feature [−Trisyllabic Shortening], which prevents the form from undergoing this particular phonological rule. The form *serenity* will be formed by the same WFR, but will not receive this particular feature. As a consequence, it will be subject to the rule of trisyllabic shortening in the phonological component, which shortens the vowel in the ante-penultimate syllable. In a similar fashion a non-compositional semantic interpretation can be associated with a particular complex form.

Halle further proposes that non-existent words produced by the WFRs, that is accidental gaps such as #*derival*, are given a feature [−Lexical Insertion], which prevents them from being inserted into the syntactic structure. This particular feature then makes the distinction between existing words (that do not have the feature) and the potential ones that get the feature in the filter. Note that for Halle's model to work properly, it is crucial that all of morphology is located before syntax. In order to prevent certain words getting inserted into the syntax, they first have to be filtered out.

In the remainder of this chapter, we will focus on theories of English morphology that locate word-formation pre-syntactically. Such theo-ries are often referred to as **lexical morphological theories**. Later in this book we will see that other theoretical positions are also possible, and indeed have been defended. In this chapter we go into the details of the lexical view on word-formation, seeing what arguments have been given for this position and what insights these theories have brought us.

The chapter is organised as follows. In Section 2.3 we will start by looking at a generalisation about the ordering of affixes that lies at the heart of many lexical theories of English morphology. A distinction is made between two types of affixes that behave differently with respect to a certain class of phonological rules and also seem to stand in a specific ordering relation. This distinction in classes only refers to affixation. In Section 2.4 we review several arguments that have been given for the inclusion of compounding in the lexicon. We are then in a position to present an influential and detailed lexical model of English morphology, dubbed level-ordered morphology, in Section 2.5. In Section 2.6 we focus our attention on the form of WFRs and the status of affixes. We then turn to some criticism of level-ordered morphology and alternatives that have been proposed in Section 2.7. Section 2.8 presents an alternative to the model discussed in Section 2.5, maintaining the lexicalist position and its explanatory goals.

2.3 Morphology and phonology

Compare the following complex forms:

(7) A   A-*ity*   A-*ness*

   ágile   agílity   ágileness
   fátal   fatálity   fátalness
   prodúctive   productívity   prodúctiveness

The adjectives in the left-hand column all have stress on the penultimate syllable. In the second column however, after attachment of -*ity*, stress shifts to a syllable to the right of this original position. However, this does not happen in the third column. Apparently, attachment of the affix -*ness* does not influence the position of word-stress in the way that attachment of -*ity* does. This difference in behaviour with respect to stress-rules and other phonological rules led Chomsky and Halle (1968) to suppose that affixes such as -*ity* are separated from their stems by a +-boundary; affixes such as -*ness* on the other hand are preceded by a #-boundary. In their cyclic theory of phonology this comes down to the following: the cyclic phonological rules view the whole word including the affix in the case of a +-boundary, whereas they will only see the domain of the stem in the case of a #-boundary. Siegel (1974) calls the affixes separated from their stem by a +-boundary Class I affixes, and the ones separated by a #-boundary affixes Class II affixes. Other examples of Class I affixes are -*ic*, -*al* and −*ian*, as is shown by the stress shift in (8a), whereas -*less*, -*ful* and -*ish* are apparently stress-neutral, i.e. Class II, as shown in (8b).

(8) a. átom–atómic   párent–paréntal   Méndel–Mendélian
         ártist–artístic   órigin–oríginal   Néwton–Newtónian

     b. átom–átomless   bóunty–bóuntiful   Méndel–Méndelish
         bóttom–bóttomless cólour–cólourful   Néwton–Néwtonish

Class I affixes differ from Class II affixes not only in their behaviour
with respect to the stress-rules, but also in their allowance for what are
known as non-automatic phonological rules. The following examples
illustrate this point:

(9) a. Class I: il-literate, im-possible, ir-rational, in-tolerable
     b. Class II: un-lucky, un-predictable, un-ripe, un-true

In case of the negative prefix *in-*, the final coronal nasal [n] is fully
assimilated to the following consonant, whereas no such assimilation
occurs in the case of *un-*. This assimilation is clearly not an automatic
phonological rule of English, as we can see in examples using the proposition *in*:

(10) a. the boys stood in line / *il line
      b. my paper is in revision / *ir revision

We never find such non-automatic phonological processes with Class II
affixes. For some more examples, consider the following data:

(11) a. Class I: divide–division; collide–collision
      b. Class II: divide–dividing; collide–colliding

Again, the phonological changes we witness in the pairs in (11a) are
non-automatic; we only find them in particular morphological contexts.
And again we see that Class II affixes (11b) behave differently in the
sense that they do not provide the appropriate context for any non-
automatic phonological rule.

Interestingly, according to Siegel (1974) this difference in phonological behaviour between Class I and Class II affixes is mirrored in
the ordering of affixes. Siegel observes that Class II affixes occur only
'outside' and never 'inside' Class I affixes, where 'inside' means 'closer to
the base'. Following Selkirk (1982), we will call this the **affix-ordering
generalisation**. Given two affixes, the generalisation states that of the
four logical possibilities, namely I–I, I–II, II–II and II–I, only the last
ordering will lead to ungrammatical results. The examples in (12) illustrate this point:

(12) atom-ic$_I$-ity$_I$ atom-ic$_I$-ness$_{II}$
      atom-less$_{II}$-ness$_{II}$ *atom-less$_{II}$-ity$_I$

Note, in passing, that the stress-patterns of these words exemplify once again the stress-shifting behaviour of Class I affixes and the stress-neutral behaviour of Class II affixes (*átom–atómic–atomícity* vs. *átom-less-ness*). More generally, the affix-ordering generalisation may be summarised as follows:

(13) a. [[[A] X] Y]   c.   *[[[A] Y] X]

    b. [[X [A]] Y]   d.   *[[Y [A]] X]
        where X = a Class I affix and Y = a Class II affix

(14) a. [[[A] ... X^n...] Y]   c.   [[[A] (X)] ... Y^n...]

    b. [[... X^n ... [A]] Y]   d.   [... Y^n ... [[A] (X)]]
        where X = a Class I affix and Y = a Class II affix

In (13a) and (13b) the Class I affix X is closer to the stem A than the Class II affix Y, which is fine according to the affix-ordering generalisation, whereas in (13c) and (13d) it is the other way around, resulting in ungrammatical structures. In (14) we see that we may also attach multiple Class I affixes or multiple Class II affixes as long as we respect the affix-ordering generalisation.

Siegel proposes a model that may account for both the behaviour with respect to the stress-rules of Class I and Class II affixes and the affix-ordering generalisation. The idea is that stress-rules operate after Class I affixation, thus accounting for their stress-shifting property, but before Class II-affixation, which explains their stress-neutrality. These affixes simply cannot change the stress-location since the stress-rules have already applied and the model allows no feedback from the output of the Class II affixation. This stipulated ordering of Class I and Class II affixation is called **extrinsic ordering**, implying that there is no grammatical reason for this ordering; it is merely stipulated.

(15) Class I affixation
        ↓
    Stress-rules
        ↓
    Class II affixation

Both the morphological levels are 'recursive', in the sense that multiple applications of affixation from the same level are allowed (see the structures in (14)). But, crucially, no feedback from Class II-affixation to Class I-affixation is allowed. Later the model in (15) became known as level-ordered morphology.

2.4 Compounding as a lexical process

So far, we have been looking at affixational processes leading to the temporary conclusion that we have to distinguish between two classes of affixes depending on their mutual order and their behaviour with respect to certain phonological rules. As we have seen in Chapter 1, word-formation is not limited to affixation but also includes compounding. So we may wonder how compounding would fit the picture sketched above. Let us start by considering some examples. The following come from Allen (1978: 86–7):

(16)   mad-man   'man who is mad'
       black-bird   'bird which is black'

       dog-house   'house which is for a dog'
       door-knob   'knob which is for a door'

       oil-well   'well which yields oil'
       water-mill   'mill which runs on water'
       field-mouse   'mouse which lives in the field'
       steam-boat   'boat powered by steam'

A characteristic of compounds in English is that they often have meanings that are only to a certain extent predictable from their constituting elements. It is true that a *field-mouse* is a mouse that lives in the field. But not just any mouse that happens to match this description is a *field-mouse*. Only a particular type of mouse that typically or characteristically lives in the field can be called a *field-mouse*. Similarly, not any black bird qualifies as a *blackbird*. A blackbird is a particular type of bird that (also) happens to be black (at least the adult males). This property of compounds that we may describe as their readiness to get specialised meanings is often called **lexicalisation**. The idea is that a lexicalised compound is no longer the result of a productive rule, but has become a frozen element in the lexicon associated with a particular meaning. Here are some more examples of lexicalised compounds (again taken from Allen 1978: 90):

(17)   bulls-eye   hot-dog
       snap-dragon   blue-print
       chair-man   green-house
       main-land   broad-side

To understand properly another reason for including compounds in the lexicon we need a little more background. Lees (1960) is a first attempt in generative grammar to account for nominalisations and compounding. Lees' is a transformational account that basically derives nominalisations and compounds from underlying sentences. So, the paraphrases in (16) are roughly the underlying structures from which Lees derives the compounds. Allen (1978) criticises such an account, acknowledging the fact that in the early days of generative grammar, transformations were the only means available. She notes, however, that a transformational account runs into trouble not only because of the property of lexicalisation, but also because of the great variety of semantic relations that the two members of a compound may have to one another. Take *water-mill*, for example. Here the relation between the elements *water* and *mill* is one of energy supply: it is a mill powered by (streaming) water. But there is no principled reason why the compound could not also mean 'a mill producing water' or 'a mill located near water'. It is only our knowledge of the world that tells us that a *steel-mill* or a *paper-mill* are not powered by paper or steel but rather are somehow producing these materials, whereas water is not something that is produced by mills (at least not in our world). Put differently, there is no grammatical reason for the different interpretations of *steel-mill* and *paper-mill* on the one hand and *water-mill* on the other, and therefore we should treat them uniformly, rather than derive them from different underlying structures. Allen proposes that the semantic interpretation of compounds is subject to the following condition:

(18) Variable R Condition:[1]
      In the primary compound $[X Y]_z$, the meaning of X fills any one of the feature slots of Y that can be appropriately filled by X.

The condition in (18) leaves open a number of interpretations for any compound. The actual meaning of existing compounds is often the result of lexicalisation. But (18) also excludes those interpretations that are grammatically impossible. The compound *water-mill* cannot mean any of the following:

(19) a mill which drinks water
      a mill which lives near the water
      a mill which grinds water
      a mill which hunts water

The reason for the impossibility of these interpretations is that the semantic features of the noun *mill* do not fit the restrictions that the different predicates in (19) require, or the predicates are incompatible with the properties of the noun *water*. For example, *mill* is inanimate and therefore it cannot be interpreted as the subject of *drink*. So, rather than a set of transformations that remove predicates such as *produce* or *made of* from the underlying representation, Allen chooses a lexical account in which the interpretation of the compounds is regulated by (18).

Allen proposes that nominal compounds all have the same structure, which can be represented as follows:

(20)

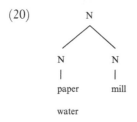

Next to the variable interpretation of the relation between the two members, there is, however, also a linguistic constant in the interpretation of such structures. Compounds of this type are all right-headed. That is, the right-hand element in these compounds is the thing modified (the **determinatum**), whereas the left-hand member modifies the head (the **determinans**). A *computer-game* is a particular type of game, whereas a *game-computer* is some kind of computer. Moreover, the right-hand member of a compound is not only semantically the head; it also determines the word-class of the compound as a whole. The compound *blackbird* is a noun since *bird* is the head and *bird* is a noun. *Bird-black* is a particular kind of *black* and is an adjective because *black* is an adjective. This generalisation is known as the **right-hand head rule** (Williams 1981).[2]

The examples discussed so far are known as **endocentric compounds**. Such compounds are characterised by the fact that they are headed structures. Next to these compounds, English also has a number of **exocentric compounds**. Here are some examples:

(21)   pickpocket
       red-coat
       cotton-tail
       cut-throat

The crucial difference between these and the examples in (16) is that these exocentric compounds do not allow parallel paraphrases such as 'a pickpocket is a pocket that . . .'. A more apt paraphrase would be something like 'A pickpocket is a *person* that picks from people's pockets.' But there is simply no morphological part of the structure that corresponds to the semantic element 'person'. In general, exocentric compounds can be so paraphrased and in all such cases, the head is absent from the linguistic structure. We will see in the next section that some of these exocentric compounds play an interesting role in the discussion about level-ordering.

2.5 Level-ordered phonology and morphology

The level-ordered model of Siegel is further developed especially in work by Allen (1978), Selkirk (1982) and Kiparsky (1982, 1985). The central idea is that word-formation processes are ordered in two or three different levels (depending on the specific model) and that these levels determine the domain for application of the phonological rules of that level. The model predicts specific correlations between affix-order (those belonging to earlier levels will be 'inside' those that belong to later levels) and the application of phonological rules. We illustrate the workings of the model with several examples that we take from Kiparsky (1982).

Before we illustrate the model and go into the morphological explanations it offers, we should stress here that at least half of the motivation for this model is phonological. Kiparsky seeks with this model of lexical phonology an alternative for the Alternation Condition as a restriction on underlying phonological forms. This is a reflection of the 'abstractness' discussion that has been on the phonological research agenda since the early 1970s. Very briefly, the question is how we should ban abstract representations such as /nɪχtVŋgeɪl/ *nightingale* from our underlying representations. The motivation behind such representations is that the words in question fail to undergo a particular phonological rule (in the case of *nightingale*, the rule of trisyllabic shortening). The underlying representations are set up in such a way that the structural description of the phonological rule is not met. The particular underlying representations need to be modified later by separate phonological rules, which are hopefully independently motivated. However, this results in highly abstract underlying representations that are often weakly motivated and simply not learnable. Kiparsky first tried to answer this problem by formulating what he called the Alternation Condition, stipulating that we may only set up underlying forms that at least have a single alternant that occurs at the surface. The reason behind this formulation is that it would otherwise be impossible for a language-learning child to construct the underlying forms from the ambient data. However, for several reasons that we will not go into here, this Alternation Condition is unsatisfactory.

The important insight is that obligatory absolute neutralisation rules, i.e. phonological rules that neutralise a particular phonological opposition, such as trisyllabic shortening, should be restricted to 'derived environments'. So this rule cannot apply in *nightingale* since this form is morphologically un-derived. In that way we do not need any stipulation with respect to the underlying form; instead, we limit the application of a particular set of phonological rules to those environments that are created by the application of morphological rules. Lexical phonology allows for an elegant formulation of the notion 'derived environment' given two further assumptions. First, we assume that lexical items are in fact also a kind of rules, called identity rules. Second, it is assumed that the ordering of rules is determined by the Elsewhere Condition. This condition reads as follows:

(22) Elsewhere Condition (Kiparsky 1982: 136–7)
      Rules A, B in the same component apply disjunctively to a form ϕ if and only if
      (i) the structural description of A (the special rule) properly includes the structural description of the rule B (the general rule).
      (ii) The result of applying A to ϕ is distinct from the result of applying B to ϕ.
      In that case, A is applied first, and if it takes effect, then B is not applied.

Consider now the application of the rule of trisyllabic shortening to an underlying form /naɪtɪŋgeɪl/. This underlying form meets the structural description of the rule. However, there is another rule, the lexical identity rule, which is of the form /naɪtɪŋgeɪl/ → /naɪtɪŋgeɪl/, whose structural description is thus also met by this underlying form. Moreover, this latter rule is more specific than the structural description of trisyllabic shortening. The lexical identity rule thus blocks, according to (22), the application of trisyllabic shortening, since, it is the more specific rule, and since its output is distinct from the application of trisyllabic shortening. In this way, Kiparsky derives the notion of 'derived environment' from a combination of the Elsewhere Condition and the assumption of lexical identity rules.

Let us now turn to the morphological side of the model. We will again see the importance of the Elsewhere Condition, and the use of identity rules. Kiparsky (1982) proposes the following model for English morphology (from Kiparsky 1982: 132).

As in Siegel's model, affixes belong to a particular level. Suffixes such as -*al*, -*ous*, -*ity* and -*th* are all level-1 affixes, whereas e.g. -*hood*, -*ness*,

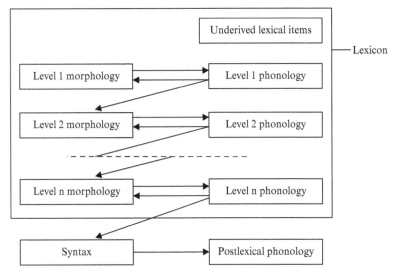

Figure 2.2 Kiparsky's (1982) model of the lexicon, redrawn after Kiparsky (1982: 132)

-*er*, -*ism*, and -*ist* are examples of level-2 affixes. But the distinction also pertains to prefixes, *in*- being a typical level-1 and *non*- being a level-2 affix (Allen 1978). This predicts the familiar ordering of affixes, as can be illustrated by the examples in (23):

(23) a. in-legible   illegible
      b. non-legible   *nollegible
      c. non-illegible
      d. *in-non-legible

The assimilation of the final nasal of the prefix to the initial consonant of the stem it attaches to is a level-1 phonological rule; therefore, although it applies in (23a), it cannot apply in (23b). The prefix *in*- being a level-1 affix can be 'inside' the level-2 prefix *non*- (as in (23c)), but not vice versa, hence the ungrammaticality of (23d).

   More generally, the idea behind the model is that irregular rules and unproductive processes are ordered at level 1, whereas more regular and transparent processes are ordered at higher levels. This ordering follows from the Elsewhere Condition discussed above. If there are two morphological processes that express identical semantics, the Elsewhere Condition tells us that the more specific rule will be ordered before the more general rule. That is, irregular unproductive processes will be prior to the general productive ones. Along these lines, Kiparsky derives the fact that inherently plural nouns such as *cattle* and *people* cannot be morphologically pluralised, that is, *cattles* and *peoples* are ill-formed (we ignore the fact that *peoples* can be pluralised in the meaning *the peoples of West Africa*). The idea is that the same rule-ordering applies. The identity rule for *cattle* and *people* will contain the feature [+plural] and therefore, the rule that derives plural nouns (ordered at level 3) cannot apply to these words, because there is a more specific rule (i.e. the identity rule) blocking its application.

Similarly, irregular plurals such as *mice, teeth, feet*, etc. are formed at level 1, whereas regular inflection is located at level 3. Irregular past tense formations of verbs as in *hit, kept, left, drew*, etc. are also all formed at level 1, whereas all regular verb inflection takes place at level-3. Kiparsky further assumes a general convention, known as Bracketing Erasure, that erases all internal brackets at the end of each level. As a consequence, the morphological structure of a particular derivation is only available within the same level. Any rule of a later level will not be able to refer to the internal structure assigned at an earlier level.

Note that Kiparsky (following Allen 1978 in this respect) also includes compounding and inflection in the model (see also Section 2.6). Compounding is located at least at level 2, since both level-1 and level-2 affixes can be found inside compounds, and inflection is located at level 3, since inflection is always outside derivation. The following examples illustrate the point:

(24) a. *brother]$_N$-s]$_N$-hood
      b. *work]$_V$-ed]$_V$-er

The affix *-hood* can be attached to nouns in order to derive a collective noun. However, it cannot attach to plural nouns. Similarly, *-er* is a productive affix after verbs, but these verbs are always non-inflected. All inflection is outside all derivation. Interestingly, there are some exceptions to this general rule. The following compounds seem to have inflected forms 'inside':

(25) mice-infested
      teeth-marks

Given the fact that irregular processes are located at level 1, the data in (25) do not come as a surprise. Rather, the model predicts that all forms made at level 1 could in principle be part of a compound. Therefore, the data in (25) support the assumption that irregular inflection is a process that takes place prior to compounding.

The same conclusion is supported by the observation that endocentric compounds of which the right-hand member requires an irregular plural retain the irregular plural in compounds. Kiparsky assumes that forms such as *milk teeth* have the structure [[milk][teeth]]. Contrary to this, in exocentric compounds, such as *sabre-tooth*, we see that irregular plurals are lost and replaced by regulars: we get *sabre-tooths* and not *sabre-teeth*. Why? Kiparsky assumes that exocentric compounds require a zero-affix (this follows from the assumption that all word-formation is essentially endocentric; see Section 2.5). This zero-affix cannot be added to a regular plural form since it is assumed to be a level-2 affix. So the exocentric compound can only be singular at level 2 and therefore may receive its plural form only at level 3.

In the same way, the model explains the irregular inflection of compound verbs that are built from irregular verbs. Words such as *forgive*, *partake*, *withstand*, *withdraw*, etc. have irregular past tenses and participles. The explanation, according to the model, is that these past tenses and participles are formed at level 1 and therefore are available for these compounds. Furthermore, the theory predicts that these available forms should be used, rather than their regular counterparts, since these irregular past tense forms will block the application of the more general past tense formation at level 3.

This prediction seems to be contradicted by the regular inflection of a verb like *grandstand*. The irregular verb *stand* has a past tense *stood* that should be available at level 1 and therefore also be available for the compound. However, the verb *grandstand* is not derived from the adjective *grand* and the verb *stand* directly. Rather, it is derived from a noun *grandstand* by way of conversion, or zero-derivation. Now, Kiparsky assumes that conversion from verbs to nouns is a level-1 process, whereas conversion from nouns to verbs is a level-2 process. Both types of conversion are involved in the construction of the verb *grandstand*. First, at level 1, the noun *stand* is formed from the verb through V-to-N-conversion. At level 2 this noun is compounded with the adjective *grand*, forming the nominal compound *grandstand*. This compound is then subject to N-to-V-conversion, deriving the verb *grandstand*. So only after level 2 can verbal inflection be attached, and at that point the level-1 inflection is no longer accessible.

(26) Level 1: $[\text{stand}]_V$ $\rightarrow$ $[\text{stand}]_N$ (by V-to-N conversion)
    Level 2: $[\text{grand}]_A + [\text{stand}]_N$ $[\text{grandstand}]_N$ (compounding)
    Level 2: $[\text{grandstand}]_N$ $\rightarrow$ $[\text{grandstand}]_V$ (N-to-V-conversion)
    Level 3: $[\text{grandstand}]_V + \text{ed}]_{V+\text{TENSE}}$ (regular inflection)

The assumption that V-to-N-conversion is a level-1 rule, whereas N-to-V-conversion sits at level 2, makes some further morphological predictions. First, note that N-to-V-conversion is far more productive than V-to-N-conversion, as the assignment to the different levels suggests. Second, we should be able to find cases of V-to-N-to-V conversion, but not N-to-V-to-N conversion, since this latter sequence would involve a level-2 rule followed by a level-1 rule. Kiparsky provides the following examples as instances of V-N-V conversion:

(27) V   N   V
      permít   pérmit   pérmit
      protést   prótest   prótest
      digést   dígest   dígest

As a result of V-to-N-conversion, we see that the stress shifts to the penult. This is to be expected if this type of conversion is a level-1 rule. The stress does not shift if these nouns (or any other nouns) are converted into a verb. This analysis is further supported by the semantics of the relevant forms. *To pérmit* is 'to issue a permit', whereas *to permít* does not necessarily require the presence of a permit; similar remarks hold for the other examples.

Third, the hypothesis makes some further predictions as to the ordering of affixes with respect to conversion. More specifically, we expect level-1 affixes to occur freely after nouns converted from verbs (being a level-1 rule), but we do not expect such affixes to occur after verbs derived from nouns (which are derived at level 2). Kiparsky (1985: 142) gives the examples in (28a) to substantiate the first claim. The examples in (28b) should support the second:

(28) a. alarm]$_V$Ø]$_N$-ist, escap]$_V$Ø]$_N$-ism, tortur]$_V$Ø]$_N$ous, segment]$_V$Ø]$_N$al, rebel]$_V$Ø]$_N$ious

      b. *gestur]$_N$Ø]$_V$ation, *figur]$_N$Ø]$_V$ive, *pattern]$_N$Ø]$_V$ance, *crusad]$_N$Ø]$_V$atory, *cement]$_N$Ø]$_V$ant

Furthermore, we might expect level-1 affixes 'inside' converted nouns, such as *a public] ise]$_V$Ø]$_N$, or *a clar] ify]$_V$Ø]$_N$. However, there are no such examples. Similarly, there are no examples of level-2 suffixes 'inside' N-to-V-conversion, such as *to sing] er]$_N$Ø]$_V$, *to free] dom]$_N$Ø]$_V$, etc. So, in general, there do not seem to be zero-derived words from affixed forms at the same level. To account for this observation, Kiparsky invokes a general constraint that forbids zero-affixes to attach to suffixed forms:

(29) *] X] Ø

Given Bracketing Erasure, which effectively wipes out the morphological structure of a level before we enter the next level, we would expect that this constraint is not obeyed by affixes attached at level 1 which are then converted to verbs at level 2. So Bracketing Erasure predicts that we will find examples like the ones in (30):

(30) to press]ure$_N$]$\emptyset$]$_V$, to commiss]ion$_N$]$\emptyset$]$_V$, to tri]al$_N$]$\emptyset$]$_V$, to refer] ence$_N$]$\emptyset$]$_V$

Summarising, Kiparsky's model, partly motivated by fundamental questions as to what are possible underlying phonological representations, is a lexical model of word-formation that incorporates not only derivation and compounding but also inflection. The heart of the model is formed by level-ordering motivated by the correlation between phonological (triggering some rules but not others) and morphological behaviour of affixes (affix order).

2.6 The form of word-formation rules

In the previous chapter we have already briefly discussed the form of morphological rules. We have seen that Aronoff (1976) proposes WFRs that perform a particular type of phonological operation (on a base), which goes hand in hand with a change in category and semantics. But different approaches are possible and have been proposed. An important characteristic of these approaches lies in the status that affixes are given. In Aronoff's proposal, affixes are mere phonological changes to the base. However, Lieber (1980) proposes that affixes are fully fledged entries in the lexicon, just as stems are. In this approach, affixes are lexical entries having a phonological, a syntactic and a semantic characterisation. For example, the lexical entry for the affix -*ness* looks as follows:

(31) Lexical Entry for -*ness*:
       Phonological representation: [nəs]
       Category: N^{-1}
       Subcategorisation: [A ___]
       Semantic representation: 'HAVING THE PROPERTY A'

The phonological and semantic characterisations of -*ness* are self-explanatory. Apart from these properties, the affix is also characterised as having the syntactic category N, which accounts for the fact that the affix 'makes' nouns. We will see shortly how the category of an affix may determine the category of the complex word as a whole. Moreover, the category N has what is called a negative bar-level (indicated by '−1' in superscript). This encodes the boundedness of the affix; that is, it prevents -*ness* from occurring without a base: only elements with bar-level 0 have the ability to be freestanding. So a noun such as *house* has the category N^0, just like any other free morpheme. Affixes are typically characterised by a negative bar-level. The affix also has a **subcategorisation frame**. This tells us what type of base in terms of its syntactic category the affix may attach to. In the case of -*ness*, the affix 'selects for' adjectival bases.

In this approach to word-formation, there are no WFRs. Instead, the idea is that lexical entries, such as stems and affixes, may freely combine provided that their subcategorisation frames are satisfied. A complex word is not the result of a particular WFR that makes nouns out of adjectives marked by a particular change in phonological form, but the result of the combination of two lexical items. Moreover, word-formation is considered an **endocentric** process: the properties of the complex word always reside in the lexical items from which it is constructed. The way this is done is with the help of **percolation conventions** that determine which properties of the constituting morphemes may determine the properties of the whole. Lieber (1980) proposes four percolation conventions; we will first illustrate the workings of the first two (Lieber 1980: 49, 50):

(32) a. Convention I:
          All features of a stem morpheme including category features
          percolate to the first non-branching node dominating that
          morpheme.

      b. Convention II:
          All features of an affix morpheme including category features
          percolate to the first branching node dominating that
          morpheme.

In a Lieber-style analysis, we first generate a structure that does not have any categorial labels, as in (33a). Next we insert lexical items into the end nodes of these structures, as in (33b), after which the percolation conventions determine the properties of the higher nodes in the structure, as in (33c).

(33) a.   b.   c.

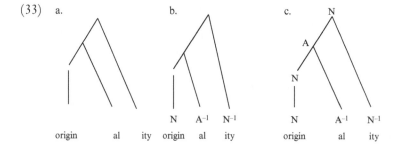

Together conventions I and II guarantee that every complex word receives a category, provided that all stems and affixes are categorised in the lexicon. Now, that may be doubtful given data such as (34):

(34) counter- intuitive$_A$, productive$_A$ counter-productive$_A$, counter-intuitive$_A$

sign$_V$, vail$_V$ counter-sign$_V$, counter-vail$_V$

offer$_N$, plot$_N$ counter-plot$_N$, counter-offer$_N$

un- interesting$_A$, just$_A$, steady$_A$ un-interesting$_A$, un-just$_A$, un-steady$_A$

do$_V$, fold$_V$, learn$_V$ un-do$_V$, un-fold$_V$, un-learn$_V$

re- do$_V$, appear$_V$, view$_V$ re-appear$_V$, re-do$_V$, re-view$_V$

The prefixes in (34) do not change the category of the base they attach to; that is, the complex words in the right-hand column of (34) all have the same category as their base. So, if we wanted to uphold the idea that affixes determine the category of the base, we would have to assume that there are three different prefixes *counter-* each with its own category and subcategorisation frame. Furthermore, we would have to accept that it would be fully coincidental that the subcategorisation of these three different prefixes is always the same as the category of the prefix, that is, *counter$_A$* only attaches to adjectives, *counter$_V$* only to verbs and *counter$_N$* only to nouns. A more explanatory approach would be to assume that the prefixes in (34) are unspecified for category.

Such a proposal has been made by Allen (1978) and Williams (1981). Even stronger, they argue that, as a rule, a prefix cannot determine the category (or any other property) of the complex word. The **right-hand head rule** states that in a morphological structure the right-hand member is the head (see also Section 2.3) (Williams 1981: 248):

(35) In morphology, we define the head of a morphologically complex word to be the right-hand member of that word.

However, Lieber notes that in some cases prefixes do have a category. For example, the prefix *en-* makes verbs regardless of the category of the right-hand member:

(36) en- bark$_N$, code$_N$, courage$_N$ em-bark$_V$, en-code$_V$, en-courage$_V$

close$_V$, fold$_V$, wrap$_V$ en-close$_V$, en-fold$_V$, en-wrap$_V$

large$_A$, rich$_A$ en-large$_V$, en-rich$_V$

Therefore, rather than a general rule such as (35) she formulates a third percolation convention, in addition to the ones in (32): (Lieber 1980: 50)

(37) Convention III:
      If a branching node fails to obtain features by Convention II,
      features from the next lowest labeled node are automatically
      percolated up to the unlabeled branching node. So, if we assume
      that the prefix *counter-* does not have a category, the structures in
      the first three examples in (34) are labelled as follows:

(38)

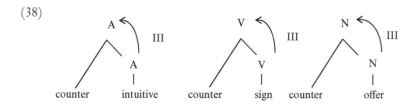

This in contrast to the prefixes in (36) that do have a category, in which
case Convention III is superfluous. Finally, Lieber has to account
for the observation that in compounds the right-hand element is the
head. This is accounted for by the following (and final) percolation
convention:

(39) Convention IV:
      In compound words in English features from the right-hand stem
      are percolated up to the branching node dominating the stems.

    The above discussion makes clear that assuming affixes to be lexical
items buys us the possibility of generalising over morphological structures by means of the percolation conventions of Lieber, or by making
crucial use of a notion 'head' as in the more general right-hand head
rule of Williams. Such generalisations are not possible in a grammar
using WFRs. These considerations form part of the motivation for
word-structures as in (33) and (38) that share certain properties with
sentence structures. As in syntax, the words are seen as endocentric
or headed constructions; just as a verb phrase (VP) always contains a
verb as its head, a noun always either is or contains a noun. This may
even lead to the assumption that there is no principled distinction at
all between word-structure and syntactic structure, but that word-
structure is simply the syntactic structure below the zero-bar level (cf.
Ackema 1995).
    However, Bauer (1990) criticises the idea that words have heads
similar to syntactic phrases. He shows that the syntactic notion 'head'
is in several respects different from the morphological notion. Many
properties of syntactic heads do not transfer to morphological heads,

or if they transfer then it turns out that it is sometimes the base that functions as the head and sometimes the affix. For example, in syntax the head of a phrase is the element which is subcategorised for other elements that go with this head in the same phrase; in English morphology we see that affixes are subcategorised for the element to which they may be attached (verb, adjective, etc.). According to this criterion, then, affixes are heads rather than stems. However, another property of heads in syntax is that they are the obligatory elements in a phrase; without the head, the phrase cannot exist. Applying this to words, we must conclude that bases, rather than affixes, are heads; without bases words cannot exist, whereas words without affixes are fully grammatical. Such considerations show that the motion 'head' in morphology cannot be equated with the notion 'head' in syntax.

The idea of level-ordering is given a different implementation in Selkirk's (1982) approach. Selkirk sees the levels of level-ordered morphology as different levels in a context-free rewrite grammar. Selkirk proposes that the distinctions between level-1 and level-2 affixes follow from a distinction between affixes that attach to roots, called root-affixes, and affixes that attach to words, called word-affixes. Furthermore, we distinguish two types of rewrite rules: those that rewrite 'Word', and those that rewrite 'Root':

(40) a. Word $\rightarrow$ Affix^{word}, Word
          Word $\rightarrow$ Word, Affix^{word}

      b. Root $\rightarrow$ Affix^{root}, Root
          Root $\rightarrow$ Root, Affix^{root}

      c. Word $\rightarrow$ Root

The rules in (40a) account for level-2 affixation, and those in (40b) account for level-1 affixation. The affix-order generalisation falls out from this schema since it is not possible to generate a structure that has a root-affix outside a word-affix, whereas the opposite ordering is possible since it is possible to rewrite the symbol 'Word' as a 'Root', but it is not possible to rewrite 'Root' as a 'Word'.

2.7 Problems with level-ordered morphology

Aronoff (1976) had already observed that the affix-ordering generalisation meets some counter-examples that cannot be explained away so easily. Suffix strings such as *-abil-ity, -ment-al, -ist-ic* and *-is-ation* are all of the forbidden type [[[X] classII] classI]. Williams (1981), Strauss (1982) and Aronoff and Sridhar (1983) further point out serious problems with the affix-ordering generalisation, and consequently with level-ordered morphology. Williams observes that the model encounters counter-examples in the form of level-2 prefixes that attach inside level-1 suffixes. Consider the form *ungrammaticality*. The suffix -*ity* is clearly, being stress-attracting, a level-1 affix. Therefore, given the affix-ordering generalisation, since -*al* is 'inside' -*ity* it should also be a level-1 affix. Allen (1978) analyses the prefix *un*- as a level-2 affix. Assuming that analysis to be correct, the only possible morphological structure for *ungrammaticality* is one in which *un*- attaches to the noun *grammaticality*. But that analysis conflicts with the subcategorisation frame of *un*-: under normal circumstances this prefix attaches to adjectives, and not to nouns (there are some exceptions, but that need not concern us here). It is also in difficulties with the semantic interpretation of the word *ungrammaticality*, which is not something like 'NOT something grammatical' but rather 'something NOT grammatical'. So, if *un*- is truly a level-2 affix, this is an example of a **bracketing paradox**. In this particular case, the presumed morphological structure does not match the semantic structure.

Fabb (1988) is another important voice in a growing choir of linguists that during the 1980s argued against the level-ordering model (e.g. Gussmann 1988). In addition to the problems observed already, he demonstrates that a fairly large number of suffix-pairs ruled out by level-ordering do in fact exist. From these examples we must conclude that the level-ordering hypothesis is too strong: it rules out too many cases. However, Fabb's most important criticism is that the level-ordering hypothesis is at the same time also too weak: far too many examples are ruled in, where they should be excluded. To demonstrate this, Fabb takes 43 suffixes into consideration, which together form a potential $43 * 43 = 1,849$ possible suffix-pairs. We wouldn't expect all of them to occur since their subcategorisation properties (a deverbal suffix cannot combine with an adjective or noun-producing suffix, regardless of any theory on levels or ordering) already reduce the number of possible combinations to 663. Some additional constraints, such as prosodic restrictions that particular affixes conform to (e.g. adjective-forming -*ful* only attaches to a stress-final base), further limit the number of expected possibilities without the level-ordering hypothesis to 614. Now, level-ordering predicts that of this 614 no fewer than 459 will lead to a grammatical result. Yet Fabb claims that of these predicted 459, only 50 suffix-pairs are actually attested. Clearly, the level-ordering hypothesis is not restrictive enough: it is too weak a constraint. Therefore, we need additional means in order to cut down the potential number of suffix combinations to a number that is closer to the actually observed 50.

Fabb's point is that once we have these additional means, we can do without the extra power of level-ordering.

These additional means are **selectional restrictions**. Affixes, apart from their subcategorisation frame, put additional requirements on their bases. For example, affixes from a Latinate origin only attach to bases from the same origin, whereas Germanic affixes may freely attach to either Latinate or Germanic bases. The examples in (41)–(44) illustrate the point:

(41)   rigid-ity   rigid-ness
       atom-ic   atom-less
       modern-ise, modernity   modern-ness

(42)   *calm-ity, *calm-ise   calm-ness
       *cool-ity, *cool-ise   cool-ness

(43)   atom-ic   atom-ic-ity   atom-ic-ness
       unit-ary   unit-ar-ian   unit-ari-ness

(44)   home-less   *home-less-ity   home-less-ness

In (41) we see Latinate bases to which Latinate and Germanic affixes may freely attach. In (42) we see that the Latinate affixes do not attach to Germanic bases. Germanic affixes on the other hand are less choosy, as can be seen from the right-hand column of (42). Similarly, looking at already affixed bases, we see again that Latinate affixes only attach to bases with Latinate affixes (44), whereas Germanic affixes may attach to either Latinate affixed forms or Germanic affixed forms (43). A large part of this observation about the distribution of affixes is covered by the level-ordering generalisation. With few exceptions, Latinate affixes are level-1, and by far the most Germanic affixes are level-2, and thus we may wonder whether we would need levels at all if the [+/− Latinate] distinction expresses precisely the same generalisation. Put differently, once we acknowledge the need for the [+/−Latinate] constraint, the fact that *homelessity* is not a possible word is no longer an argument for level-ordering; it simply follows from the restriction that -*ity* only attaches to Latinate bases. Moreover, as can be seen from the data in (41) and (42), the [+/−Latinate] constraint does more work than level-ordering. Level-ordering has nothing to say about the ungrammaticality of the data in (42). Since only affixes, and not roots or stems, belong to a particular level, level-ordering is simply irrelevant for these cases, and therefore we need to invoke the [+/−Latinate]-constraint in order to rule out these data.

In addition to the importance of the [+/−Latinate] constraint, Fabb also makes some observations about the distributional properties of affixes. First of all, he notices that some affixes never attach to an already suffixed word. Affixes such as *-age*, *-ify*, *-ism* and *-ist* are among these suffixes. The fact that they do not attach to level-2 affixed bases can therefore no longer be seen as an argument in favour of level-ordering, since they do not attach to level-1 affixed bases either. Second, there is a handful of affixes that only occur outside one and the same suffix. For example, the affix *-ary* is always found outside *-ation*. This is a much more stringent condition than the constraint that *-ary* is a level-1 affix. That would allow for a number of combinations that are never attested. So, Fabb therefore concludes:

> To conclude, one of the strongest, most frequently stated, and most historically important arguments for level-ordering is that level-ordering of suffixes makes new predictions about non-occurring pairs in English. In this paper I have suggested that this argument can no longer be made, thus weakening the overall evidence for the level-ordering of morphemes. (Fabb 1988: 539)

A final argument against level-ordered morphology is that many affixes cannot be uniformly assigned to a particular level. Many affixes have a dual status. Selkirk (1982) had already assumed that some affixes have dual status, but Giegerich (1999) shows in great detail that at least 20 per cent of English affixes cannot be assigned to a single level but have a dual nature. For example, take the suffix *-y* (Giegerich 1999: 48–9). The suffix can occur after words and compounds as in (45a), but also after bound roots as in (45b):

(45) a. sun-y   headach-y   b. empt-y   worth-y
        bush-y   open-air-y   dizz-y   louse-y
        rock-y   other-world-y   paltr-y

The examples in the right-hand column of (45b) show that *-y* sometimes gives rise to a(n unpredictable) voicing alternation. If attachment to bound roots (i.e. roots that do not occur freestanding) is taken as an indicator of level-1 status (as it is by Giegerich), and if the fact that it can attach to compound-like constructions in (45a) is indicative of a level-2 status, then there is no escapeing the conclusion that *-y* has dual status. Of course, this all depends on a theory or list of criteria that tells us when a particular form should be considered level-2 and by what criteria we may come to the conclusion that a form is a level-1 construct. Giegerich starts out with a thorough discussion of the criteria that have been mentioned in the literature to argue for level-1 or level-2 status (see also Szpyra 1989). We summarise this list here very briefly:

- Affix-order: this is very doubtful since so many affixes seem to have dual status, and given the critique of the affix-ordering generalisation above.
- Categorial status of the base: bound roots cannot have a category. Since bound roots only occur at level 1, the fact that a particular affix can occur on bound roots shows its level-1 status.
- Productivity and semantic uniformity: as we have seen above, lack of productivity and semantic irregularity may be taken as indicators of level-1 status.
- Stress behaviour: stress-attracting suffixes are level-1, whereas stress-neutral ones are level-2. However, note that in cases such as *escapee*, *payee*, *Turneresque*, *Faroese*, etc. where the suffix itself is stressed, this final stress is exceptional. Thus, the affix would have to be marked as being stress-bearing, which would also be possible if it were a level-2 affix, assuming that it leaves the stress of the base intact.
- Syllabification behaviour: compare the following forms: *cylinder*, *cylindric*, *cylinderish*. The second form is the only one of the three in which [r] is non-syllabic. We may explain this as follows: at level 1 these final sonorants cannot be the nucleus of a syllable. So they remain unsyllabified at this level, unless a particular affix is attached that allows them to be syllabified as an onset (as in *cylindric*). At level 2 the final sonorant triggers schwa-epenthesis, which accounts for the other forms. This can be used as a diagnostic for level-1 status (of -*ic* in this case), or level-2 status (of -*ish*).

2.8 Base-driven strata

Giegerich (1999) offers an alternative model that maintains the claim that the (English) lexicon is organised in different strata, but at the same time tries to answer the empirical problems that the model of Siegel, Kiparsky and others encounters. Giegerich's central claim is that the different strata or levels cannot be defined on the basis of the properties of affixes, but have to be defined in terms of the properties of the morphological bases.

Stressing and adding to earlier observations of Aronoff (1976), Fabb (1988), Szpyrza (1989) and others, Giegerich demonstrates that many affixes in English do not exclusively belong to level 1 or level2, but that a large proportion of the English affixes has a dual status: in some words they act as level-1 affixes, whereas in others they have level-2 status. For example, the affix -*able* attaches to bound roots in (46a), whereas it attaches to words in (46b) (compare Giegerich 1999: 28–9):

(46) a. navig-able   b. navigat-able
         appreci-able   appreciat-able
         demonstr-able   demonstrat-able
         toler-able   tolerate-able
         c'ompar-able   comp'ar-able
         r'epar-able   rep'air-able

The forms in (46a) have non-transparent semantics, whereas the ones in (46b) are fully compositional. Furthermore, the forms in the left-hand column may show different stress-patterns from the ones in the right-hand column, as the last two examples illustrate. These properties together are taken as evidence for the dual nature of the affix -*able*: it is a level-1 affix in the left-hand column, but a level-2 affix in the right-hand column.

As a second example of an affix that has dual status, consider the affix -*er*. This affix clearly has level-2 status, since it is fully productive and attaches to both Latinate (47b) and Germanic (47a) bases:

(47) a. diver   b. contracter
         killer   consumer
         singer   producer
         worker   publisher

Furthermore, Giegerich notes that Marchand (1969) observed that -*er* also attaches to bound roots:

(48) astronom-er
      astrolog-er
      adulter-er
      philosoph-er
      presbyt-er

This points to a level-1 status. Therefore, Giegerich concludes that the affix -*er* also has dual status in the English lexicon.

This dual nature is a property that is not only found in -*able* and -*er* but that Giegerich argues also holds for many other affixes, such as -*ant*/-*ent* (as in *irritant*, *pollutant* and *president*), -*ee* (as in *nominee* and *trainee*), -*(e)ry* (as in *winery* and *monastery*), and several more. The fact that many affixes cannot exclusively be pinpointed as either level-1 or level-2 seriously undermines affix-driven level-ordered morphology, for if many affixes can be either level-1 or level-2, the model loses its predictive power.

Let us now turn to Giegerich's proposal. Giegerich claims that strata in the English lexicon do not stem from different types of affixes but result from different types of morphological bases. The defining characteristics of level 1 are unproductivity, phonological irregularity and semantic opaqueness. Giegerich observes, following Aronoff (1976), that these three properties go hand in hand. The results of unproductive morphological processes very often have a non-compositional interpretation and/or display an allomorphy that is unexpected. Or, to put it the other way around, the more productive a morphological process, the bigger the chance that the process is phonologically regular and semantically transparent. This three-way correlation can be understood in terms of **listedness**. Listed forms may have idiosyncratic semantics and may display phonological irregularities. If the output of a particular morphological process cannot be listed, it is necessarily regular and fully productive. Giegerich claims that the defining characteristic of level 1 in the English lexicon is listedness. All roots, affixes and complex forms at this level are listed, and consequently, they are open to semantic idiosyncrasy or phonological irregularity next to their unproductivity.

The bases of level-1 formations are always **roots**. Since multiple affixes can be attached at level 1 (for example *sens-ation-al-ity*), the output of level-1 processes is also always a root, with the exception of a somewhat special rule to which we turn shortly. Note that the notion 'root' receives an interpretation that differs from previously discussed morphological theories. Usually a root is a non-affix that is bound, i.e. it cannot occur as a freestanding form. An example would be the form *matern-* in *maternity* and *maternal.* Giegerich defines roots as bases that do not have a category. As such, Giegerich's definition includes all forms that are traditionally called roots but also encompasses many more. To see why all 'traditional' roots are included in the definition, we have to establish that we cannot undisputedly assign a category to bound roots such as *matern-*. Since it is not a freestanding form, the only way to decide the issue is to consider the subcategorisation frames of affixes that attach to this root. Since *-ity* normally attaches to adjectives (*grammatical-ity, reparabil-ity*) we would have to decide on the basis of *maternity* that the root *matern-* is an adjective. However, by the same reasoning the form *maternal,* since *-al* attaches to nouns elsewhere (*convention-al, magic-al*), would bring us to the conclusion that *matern-* is a noun. Because the form cannot be used without an affix, there is no independent means to arrive at its category. Giegerich concludes that *matern-* does not have a category. The same reasoning applies to many more roots, and therefore this conclusion generalises to the category root.

Now, consider the example *sensationality*. This form is a level-1 formation since the affix *-ity* is not fully productive and may produce semantic idiosyncrasies. Consequently, *sensationality* is a root, which

seems to contradict the definition just given, since this form has a category. From its syntactic behaviour, there can be no doubt that it is a
noun. However, Giegerich assumes that this category does not come
about at the point where *-ity* attaches, but later, at a point where the
form is turned from a Root into a Word. Since level-2 processes only
operate on words, in order for a level-I form to become available for
level-II processes it has to be converted from a Root to a Word. This
conversion is done by means of a special rule of the following form
(Giegerich 1999: 76):

(49)   Root-to-Word Conversion:
       $[]_r \rightarrow [[]_r]_L$ (L = N, A, V)

The rule simply assigns a category (noun, adjective or verb) to the
root, and as a consequence the root is no longer a root, but becomes a
word that is eligible for insertion into a syntactic node of the category
assigned to it by rule (49). Or, alternatively, it can be further affixed by
word-affixes. Bound roots, such as *matern-*, are not subject to the conversion rule and therefore cannot be words. As will be clear from this
exposition, it needs to be stipulated per root whether a category will be
assigned by (49), and if so, which one.[3]

As we have seen at the beginning of this chapter, precisely these
properties were the motivation for a lexical treatment of morphology,
'lexical' referring here to the property of listedness.

2.9 Lexicality, productivity and the existence of words

We started this chapter by pointing to idiosyncratic properties of words
that would motivate their listedness. In many lexical models of word-
formation the listedness of 'existing' words is almost taken for granted,
but not all morphologists are equally convinced that morphology is
all that different from syntax in this respect. Compare again a phrase
such as *kiss a girl* to a word such as *kissing*. In many lexical approaches
to word-formation it is assumed that *kissing* is stored in the lexicon,
since it is an existing word. Phrases such as *kiss a girl*, on the other
hand, are not listed or memorised but are assumed to be constructed
by rule. DiSciullo and Williams (1987), for example, argue that there
is no reason for this bifurcation between listed words and constructed
phrases. In their words: 'Our overall point is that listedness is no more
intrinsically characteristic of words than it is of phrases' (1987: 3).
In order to show that listedness is not an intrinsic property of words
they first show that there are also phrases that need to be listed. Every
phrasal idiom needs to be listed, since in those cases meaning cannot

be compositionally derived from the constructing elements. Consider Jackendoff's (1975) view, which we briefly explained in Chapter 1, that WFRs are redundancy rules over the list of words. (This view is now taken further in 'construction morphology'; see Booij 2010.) In this view, storage (or listing) of words that are fully regular does not add to the information load of the lexicon. However, according to DiSciullo and Williams there does not seem to be anything that prevents us from saying that rules for constructing phrases are redundancy rules over existing phrases. Phrases such as *kiss a girl* are completely regular and therefore can be stored without any additional cost, whereas storage of idiomatic phrases such as *kick the bucket* would be more costly since it requires additional memorisation of the non-compositional semantics. So there is no need to separate phrases from words in terms of listedness.

Second, DiSciullo and Williams point out that there is also a principled reason why not all words can be stored. To see this, consider the words in (50):

(50) a. missile
      b. anti-missile missile
      c. anti-anti-missile missile missile

The word *missile* is a noun. An *anti-missile missile* is again a noun referring to a particular type of missile aimed against missiles. Much more difficult to understand is the form in (50c). However, although it may put quite a burden on the morphological parsing capacities of the language user, in principle nothing is wrong with this word. We can think of a missile that is aimed against anti-missile missiles (it probably even exists), and such a device would be called an anti-anti-missile missile missile. This goes to show that in principle there is no end to the list of words in the English language, in the same way as there is no end to the list of possible phrases (sentences). We could go on by adding *anti*s and *missile*s and still end up with only grammatical forms (see the discussion in Langendoen 1981 and Carden 1983). Since the list of grammatical forms is without end, it cannot be a list.

Note that this reasoning also has consequences for the notion 'productivity'. From a grammatical point of view a rule is either productive or non-productive. If it is productive, speakers will be able to make new forms with it. If the rule is unproductive, there is only a limited number of forms that (thus) can be listed.

We may ask why language users somehow have the intuition that a word such as *intuition* is an 'existing word', whereas *kiss a girl* is not an 'existing phrase'. The first answer is of course that if there is anything idiosyncratic about the word *intuition* then this will be a reason for listing, and that may be the cause for the intuition that the word 'exists'. However, for that same reason phrases will also be listed, and indeed, idiosyncratic phrases (*kick the bucket, draw a line*) will trigger the same kind of response that they 'exist' as does any (idiosyncratic) word. Second, note that this intuition of 'existence' is much less present in a word such as *kissing*, or *colourless*. Such words have no idiosyncrasies whatsoever and therefore there is no reason to list them, hence the intuition of 'existence' is absent.

Exercises

1. Give some examples of potential (but non-existing) words. Give at least two compounds, two suffixed forms and two prefixed forms.

2. A phonological rule that is more or less comparable to trisyllabic shortening, in the sense that it is a lexical rule that does not apply in any English word, is the velar softening rule. Some relevant examples are given below:
   electric [k]   electric[s]ity
   critic [k]   critic[s]ism
   medic[k]al   medic[s]ine

   How would you formulate the velar softening rule (given these examples)? Give some examples in which the rule apparently does not apply (despite meeting the conditions for its application that you formulated).

3. Demonstrate that compounding should be at least a level-2 process in Kiparsky's model.

4. Draw tree-structures (in the way that Lieber does) of the words *learnability*, *encompass* and *rechargable*. Indicate in these tree-structures how the percolation conventions take care of the correct categorisation.

5. Show the tree-structure that Selkirk would assign to the following words: *organisational, retrieving, colourlessness, atomicness*.

6. In Section 2.6 it is explained that the word *ungrammaticality* forms a problem for the affix-ordering generalisation (and consequently for level-ordered morphology). Demonstrate that the word *reorganisation* is a counter-example of the same type.

7. Try to think of a way that Giegerich's theory could deal with the conversion data in (27).

Further reading

Bermúdez-Otero, Ricardo (2012) 'The Architecture of Grammar and the Division of Labor in Exponence', in Trommer, Jochen (ed.), *The Morphology and Phonology of Exponence*, Oxford Studies in Theoretical Linguistics 41, Oxford: Oxford University Press, pp. 8–83.

Booij, Geert (2010) *Construction Morphology*, Oxford: Oxford University Press.

Scalise, Sergio and Emiliano Guevara (2005) 'The Lexicalist Approach to Word-Formation and the Notion of the Lexicon', in Lieber, Rochelle and Pavol Štekauer (eds.), *Handbook of Word-Formation*, Dordrecht: Springer, pp. 147–87.

Notes

1. This is a somewhat more transparent formulation, which we have taken from Ten Hacken (2009), than Allen's original. However, the intention is exactly the same.
2. Allen (1978: 105) formulates the IS A Condition, which is more or less identical and prior to Williams' right-hand head rule. Williams' formulation, however, is intended also to cover suffixation, whereas Allen's generalisation is confined to compounds. (See also Section 2.5 of this chapter.)
3. Note that there is a clear parallel, despite many differences, between Giegerich's root-to-word conversion and Selkirk's rewrite rule, shown in (40), which rewrites words as roots. The opposite directions of the arrows results from the top-down reasoning applied by Selkirk and the bottom-up logic that is typical of level-ordered approaches.

3 Inflectional morphology

3.1 Introduction

Science often replaces well-known and familiar concepts with different concepts that seem strange and even counterintuitive to the layperson at first. For the chemist the substance that comes out of your tap isn't water, scientifically speaking. Water for the chemist is a pure substance of molecules that consist of two hydrogen atoms and one oxygen atom. Tapwater may contain other ingredients such as carbon. That makes tapwater a mixture and not the pure substance. So what is water to the layperson is not exactly the same as what is water to the scientist. The same is true for linguistics. In Chapter 1 we have already started by making the well-known and all-too-common notion 'word' a bit more complex by asking what it means to say that one knows a word. At the start of this chapter on inflection, we need to complicate this notion a little further. Consider the following forms:

(1) a. (I) work
     b. (she) works
     c. (he is) working
     d. (they) worked

In everyday speech, one would say that these are four different words. However, several observations show that this set differs from the by now familiar set in (2):

(2) a. equal
     b. equality
     c. equalise
     d. to equal

First, compare the different meanings of the words in (2) to the (lack of) differences in meanings of the words in (1). It is true that the meanings of the words in (2) have some relation to the meaning of the word *equal*. But, as we have seen in Chapter 2, the semantics of these complex words is not always fully predictable, and the relation to the meaning of the base can be rather loose. Part of the semantics of these words may be specific to the word itself and cannot be related either to the stem or to the particular word-formation process. This differs completely from the forms in (1). In a sense, these words all have the same meaning. The only difference between these forms lies in their syntactic usage. For example, the form in (1b) can only be used as a third person singular present indicative, whereas (1a) is used for any combination of person and number but the third singular. One may argue that part of the 'meaning' of the form in (1b) is 'third person', but such a move merely turns a (morpho)syntactic distinction into a semantic one. This becomes even more evident if we think about assigning a similar 'semantics' to the form in (1a). This reasoning would force us to assign a meaning 'NOT 3rd person'. This may be taken as an indication that it is not semantics but syntax that we are encoding. It would also not do justice to the qualitative difference between the semantic richness of the derived forms in (2) compared to the strict and meagre 'semantic' differences in (1).

Second, note that the forms in (1) only differ in their syntactic usage. We could design a little test (familiar to those who acquire English as a second language), in which the subject is asked to fill in the right form of the word on the dotted line in (3):

(3)   She always . . .(work). . . late hours.

It would be rather awkward (and one never sees such exercises in second language teaching) to do a similar test for the words in (2). What allows us to run such a test as the one in (3) is the fact that there is only a single answer.

Third, note that the word-class of the forms in (1) does not change: these are all verbs. In contrast, the forms in (2) belong to different word-classes: *equal* is an adjective, *equality* is a noun, and *equalise* and *to equal* are verbs.

These observations together have been taken to show that the forms in (1) are just different 'instances' or 'realisations' of the same 'word', whereas the different forms in (2) are all different 'words'. But that requires a new definition of the notion 'word'. As we have seen in Section 1.6 morphologists use the term 'lexeme' to refer to this notion of 'word'.

So far, we have talked about morphology as the study of word-formation. After this brief introduction, we can now be a little more precise. In the previous chapters, we did not look at the formation of word-forms as in (1), but we looked at some of the properties of lexeme-formation, as in (2). Word-formation of which the forms in (2) are examples is called **derivation**, or derivational morphology. In this chapter we will focus on a different part of morphology, which involves data of the type exemplified in (1). As we saw in Section 1.6, these examples concern inflectional morphology. Inflection produces not new lexemes, but different word-forms of a particular lexeme.

In this chapter we will focus on the inflectional morphology of English. Different approaches towards inflectional morphology have been taken. Before we turn to a discussion of the different approaches towards inflection, we will first ask whether the difference between inflection and derivation is a real one. Arguments for a distinction between inflection and derivation are discussed in Section 3.2. In Section 3.3 we will give an overview of the different types of inflection in English. It will become clear that English is not a language with a rich inflectional structure. On the contrary, all neighbouring languages have richer inflectional means. After this exposition of the empirical basis, we will go into some theoretical questions that have been raised in the linguistic literature on inflection. The first theoretical question addressed is where inflection is located in the grammar. Different theories of inflection give different answers to this question. Some view inflection as part of the word-formation component, whereas others locate inflection elsewhere in the grammar. In Section 3.5 we discuss a different, although related, issue that pertains to the type of operations that may mark inflectional properties. Is it just affixes that mark inflectional features, or can other phonological operations also mark inflection? Again, both views are defended in the literature and we will review their arguments.

3.2 Inflection versus derivation

The morphological literature gives several criteria that we could use to distinguish inflection from derivation. However, many (if not all) of these criteria are not watertight on close scrutiny. In this section we will review some of these criteria and see what they may tell us about the English data.

The first criterion to be discussed is the above-mentioned category-changing property of derivation. In (4), we have given some derivations:

(4)   a.   work$_V$ b.   equal$_A$
            work-er$_N$ equal-ity$_N$
            work-able$_A$ equal-ise$_V$
            to equal$_V$

In these examples, it is indeed the case that the derived form is of a different word-class from the base. But if the examples in (5) are examples of derivation – and we cannot see any reason why they should not be – category changing is clearly not a defining characteristic of derivation:

(5) draw$_V$ re-draw$_V$
    green$_A$ green-ish$_A$
    cover$_V$ un-cover$_V$

In these examples the category does not change, despite the morphological operation that takes place. Now, of course, we could conclude from this that the prefixes *re-* and *un-* and the suffix *-ish* are inflectional suffixes rather than derivational ones, but that goes against some of the other criteria as we will see shortly.

Now consider the following data:

(6) a. kill   killing   The killing of Mary was brutal
       leave   leaving   John's leaving of the room, left us stupefied

    b. John's *recently/recent killing of Mary
       John's *recently/recent leaving of the room

From the examples in (6b) we may conclude that the *-ing* forms can be nouns, for they allow modification by an adjective, as nouns in general do, but not by adverbs. Furthermore, the object has to be part of a prepositional phrase rather than a direct object as we find with the verb *kill*. Therefore, on the basis of the category-changing criterion, we would have to conclude that these *-ing* forms are derivations, rather than inflections. But there are other reasons to doubt this. There does not seem to be a real lexical semantic difference between the nouns in (6) and their verbal bases. Furthermore, anticipating another criterion to be discussed, the formation of these *-ing* nouns is completely productive: there is no single verb in English (apart from modals, which seem to form a separate class) that does not have such a nominal. As we have seen before, derivation is often characterised by accidental gaps and therefore we would not expect full productivity, as we witness here. So the category-changing criterion seems to fail on both sides: it indicates that the category-changing data in (6) are derivational where there is good reason to doubt that that is actually the case; furthermore, it indicates that the data in (5) are inflectional, which also seems to go against our understanding of this notion thus far.

Let us now turn to a second criterion: the notion that inflection is semantically neutral. We have already seen some examples of this in the introduction to this chapter. So far, we have said that derivational morphology changes the lexical semantics, whereas inflectional morphology does not seem to affect the lexical semantics, but merely changes some morphosyntactic features, such as person and number. Before we evaluate this criterion let us first clarify the notion 'morphosyntactic feature'. A **morphosyntactic feature** is a feature of a particular word-form that limits the syntactic context in which this form can be used. For example, the form *is* is characterised by the morphosyntactic features '3rd person', 'present tense' and 'indicative'. The form *is* therefore cannot be used in a syntactic context that requires '2nd person', or 'past tense', or any other non-compatible feature. We thus may say that morphosyntactic features link a particular morphological form with a particular syntactic context. Inflection can now be seen as that part of morphology that relates (or marks) forms to a particular set of morphosyntactic features.

The notion that inflection does not affect lexical semantics but merely changes morphosyntactic representations needs some further modification. First of all, we should point out (following Anderson 1992: 79) that inflection sometimes does have a semantic effect. Above, we observed that there are no real semantic differences between the forms in (1). Although this may intuitively be clear for the cases of verbal inflection, in the case of plural morphology on nouns, inflection has a clear semantic effect. The noun *dog* differs in meaning from its plural counterpart *dogs*. One might wish to say that [plural] is not a real lexical semantic difference, but that begs the question. It calls for an explicit theory about what would constitute 'lexical semantics' as opposed to 'inflectional semantics'. As far as we are aware there is no such theory, and therefore it remains quite problematic to nail down the different semantic contribution of inflection versus derivation. There is another closely related difference between the plural of nouns and the plural of verbs that has caught the attention of some theoretical morphologists.

Booij (1996b) proposes a distinction between so-called 'inherent' inflection and 'contextual' inflection. We would like to explain the opposition by comparing a verbal plural form with a nominal plural form. However, since English inflection is almost lacking, we can hardly talk about the plural verb-form. The form used in the present tense plural is the same form for the 1st and 2nd person singular. Nevertheless, let us assume that *are* is the plural form of the verb BE (in fact it also happens to be used in the second person singular; we will come back to this point later). In the context of a plural subject, we need to use the form *are*; there is no choice for the speaker in this case. In contrast to this, in nominal inflection a speaker may freely choose to express the plural of *dog* or to use the singular; there is no context that forces a particular choice in this case. Of course one may point out that in the context in (7), the choice for the noun needs to be plural, since otherwise the verb-form does not match the number of the subject:

(7)   The DOG in the garden bite.

However, such reasoning turns things upside down. The form of the verb depends upon the number of the subject, and not the other way around. Therefore, the speaker may decide whether the subject is plural or singular, and that choice determines the form of the verb. For this reason, Booij proposes calling nominal plurals an example of **inherent inflection**, and verbal inflection in English an example of **contextual inflection**.

Booij's point builds upon the difference in semantics between verbal inflection and nominal inflection. Verbal inflection is merely contextual, since the primary source for the meaning component [plural] is not located on the verb itself, but lies somewhere else in the structure, in this case in the subject with which the verb agrees. Put differently, the plural form of a verb does not have a plural meaning in the sense that it expresses more instances of the particular event that is expressed by the lexical meaning of the verb. The verb-form *are* does not mean 'different instances of being'. In the case of nominal inflection, the noun is the primary source for the plural meaning; the form *dogs* really has plural semantics, hence the difference between the two. Booij does not go so far as to claim that inherent inflection is derivation rather than inflection. This criterion therefore can only be used to separate different types of inflection.

A third criterion that has been proposed in the literature is that of the paradigmatic nature of inflectional morphology as opposed to derivational morphology. The claim is straightforward: inflectional morphology forms paradigms, whereas derivational morphology does not. A **paradigm** is a multidimensional data-structure that allows one to organise all inflectional forms of a particular lexeme. Here is an example:

(8)   BE

		Present	Past	Participle	Infinitive
Sing.	1st	am	was	been	be
	2nd	are	were		
	3rd	is	was		
Plur.	1st	are	were		
	2nd	are	were		
	3rd	are	were		

The morphosyntactic features, such as [singular], [plural], [present], [past], etc., define a multidimensional space that consists of a set of cells. So in (8) the terms in bold print define a three-dimensional space (that we have to represent here in two dimensions, but see Figure 3.1 below). The dimensions correspond to the morphosyntactic categories *number* (valued singular or plural), *person* (valued 1st, 2nd or 3rd) and *tense* (present, past and participle). So, for example, the cell defined by the morphosyntactic features [number: sing.], [tense: present], [person: 3rd] is filled with the form *is*. Each cell in this three-dimensional space is filled by a particular inflectional form and each inflectional form is located in a particular cell. In this sense a paradigm is complete.

Now, let us compare this with derivation. First of all, it is not at all obvious what the dimensions of a particular derivational paradigm would be. Given an adjective such as *equal*, would 'nominalisation' be a candidate 'feature' that sets up a dimension in the paradigmatic space? But immediately a problem arises, because we could fill this particular cell with two forms: *equality* and *equalness*. That may suggest that we should see affixes as defining the rows and columns in a paradigm, but the consequence of such a move will be that we have paradigms with lots of gaps, since many affixes do not attach to large sets of stems even if they match their subcategorisation frame. This brings us automatically to a fourth criterion that is often mentioned in the literature: full productivity. However, as we will see below, this criterion also is not watertight: there are examples of incomplete inflectional paradigms and also of fully productive derivations.

If inflectional paradigms are complete in the sense above, that is, every cell in the paradigm is filled by a particular form, then that situation contrasts with the accidental gaps that we encountered in derivational morphology. Put differently, inflection seems to be fully productive; derivation is not. The latter statement needs some modification, however. Consider again the case of the nominalisations in (6) above, repeated here for convenience in (9):

(9)   kill   killing
      leave   leaving

Above we noted that the formation of *-ing* nominals is completely productive. We have already indicated that this might be taken as an argument that these nominalisations are cases of inflection rather than derivation despite their category-changing behaviour. On the other hand, we could also reason the other way around. If we assume that inflection is really never category-changing, the cases in (9) are clear instances of derivation. But in that case, there is at least one derivational process that is fully productive and seriously weakens the productivity criterion.

Second, consider the nominal forms in (10):

(10) a. information   *informations
        dust   *dusts
        wealth   *wealths
        water   *waters

     b. *scissor   scissors
        *clothe   clothes
        *measle   measles
        *mean   means
        *oat   oats

As we see from these examples, it is simply not true that nominal plural formation is fully productive: there are nouns that just do not have a plural form. It might be the case that the semantics of the noun is such that a plural is simply impossible. This is certainly the case for mass nouns such as *water*, or *sand*. If we do pluralise these nouns we get what is called a coercion effect: the semantics of the noun gets a different interpretation. It no longer means 'sand', but the plural forces the interpretation 'type of sand'. Plurality is only possible for count nouns; so this is a semantic condition on this morphological operation. But if there is a semantic condition on this morphological operation, is it then still a case of inflection? We will come back to this question in Section 3.3.1. Furthermore, the forms in (10b) show that not all nouns have a singular form. These 'pluralia tantum' are nouns that only have a plural form (which in itself is an interesting morphological phenomenon; see Acquaviva 2004, 2008 for extensive discussion). Note that at first sight there are forms that may be seen as the singular forms of these 'pluralia tantum', such as *mean* and *oat* as in 'common oat'. However, these forms cannot be taken as the singular forms of *means* and *oats* since they have an unrelated meaning. Therefore, it seems safe to say that the lexemes in (10b) only have a plural form.

The above observations that distinguish derivation from inflection do not necessarily force us to the conclusion that we also need to separate the two notions theoretically. It could be the case that the observed differences are epiphenomenal, that is, that these differences follow from another property and that in principle the two make use of the same linguistic mechanisms.

3.3 Inflection in English

Inflection is category-specific. That is, the inflection in verbs is sensitive to different morphosyntactic categories from those nominal inflection is sensitive to, and the form it takes is different in both categories. In fact, the origin of separating different word-classes such as nouns and verbs lies in their different behaviour with respect to inflection.

First, we will look into nominal inflection. English has almost no nominal inflection as compared to many of the world's languages. To compare, English has no case system, that is, the form of a noun (apart from its number marking) is always the same whatever the syntactic context may be. In a language such as Finnish, the form of a noun is dependent upon the syntactic context in which it occurs, and the noun may take one of fourteen different forms. Even one of the closest neighbours of English, German, has different inflectional forms of nouns. The form of a noun in these languages is partly dependent upon its 'case'. This case is determined by the syntactic function of the phrase of which the case-marked noun is the head. 'Case' is thus a morphosyntactic category, just like 'person' or 'number', but a morphosyntactic category that English altogether lacks.

Similarly, where other West Germanic languages such as Dutch, Frisian and German have a gender system, English does not. In German each noun belongs to one of three 'gender classes': a noun is either masculine, feminine or neuter. Standard Dutch has a two-gender system: nouns belong either to the class of neuter or to the class of non-neuter nouns. The gender of a noun determines such things as the inflection on an (attributive) adjective, the form of determiners and the form of relative pronouns. English nouns are of a single type; there are no morphological subclasses. This implies that the only inflectional dimension left in the nominal domain is number. Although this is meagre with respect to other languages, we will see that even the little that there is may give rise to interesting observations.

Second, we will look into adjectival inflection. In general in the Germanic languages, adjectives are inflected for number and gender when these adjectives are used in what is called attributive position. Below we have given a few examples from German, just to show what English is lacking:

(11) ein   jung*er* Mann   'a young man'   (masc., sing., 'strong', nom.)

      eine jung*e*   Frau   'a young woman' (fem., sing., 'strong', nom.)

| ein | jung*es* | Mädchen | 'a young girl' | (neuter, sing., 'strong', nom.) |

(12) | der | jung*e* | Mann | 'the young man' | (masc., sing., 'weak', nom.) |
| die | jung*e* | Frau | 'the young woman' | (fem., sing., 'weak', nom.) |
| das | jung*e* | Mädchen | 'the young girl' | (neuter, sing. 'weak', nom.) |

The different forms of the adjective depend on four different morpho-syntactic features that together determine the full paradigm for the prenominal adjectives in German. These features are *gender*, which can have one of three different values (masculine, feminine or neuter); *number*, which can be either singular or plural; *case*, which can be one of four (nominative, genitive, dative or accusative); and finally, there are two series, traditionally referred to as 'strong' (11) and 'weak'(12), depending on other properties of the NP (or maybe better: DP) in which the adjective occurs. If we compare this situation to English, we must say that English is truly meagre in this respect: there is exactly one and no more than one form of the attributive adjective.

However, there is another property of adjectives that is expressed in English and that could be seen as a form of inflection. We will discuss comparative and superlative forms in Section 3.3.2.

Third, we will discuss verbal inflection. Obviously, this is the richest of the inflectional paradigms in English, but here also a brief comparison to a neighbouring language such as German is enough to show that in the course of history English has lost many of its inflectional distinctions that in the past apparently also belonged to the language. That is, it is not the case that the relative richness of inflection in German must be attributed to a later rise of inflection in this language. Rather, English has lost many of these inflections, as is immediately clear from a brief comparison to older stages of the language. For example, Old English also has gender, case and different person markings on the verb, such as *-eth* for third person singular, and *-est* for second person singular. But in the period between 1200 and 1400 most of these different inflectional markings disappeared. What is left of verbal inflection will be discussed in Section 3.3.3.

At this point one may wonder what has happened in the history of English such that so many of its former inflectional distinctions have disappeared. This question defines an entire separate field of inves-tigation. An important factor that plays a role in language change in general and that has certainly played a role in this deflection process is language contact. English has a history characterised by different types of contact in different periods. Starting with the invasion of the Vikings in the ninth century, which according to the standard opinion changed English from an OV-language (with the verb at the end of the verb phrase) to a VO-language (with the verb at the beginning of the verb phrase), through to the French conquerors in the eleventh century, and the subsequent influence of French on the English language, the early history of English is indeed one of contact and mixture. No doubt this has played a decisive role in the loss of the inflections, although the exact workings of this process of loss are still the subject of research.

3.3.1 Nominal inflection

English nouns are specified for the category 'number'. There are two values: singular and plural. This is not the only possible option in natural languages, though. There are languages in which the category 'number' is split up into more dimensions, so that we find languages that, apart from a singular and plural, also have paucal (used to mark few entities), dual (for pairs) and trial (for triplets) forms. We will follow a particular notational convention to write down the value of a morphosyntactic feature. We write between square brackets the name of the morphosyntactic feature followed by a colon and the value of that feature. English nouns are thus characterised as either [number: singular] or [number: plural]. Conceptualised in this way, the category [number] is a feature with two possible values. However, we could also assume that singular is just the absence of plural. That would imply that [number] is just a single-valued feature as in (13):

(13) a.   [number: __]   Interpretation: 'singular'
      b.   [number: plural]   Interpretation: 'plural'

The way the morphosyntactic feature [number] is conceptualised in (13) is referred to as **privative**. The absence of the feature implies that the feature gets a 'default' interpretation, in this case [singular].

In most cases, plurality of nouns in English is morphologically expressed by a suffix /-z/ (spelled as -s). This /-z/ may take different forms depending on the phonological form of the stem. We say that there are three different **allomorphs**. That is, the plural may take the form [-ɪz], [-s] or [-z], depending upon the phonological context in which it appears. In this particular case, the choice for an allomorph depends on the final phoneme of the stem it attaches to. The form of the plural allomorph is [ɪz] if the final consonant is a sibilant (14).

(14) moose   mooses   [ɪz]
    bus   buses   [ɪz]
    bush   bushes   [ɪz]
    witch   witches   [ɪz]

If the stem ends in a (non-sibilant) voiceless obstruent, the plural allomorph is [s] as in (15a); if it ends in any other phoneme, the allomorph is [z] as in (15b–d):

(15) a. cat   cats   [s]
      step   steps   [s]

    b. dog   dogs   [z]
      band   bands   [z]

    c. girl   girls   [z]
      boy   boys   [z]

    d. bee   bees   [z]
      flower   flowers   [z]

So we may say that the three allomorphs are in fact just one and the same morpheme at a more abstract level. But that is only part of the story.

First, note that with respect to this allomorphy there are some exceptions. For example, the plural of the word *life*, despite the stem-final voiceless fricative [f], is *lives* [laɪvz], in which we, unexpectedly, find the allomorph [z], but at the same time, we observe voicing of the final stem consonant (f → v). The same thing happens in *bath–baths* and also in *house* [s] – *houses* [zɪz]. As Halle and Marantz (1993: 131) point out, these are cases of 'double marking'. The plurality of these nouns is expressed not only by the plural affix, but also by a phonological change in the stem.

Second, apart from the large majority of nouns in which the plural is expressed by one of the allomorphs discussed so far, there are also several irregular cases. The plural forms of these are expressed by either a different allomorph as in (16a), or by no affix at all as in (16b). In the latter cases, plurality sometimes goes hand in hand with a change of the stem vowel as in (16c):

(16) a. ox   oxen
      child   children

    b. fish   fish
      sheep   sheep

    c. goose   geese
      foot   feet

Furthermore, there are still a few other possibilities for making a plural noun in English. These forms originate in other languages but have been 'borrowed' with their original way of making the plural. Some examples are in (17):

(17) alumnus   alumni
      symposium   symposia
      thesis   theses

Admittedly, these latter cases have a highly 'learned' or 'academic' character, but they serve to illustrate the point that the same notion [plural] may be expressed by different affixes.

A rather simplistic way to analyse the whole range of different plural forms would be to say that there are several different affixes in the lexicon that are exactly synonymous: they all carry the feature [number: plural]. However, that poses some difficulties. First, note that the usual meaning of synonymy implies that forms can be freely exchanged. Clearly, that is not the case here. So, despite the fact that the different affixes have exactly the same meaning, only one affix can be chosen given a particular stem. In this view, the lexicon will contain the representations in (18):

(18) a. -en   [number: plural] in {child, ox, . . . }
      b. -Ø   [number: plural] in {fish, sheep, . . . }
      c. - i   [number: plural] in {alumn, temp, . . . }
      d. - a   [number: plural] in {symposi, bacteri, . . . }
      e. -iz   [number: plural] / [sibilant] _____
      f. -s   [number: plural] / [voiceless obstruent] _____
      g. -z   [number: plural] / ?

The affixes all share exactly the same morphosyntactic characterisation, i.e. [number: plural], and furthermore, they contain information about the stems they may be combined with.

However, this idea also immediately runs into trouble. To begin with, there is no obvious way to characterise the environment in which the allomorph -z in (18g) applies. It is the typical 'elsewhere' case: if none of the allomorphs (18a–f) attaches, the allomorph -z steps in. But such a formulation is only possible if we can order the affixes in (18) with respect to each other. However, such ordering is not in accordance with our assumption that the different plural allomorphs are independent affixes in the lexicon. Furthermore, this idea of independent affixes cannot explain the complementary distribution of the different allomorphs: the environments in which the affixes may attach do not overlap, nor do they leave any gaps. If the allomorphs indeed were independent affixes, this would be a fortuitous circumstance that would receive no explanation. As a third objection to the analysis in terms of independent affixes, it is necessary to point out that if that were the case it would also be purely coincidental that the affixes are completely synonymous. Why would there be five affixes with exactly the same meaning that cannot be exchanged with one another but have made a strict division among the stems to which they attach? Clearly, we must put the idea of independent affixes in this case aside. We need some other, deeper explanation as to the plural allomorphy in English.

To this, we turn to a variant of the idea of an underlying representation. Phonology is not the only possible level at which different allomorphs may have a single representation. Suppose that one separates morphological processes (such as 'pluralisation') from the specific phonological realisation. Rather than assuming that there are seven different affixes (18) that nicely divide the lexicon, assume that there is a single morphological process – call it pluralisation – that can be realised by (at least) seven different affixes. This idea is also known as the Separation Hypothesis (Beard 1995) (see also Chapter 1). Under that hypothesis morphological processes are not identical to the different affixes that we observe, but these affixes are merely the spell-out or realisation of more abstract processes that do the actual morphology. The rules in (18) can then be viewed as the rules that spell out the abstract pluralisation operation.

(19) a. insert -en in [number: plural] / {child, ox, . . . }_____
     b. insert -Ø in [number: plural] / {fish, sheep, . . . }_____
     c. insert – i in [number: plural] / {alumn, temp, . . . }_____
     d. insert - a in [number: plural] / {symposi, bacteri, . . . } _____
     e. insert -iz in [number: plural] / [sibilant] _____
     f. insert -s in [number: plural] / [voiceless obstruent] _____
     g. insert -z in [number: plural] / _____

It is easy to see how this view answers the problems that we face under the assumption that each plural affix is a separate entry in the lexicon. The complementary distribution of the affixes can now be understood; there is just a single pluralisation operation and the spell-out rules guarantee that each stem may receive one and only one of the set of allomorphs. Every noun can be subject to pluralisation – apart from the semantic restriction that we mentioned above – and the spell-out rules in (19) determine in which environment which allomorph should be chosen. Furthermore, the fact that the affixes are fully synonymous is also explained: the affixes themselves are not the locus for the semantic interpretation. It is the abstract morphological operation that carries the

meaning 'plural'. The affixes themselves are mere meaningless phonological strings inserted under specific morphological and phonological
conditions, made explicit in the spell-out rules.

This leaves open the issue of the 'elsewhere' case. First, consider
rules (19a) and (19e). The second rule is blocked as soon as the first
rule is applicable. If we do not stipulate that ordering, rule (19e)
could apply in a form like *ox* with the unwelcome result *oxes. By
stipulating that (19a) applies before (19e), and that the latter does
not apply as soon as the former applies, we prevent this result. This
specific rule-ordering is known as **disjunctive rule-ordering** (also
see Chapter 1). It rests on one of the oldest insights in the workings
of a grammar and dates back to the fourth-century BCE grammarian
Panini. The insight is that the most specific rule applies first, and only
if it is not applicable (because its structural description is not met)
does a less specific rule apply. This rule may in turn block the application of a following rule with a yet more general structural description, until we reach a point where the elsewhere rule applies. This
is the 'catch-all' statement at the end, which guarantees that every
possible environment receives an output. This type of rule-ordering
is therefore also commonly known as the **Elsewhere Condition** (cf.
Kiparsky 1973, 1982).

This concept in which a more specific form 'goes before' a more
general form is also known under the name 'blocking'. The more specific form, e.g. *symposia*, blocks the more general form, e.g. *symposiums*.
We will come across another example of blocking in the next section.

3.3.2 Adjectival inflection

As we have seen above, English does not have the adjectival inflection
we encounter in German or Dutch where the form of the attributive
adjective partly depends on the gender and number of the noun it modifies and on the definiteness of the determiner phrase it is part of. Nor
does English show the adjectival inflection we encounter in Romance
languages in which a predicative adjective is inflected for gender and
number. Compare the examples from Dutch in (20) and French in (21)
with the English glosses: English adjectives only come in a single form.

(20) Dutch:

een	aardig-e	jongen	[non-neuter; singular; indefinite]
a	nice	boy	
een	aardig-Ø	meisje	[neuter; singular; indefinite]
a	nice	girl	

(21) French:

L' étudiant	était	très	beau	[masc.; sing.]
the student-masc.	was	very	beautiful	
L' étudiante	était	très	belle	[fem.; sing.]
the student-fem.	was	very	beautiful	

Apart from this clear lack of adjectival inflection, there is another morphological process operating on adjectives that might be considered inflectional. Some examples are in (22):

(22) a. The *big* car is in front of the house.
  b. The *bigger* car is next to it.
  c. The *biggest* car is yours.

The adjective in (22b) is called the comparative form and the one in (22c) is the superlative. The process is productive: many adjectives have a comparative and a superlative form, the only restriction being that the adjective must be gradable. In a variety of cases the semantics of the adjective is non-gradable, and these do not allow the comparative and/or superlative. Some examples are given in (23):

(23) a. This is the former president of our company, but the president before that one is the *formerer.
  b. This is a Roman coin, but that one is even *more Roman.

Now note that the formation of the comparative with the -er suffix and the superlative with -est in English is subject to a particular, and well-known, phonological condition: only those adjectives that have one and no more than one syllable (apart from those ending in -le, -er, -ow, -y and -some) can be affixed in this way. So, *big–bigger* is fine, but *intelligent–*intelligenter* is not. Stems such as *happy* and *brittle* have endings such that they also allow for the comparative -er. The reason why exactly those stems allow for the comparative in -er need not concern us here. What about those adjectives that do not allow a comparative in -er? Is it altogether impossible to make comparative forms of these stems? It most certainly is possible, but these comparatives are **periphrastic** forms. That is, they do not consist, as the **analytic** forms do, in a single word, but they are syntactically complex. See the examples in (24):

(24) a. intelligent b. more intelligent c. most intelligent

Here we witness another blocking relation. We may say that the forms *bigger* and *biggest* are the special forms: they block the formation of the more general cases *more big and *most big.

3.3.3 Verbal inflection

As we have said above, English inflection is almost non-existent as compared to the inflectional systems of many other languages in the world. To give just an idea: in a language such as Finnish, any native speaker may have hundreds of inflectional forms of a verb at his or her disposal, but even in other Indo-European languages, such as Bulgarian or Latin, verbal inflectional paradigms can be substantially larger than in English. Often a distinction is made between what are called 'agglutinating' languages and 'fusional' languages. In an agglutinating language each and every inflectional affix adds, or realises, a particular morphosyntactic feature, whereas in fusional languages more than one morphosyntactic feature is 'fused' in a single inflectional affix. To see this, compare the Turkish nominal inflectional paradigm in (25a) to the Latin inflectional paradigm in (25b):

(25)   a. Turkish: b. Latin:

	Sing.	Plur.	Sing.	Plur.
Nom.	ev	ev-ler	mens-a	mens-ae
Gen.	ev-in	ev-ler-in	mens-ae	mens-arum
Dat.	ev-e	ev-ler-e	mens-ae	mens-is
Acc.	ev-i	ev-ler-i	mens-am	mens-as
Abl.	ev-den	ev-ler-den	mens-a	mens-is

The Turkish plural paradigm is clearly the combination of the realisation of the number feature (by the affix *-ler*) and the realisation of a morphosyntactic case-feature (*-Ø*, *-in,-e,-i* and *-den* respectively). The equation in (26) holds for this paradigm:

(26) Plural case form of a stem = Stem + Plural-affix + Case-affix.

However, in Latin we see that a particular plural case form does not equal the singular form of that particular case plus some identifiable plural affix. Rather, case and number are fused in Latin, giving rise to different endings for each number/case combination.

English has no case, and therefore the issue of whether English is fusional or agglutinative does not arise in nominal inflection. However, it does play a role in verbal inflection, as we will see shortly.

Let us start by giving a list of forms that an English regular verb such as WORK can take:

(27) a. work
      b. work-s
      c. work-ed
      d. work-ing

Not very impressive, is it? Given the fact that, as we already remarked above, a Finnish native speaker may give you hundreds of different forms for one verb, four is a rather disappointing figure. However, this figure underestimates somewhat the real complexity, since a highly irregular verb such as BE shows eight different forms:

(28) a. am
 b. is
 c. are
 d. was
 e. were
 f. be
 g. been
 h. being

Now we may wonder why some verbs have only four different forms, whereas another may have eight. Relating these two lists of forms can be made more insightful if we consider the morphosyntactic categories that play a role in English verbal inflection. These categories are by no means pre-given, but we need to find empirical evidence that may tell us what categories play a role.

First, it will be quite clear that the morphosyntactic category [person] somehow plays a role in the verbal system. In regular verbs, the third person has a different form from the first and second persons. These latter two have the same form in regular verbs (27), but in the case of the verb BE, three different forms appear: I *am*, you *are*, he *is*. That simple observation tells us that English has three different values for the morphosyntactic category [person]; without these three different values we would not be able to distinguish these forms of the verb TO BE. This implies that in regular verbs, the same form (27a) is used for two different morphosyntactic feature values.

Second, [number] plays a role, as can be seen from the third person singular (which requires the suffix -*s*). In the plural, however, [person] features do not seem to play a role at all: there is only a single plural form.

Third, it doesn't take a grammatical wizard to conclude that the morphosyntactic category [tense] plays a role. Verb-forms in English have a different form in the past tense from that in the present tense. But we can see that in almost all verbs neither [person] nor [number] plays a role in the past tense: there is only a single past tense form.

Before we further complicate things, it may be helpful to think of inflectional forms as ordered in a multidimensional space of which the dimensions are defined by the morphosyntactic categories. The

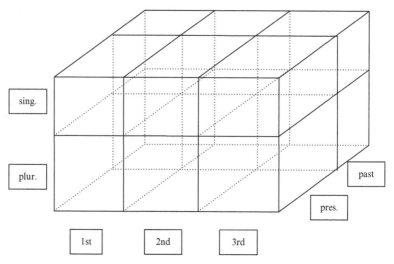

Figure 3.1 English inflection as a three-dimensional space

different feature values that such a category can take further split up each dimension into several 'cells' that may each contain one and only one inflectional form (see Figure 3.1).

The multidimensional space in Figure 3.1 is a way to represent the paradigm of the English verb. The paradigm contains 3 * 2 * 2 = 12 cells. However, as we have seen above, no verb of English actually has twelve different verb-forms. This implies that in many cases a single form fills more than one cell. Or we could say that the cells are merged. If a single form is used in more than one cell, this is called a **syncretism**. In the English verbal paradigm many such syncretisms occur. For example, in all verbs except TO BE, first and second persons singular in the present tense are syncretic. In the past tense, no distinction is made between either person or number, again with TO BE as the only exception. And, as we have already seen, in the plural, person does not make any difference.

There are a few verbal morphosyntactic categories that do not fit in the structure in Figure 3.1. Put differently, if we would like to represent the complete paradigm of the English verb, a little more is necessary than this three-dimensional structure. English verbs are also sensitive to the category [mood]. Mood can have the value indicative (that is, the mood used in ordinary declarative sentences), and it can also have the value imperative (which we encounter in orders and commands). Consider the examples in (29):

(29) a. You *are* silent.
      b. *Be* silent.

The form of the verb *to be* in (29a) is an indicative; the form in (29b) is an imperative, which happens to be syncretic with the infinitive, yet another morphosyntactic category that is not part of Figure 3.1.

Going briefly back to the question of whether English verbal inflection is fusional (as in Latin) or agglutinative (as in Turkish), one might want to say that English is fusional since there are no cases of stacking of person and number affixes, or person and tense affixes. On the other hand, the whole paradigm is so meagre that it is also difficult to argue that English verbal inflection is fusional: there is only a single affix in the past tense, and there is only a single affix in the present tense to mark (third) person. That is a very small basis on which to argue for a fused tense and person. We will come back to this issue in Section 3.4.

There is one more empirical issue we need to address here. Generalising somewhat, we may say that English verbs fall into two separate classes: the regular verbs and the irregular verbs. Clearly, the verb BE belongs to the (highly) irregular ones, whereas WORK is an example of a regular verb. But apart from BE English has many more irregular verbs that are characterised by the fact that they do not take the affix -*ed* either in the past tense or in the past participle. They exhibit deviant past tense forms, which are sometimes identical to the past participle. Depending on this form, we may distinguish between separate subclasses of irregular verbs.

Below we have listed several types of irregular verbs and their past tense and past participle forms:

(30) | Present | Past | Participle |
| --- | --- | --- |
| hit | hit | hit |
| keep | kept | kept |
| sing | sang | sung |
| draw | drew | drawn |
| bring | brought | brought |
| write | wrote | written |

In principle there are two different ways in which we can derive these irregular forms. One is simply by storing the forms, as unanalysable wholes, with the appropriate lexeme. The picture of the derivation of the past tense forms of English verbs would then be as follows. Regular forms are derived by a rule that adds a suffix -*ed* to the stem of the verb. This rule is blocked, however, by the more specific verb-forms stored in the lexicon with a past tense feature. So a form such as **hitted* could not arise since the stored form *hit* [+past] would block the past tense rule.

Another way is to assume that the irregular verbs are also derived through rules. It may seem odd to assume rules for the irregular cases. The rules often have only a very limited domain of application, indicated by the listing of verbs to which the rules apply (the verbs that have similar past tense forms). However, there is a price to pay for the 'storage' account that is not immediately apparent from our exposition so far. Note that a 'storage' account in principle could also 'derive' past tense forms that are completely deviant from their co-lexemic stem. That is, there is no explanation in this account for the fact that the past tense forms do not differ wildly from the base-forms, but share most of the phonemic content of these stems. Furthermore, the 'storage' account also has no insight to offer as to the different classes of irregular verbs. It is clear that among the irregular verbs certain patterns can be observed in the past tense forms and the forms of the participles. To mention just some of these patterns: some verbs only display a change in the stem vowel, which is copied in the past participle (*fling–flung–flung*, likewise *bind*); some verbs display a vowel-change in the past tense and yet another vowel-change in the past participle (*drink–drank–drunk*; likewise *sing, ring,* etc.); there are verbs with vowel shortening and a suffix *-t* (*keep–kept–kept*, likewise *creep, leap, sleep, weep,* etc.); yet others have identical forms in present, past and past participle (*hit–hit–hit*, likewise *cut, hurt, let, put,* etc.). Third, the storage account also has no story to tell as to the fact that these patterns are not randomly distributed over the irregular verbs, but that verbs that have a similar phonemic make-up tend to have a similar pattern of past tense and participle forms. In other words, there is a lot of regularity or patterning in the irregular verbs that goes unnoticed in a pure 'storage' account.

The rule account offers a clear explanation for the fact that in most cases the past tense forms and participles do not differ too much from their stem forms; a rule may change a particular vowel feature, may add a suffix (such as *-t*), but cannot replace the whole stem by a completely different stem (as in *was* or *went*). A rule always leaves the non-focus part unchanged. Furthermore, it may also explain why certain patterns recur. There is a limited set of rules and verbs may undergo one or more rules, thus leading to subclasses and subsubclasses. However, it also seems beyond the rules to account for the fact that similar stem-forms in terms of their phonemic make-up tend to undergo the same rules. For example, even in the rule account there is no explanation for the fact that verbs ending in *-ing* are particularly prone to the pattern *-ang, -ung*.

The proper treatment of the morphology of the English past tense has given rise to a long and wide-ranging discussion among cognitive scientists from different strands of research. We will come back to this discussion and the issues briefly touched upon above in Chapter 6.

3.4 The problem of underdetermination

There is a great variety of theories on morphological inflection that result from an ongoing theoretical discussion about the proper treatment of inflectional phenomena. In order to give some insight into this complex debate, we will organise our presentation around two central questions. Both questions have a long history in the field, which we are unable to sketch in just a few paragraphs; rather we will try to present the issues in such a way that, after having read this chapter, one can fruitfully read current contributions to this field of inquiry. The first question is whether inflectional morphology should be dealt with in the lexicon or in the syntax. The second, to which we will turn in Section 3.5, concerns the question of whether inflectional morphology always involves affixation, or whether other operations are also possible instances of inflection.

The model of the grammar that is generally accepted by generative grammarians can be depicted as follows:

(31)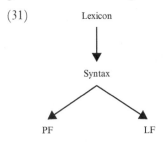

The lexicon contains the basic elements for the construction of sentences. These are put together in a syntactic structure by syntax. This structure is in turn interpreted semantically (at LF, logical form), and phonologically (at PF, phonological form). Given this model we may ask: 'Where's morphology?' This is the exact title of a paper by Stephen Anderson published in 1982. Different answers have been given by morphologists over the last decades. Some locate morphology 'in the lexicon', whereas others claim that there is no strict division between morphology and syntax. Yet others make a distinction between derivational morphology and inflectional morphology and claim that derivational morphology is 'in the lexicon', whereas inflectional morphology is 'in the syntax'.

What kind of arguments have been put forth to claim that inflectional morphology is lexical, or just the opposite, that it is syntactic? If we assume that there is a division of labour in the grammar between morphology (building words) and syntax (building phrases), it is clear that there must be a point where the two meet. A common and well-respected theory is that words enter the syntax as atoms and no syntactic operations may refer to any of the parts of the words, since for the syntax, there are no parts 'visible'. This idea is known as the **Lexicalist Hypothesis** (Chomsky 1972). It puts strong limits on the way that morphology and syntax may interact. To give an example, the Lexicalist Hypothesis directly explains why we cannot have a *wh-* word referring to a part of a word. Consider the following examples (Williams 2007: 354):

(32) a. How complete are your results?
      b. *How completeness do you admire?
      c. [how complete]-ness do you admire?
      d. What degree of completeness do you admire?
      e. How complete a record do you admire?

The crucial fact is the ungrammaticality of (32b). The examples in (32d and e) show that from a semantic point of view it is perfectly possible to ask such a question. There are no semantic (or pragmatic) reasons that rule out (32b). The real reason for its ungrammaticality is that syntax cannot address the part *complete* because this part is encapsulated in the word *completeness*. The syntactic rule that is needed to make the question cannot look into this word, or any other word for that matter.

A way to derive the Lexicalist Hypothesis from the organisation of the grammar as depicted in (31) is to assume that the insertion of lexical material only takes place after the syntax has done all of its work. This is known as **the Late Insertion Hypothesis**. The idea is that the syntax first builds structures, and only after all syntactic operations have taken place does a special operation, called 'lexical insertion', take place that inserts lexical material (words) into the end nodes of the syntactic structure. In this way the atomicity of words for syntactic operations does not need to be stipulated somehow, but follows from the fact that words are simply not part of the structure at the time syntactic operations do their work.

Despite this atomicity of words for syntactic operations, it is clear that the syntax sometimes does also need information about the properties of a word. To begin with, the syntax needs to know the word-class or category of words in order to construct larger phrases. Furthermore, in cases of agreement, in which for example a verb agrees with its subject in person and number, the syntax needs to know what the person and number features of the subject are, and this information needs to be copied or transferred somehow to the verb. Given the Lexicalist Hypothesis, we could argue that the point where morphology meets syntax is in the top node of the word. We have seen that words have a hierarchical structure. So we may represent a word such as *equality* as in (33):

(33)

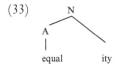

The top node contains the information that we are dealing with a (singular) noun, and that suffices for the purposes of syntax. According to the Lexicalist Hypothesis, the structure below this N is simply invisible for syntax. Whatever the structure of the material below this N-node, the N will be treated the same by syntax. The N-node corresponds to what syntacticians may call the X^0, the lowest level in X-bar theory, basically the level of words. The X^0-level is then the level where syntax meets morphology.

If we are dealing with inflection, as in the agreement example above, more information than just the category of the word needs to be made visible for syntax. Consider the structure of the inflected verb *works*:

(34)

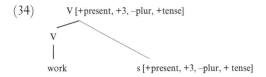

Under the Lexicalist Hypothesis, the structure in (34) is built in the lexicon and can be inserted as such in the syntax. The idea is that the affix -*s* carries the information [+present, +3, −plur, +tense]. Since the -*s* is the head of the word according to the right-hand head rule, this information percolates to the top node of the word, and can be read off in that position by the syntax. The syntax will make sure that the person and number features of the subject actually match the features of the verb. If not, the sentence is ill-formed; otherwise, it will be fine, at least as far as agreement is concerned.

It has been argued that this picture is too simple and cannot account for essential properties of inflectional morphology. One of these properties is that morphology underdetermines inflectional information. We have seen above that the form *worked* in English may be used in the past tense in all persons, including the plural. If we were to make a representation of this form analogous to the one of the form *works* in (34), how should we go about it? The form does not seem to contain any information as to number or person. Therefore, the representation in (35) seems to be the most accurate from a morphological perspective.

(35)

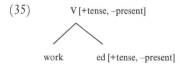

Again, the features of the affix *-ed* percolate to the top node of the verb (*-ed* being the head of the word). The problem is that at the top node, where morphology and syntax interact, there is no information on the person/number properties of this form. So how does the syntax know whether this is the correct form to agree with any particular subject? The problem seems to be that the morphological structure cannot be the source for the syntactic feature specifications, since the morphology underdetermines these feature specifications. The morphology is simply not 'rich enough' to provide the information needed by the syntax. Several solutions present themselves, which we will run through before we draw any conclusion.

First, one might assume that there are zero-affixes that add the missing featural information. In the case at hand, we would have to assume six different zeros for the six combinations of [1/2/3 person] and [±plural] in order to get 'complete' featural information at the top node. Of course, such a move would be totally ad hoc and the explanatory value is close to zero in this particular case. However, that conclusion does not automatically generalise to all instances of zero-affixation. It might be that such an analytic move is necessary and helpful in particular cases.

Second, and in our view somewhat more promising, is to assume that the syntax does not get any information as to the person/number features of this form (since it does not contain this information). Maybe we do not need fully specified feature matrices in the syntax. We would have to assume that agreement works in such a way that a particular feature-set 'agrees' with another feature-set if and only if there are no conflicting feature values between the two sets. Since the past tense form does not have any person/number features, it simply 'agrees' with any subject. However, this strategy may fail in some cases. Take, for example, English nouns. English singular nouns have no affix that provides the feature [−plural]. If we simply leave the nouns unmarked for number, then in cases of subject–verb agreement there is no way to decide what verb-form to choose. Put differently, we would predict that it would be fine to have a singular third person subject (such as the noun *car*) agreeing with a plural verb-form.

Third, it has been proposed that there are 'default' rules that fill in the 'unmarked' values of morphosyntactic features. Such rules would add featural information to those matrices that are incomplete. For example, one could argue that English nouns receive a feature [number: singular] 'by default' if there is no morphology that says differently. Such a rule guarantees that in the absence of a plural suffix, nouns are singular.

These solutions to the problem of underdetermination may in different circumstances be more or less successful in describing the relevant data, but some researchers have concluded from this property of underdetermination that a more radical change in perspective on inflection is needed. In their view, underdetermination tells us that a theory deriving the properties of complex words by 'adding up' the features of each individual morpheme cannot be right. These morphologists argue that morphology only 'spells out' or 'realises' the features that are borne by the syntax. In a way they turn the picture that we have used so far upside down. Rather than words being the source for the features at the X^0-level, it is the syntax that offers the feature-specifications of these top nodes, and the morphology only needs to find the correct form that 'realises' these features. So, for example, in the case of agreement, it is the syntactic module of the grammar that ensures that at the X^0-level there is a complete feature-set. The only thing that the morphology needs to do is to find the right form that matches these features as well as possible.

These theories are often identified with the Late Insertion Hypothesis: first the syntax builds the structure and provides the correct feature-matrices and only after that does the morphology come into play and provides the syntactic end nodes with phonological material. It seems clear that under such a view, and given the model of the grammar in (31), inflectional morphology cannot be 'in the lexicon', since it should be operating 'after syntax' that needs to provide the feature-bundles that morphology spells out. So we should then amend the picture in (31), and inflectional morphology would sit somewhere on the way to phonetic interpretation.

Underdetermination may not be the only argument for a realisational theory of morphology. Depending on one's syntactic theory, there may be mismatches between the morphological form that inflection takes in a particular language and the syntactic structure that it is assumed to have. As an example, let us go back to the difference between Turkish and Latin as exemplified in (25). In Latin the realisation of [case] and [number] is done by one and the same affix, whereas in Turkish these different morphosyntactic categories are nicely kept apart and spelled out by different sets of affixes. Now, one may want to argue that this difference between Turkish and Latin in is not so much a syntactic as a morphological difference. It seems that Turkish is the 'simpler' case in the sense that what is syntactically different is also morphologically different. That is, there is a one-to-one correspondence between syntax and morphology. In Latin, however, the syntactic nodes that are different by hypothesis ([case] and [number]) are morphologically one. In late insertion models, we can now say that Latin has a morphological rule of fusion that merges the [number] and [case] node into one and the same morphosyntactic node, which is then realised by a set of affixes. Turkish simply lacks such a fusion rule and the two separate syntactic nodes are spelled out by different sets of affixes.

There is one more property of realisational models that we need to address, and that involves the way spell-out of morphosyntactic feature bundles is organised. Recall from Section 3.3.1 that in discussing plural nouns we assumed there is a single morphological process 'pluralisation' that is realised by different affixes. In a realisational model of morphology we may assume that the syntax is responsible for a separate node that contains the feature [number: plural]. Different affixes will be in competition for the realisation of that particular node. Furthermore, the competition is decided by the Elsewhere Condition, which states that the most specific affix matching the structural description goes first, and if that does not match the next most specific comes into play, etc. until, if all special forms are discarded, a 'default' affix steps in.

Summarising thus far, we have seen that lexical models of inflectional morphology face the problem of underdetermination. This is an important reason (among others) for proposing realisational models of morphology. These realisational models leave the specification of the featural content of a particular inflectional form to syntax, and the morphology merely 'realises' or 'spells out' this particular feature-set. Affixes are in competition for the realisation of the morphosyntactic nodes. This competition is decided by the Elsewhere Condition.

Edwin Williams, in a series of papers and books (Williams 1981, 2007, DiSciullo and Williams 1987), has argued that it is not necessary to give up a lexical view on inflection given the underdetermination problem. We will explain his view in somewhat more detail below. In the course of this exposition, we will see that the notions 'lexicon' and 'lexical' have different meanings, which, according to Williams, has caused some confusion in the literature.

As we have seen above, the verbal paradigm of English has many syncretisms. Such syncretisms can be found in almost any inflectional system of any language. Williams' (1981) theory deals with these syncretisms in the following way. Williams assumes that the morpho-syntactic features, such as [±tense], [±present], [±plural] and [1/2/3 person], define a matrix. This matrix is defined by ordering the features as follows: tense > present > plural > person. The figure in (36) is a representation of the matrix (Williams 1981: 267):

(36)

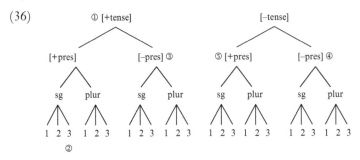

Williams assumes that there are five 'entry points', indicated by the numbers in circles in (36). Any terminal in the tree, i.e. any syntactic category, is realised by the entry point that dominates it. So the syntactic category that consists of the features [+tense, +pres., 1pers., sg] ('first person singular') is translated into the morphological subcategory ①, since that is the first so-called 'entry point' sitting above that particular syntactic category. The entry point corresponds to a particular morphological form. In the case at hand it is realised as the stem of the verb without any inflectional marking.

There are several points in this analysis that we would like to draw your attention to. First, Williams' theory is a lexical theory of inflection. It is lexical in the sense that the actual morphological forms are produced without any recourse to the syntactic structure. The matrix in (36) mediates between the syntactic structure, which yields complete feature-sets, and the morphological structure, which lumps together many syntactic distinctions under a single morphological category. Underdetermination is explained by this lumping.

Second, this theoretical idea makes clear that the essence of the problem of underdetermination is not the ordering of the lexicon before the syntax, but lies in the assumed incremental nature of inflectional morphology. According to Williams, it is wrong to assume that each inflectional affix contributes a (sub)set of inflectional features that percolate to the top node. It does not necessarily follow, as Williams shows us, that this 'feature-delivering' system is syntax itself. This system can also be located in the word-formation component.

It is important to see that in Williams' view the lexicon is a module of the grammar on a par with 'syntax'. That is, the lexicon may contain rules that actually construct forms, i.e. words. Syntax builds phrases, whereas words are built in the lexicon. Williams points out that this function of the lexicon is completely different from the lexicon as a warehouse in which all kinds of irregularities are stored. An expression one often finds in the literature is that a particular property of a word is 'lexical', meaning that that particular property should be stored in the lexicon since it cannot be predicted of that form. For example, as we have seen in Chapter 2, words have a lot of unpredictable properties, which should all be stored in the lexicon. These are often called the words' lexical properties. 'Lexical' in this sense thus means 'lawless', 'irregular' or 'unpredictable'. This sense of the notion 'lexical' is completely different from the notion 'lexicon' as the module of the grammar where words are constructed. Williams points out that there is a priori no reason to identify these two notions. Put differently, there is no reason to assume that words and only words have idiosyncratic properties. Phrases such as *kick the bucket, tear a strip off somebody* and *fly by the seat of your pants* also all have a clear idiosyncratic meaning, and should thus be stored. The only reason that in general more words than phrases have idiosyncratic properties may result from the fact that phrases are 'bigger'. Since they are bigger, they will be less frequently used, and that may turn out to be an important factor in being able to have idiosyncratic properties.

3.5 Pieces or rules?

In Section 3.4 we have seen that different answers to the place of morphology, and inflectional morphology in particular, lead to different theories of morphology. A second question concerning inflectional morphology that has received different answers in the literature and partly determines the landscape of morphological theories is whether morphology is piece-based, or whether other rules may play a role that spell out inflectional properties.

As we have seen in many examples above, a particular inflectional feature may be spelled out by an affix. Think of -*ed* as spelling out the feature 'past tense'. Although undoubtedly affixation is the most common way for languages to spell out inflectional properties, affixes do not seem to be the only possible exponents. Take, for example, the past tense of the verb *to sing*. The form *sang* does not seem to have an affix; instead, the past tense is expressed by the change of vowel from [ɪ] to [æ]. This seems to be a clear indication that affixation is not the only means for inflectional exponence. Apparently, processes other than the attachment of an affix can also mark an inflectional change.

Anderson's 'a-morphous morphology' is a realisational theory of inflectional morphology that claims that inflectional changes can be brought about by just any phonological change to the stem. According to this theory, there are no morphemes, or building blocks that construct the inflectional forms, but the morphosyntactic representation is realised by a set of disjunctively ordered rules that spell out the inflectional features.

Others have argued that although it may appear that processes other than affixation may realise inflectional features, appearances are misleading in this case. In order to understand that particular reasoning properly, we need to make a little detour to languages with morphological patterns that seem to be completely deviant from what we see in English. Consider the following forms from Arabic (data come from McCarthy 1981: 374):

(37) a. kataba   'he wrote'
    b. kattaba   'he caused to write'
    c. kaataba   'he corresponded'
    d. ktataba   'he wrote, copied'
    e. kitaabun   'book' (nom.)

The forms in (37) all share a core meaning 'write'. In form they share the consonants /ktb/, known in Semitic languages as the consonantal root. We can safely assume that the meaning 'write' is associated with this consonantal root. As one can see from this example, in Semitic languages morphological changes are not (only) brought about by affixation, but rather, patterns of vowels are 'woven' into the consonantal root and each of these patterns corresponds to a different morphological operation on the root. At first sight these patterns of vowels and consonantal roots seem completely different from our ordinary affixational patterns in which a stem receives a suffix or a prefix. However, McCarthy (1981) analyses these patterns by means of a technique known from autosegmental phonology that reduces this pattern to the ordinary stuff that is so familiar to native speakers of English.

The idea is that the consonantal root and the vowel pattern are represented separately in different planes. These planes share a core axis, or tier, that consists in a consonant–vowel pattern. Basically, and without going into any details, the rules of autosegmental phonology tell you which element from the different planes is linked to which element on the central tier. The representation in (38) makes this idea visible:

(38)

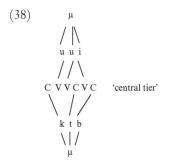

'central tier'

With this idea in mind, let us go back to English pairs such as *sing–sang*. One could assume that the vowel-change in this particular case is made in more or less the same way as it is in Arabic. To see this, we assume that there is an autosegmental element (for example, the combined phonological features [+back, +low]) that can be linked to the stem vowel of the verb, more or less as in (39):

(39)

$$\mu$$
$$|$$
$$[+\text{back}, +\text{low}]$$
$$|$$
$$\text{s V ng}$$

We could then assume that the element consisting of the features [+back, +low] is an affix (indicated by μ). This seems to imply that we may reduce all phonological changes that we may observe to affixation.

In Section 3.3 we briefly discussed cases of 'double marking'. We give some examples in (40).

(40) a. bath   baths
        life   lives
        wife   wives

     b. keep   kep-t
        weep   wep-t
        deal   deal-t

Apart from the standard plural suffix -*z*, the nouns in (40a) also exhibit voicing of the stem-final consonant. Similarly, the past tenses of the irregular verbs in (40b) display a change in stem vowel, just as we have seen in *sing–sang*, but on top of it, we also see the attachment of a suffix -*t*. In both cases a single morphological change, pluralisation or the formation of the past tense, is marked by two different changes to the stem. Note in passing that in an 'incremental' theory in which each morphological change adds (or changes for that matter) a morphosyntactic feature of the form it applies to, double markings pose an immediate problem, since it is unclear in such a theory how a second or double marking would arise. Why make some further changes to a stem if the affix that is attached provides all the inflectional information needed?

Given these double markings, a problem also arises in a 'realisational' theory of morphology. A crucial element in these theories is that the insertion of affixes is organised by competition in which the most specific affix that is compatible with the features of the morphosyntactic node wins. It will be clear that such an organisation predicts that forms are never 'doubly marked' because that would require a competition in which two rules apply at the same time. This ruins the idea of competition.

In order to circumvent these problems, some morphologists have argued that we should make a distinction between primary exponence and secondary exponence. The idea is that during spell-out, features that are part of the morphosyntactic representation of a form are 'discharged'. So, once spelled out, the feature is no longer visible or available at the level of morphosyntactic representation. This conception of discharge excludes double markings in a principled way: there is simply no way a double marking can arise. The first affix that spells out the morphosyntactic feature will make any further potential spell-outs impossible since it removes the trigger for the application of any further spell-out rules. The affix that is responsible for this discharge is called the **primary exponent**. Applying this idea to the examples in (40), we get the following picture.

Apparently, -z is the affix that realises – that is, 'discharges' – the feature [+plural] from the morphosyntactic representation. It is the primary exponent of plurality. Similarly, the affix -t in *kept* and *dealt* is the primary exponent of [+past]. That implies that the other changes to the stem in these forms result from a different type of rule altogether; it cannot be a case of spell-out in this particular theory. In addition to discharge of features, morphology apparently also hosts a number of rules that may make changes to the stem under specific circumstances. These are the rules that bring about secondary exponences. These rules are often called **readjustment rules**.

In order to exemplify this idea, let us take a look at the analysis of irregular verbs in English by Halle and Marantz (1993), who argue for a 'realisational' theory of morphology. In the first step of the analysis (the rules in (41)), the primary exponents are being inserted. That is, a morphosyntactic node *I*, which results from the fusion of the syntactic nodes *Tns* (Tense) and *Agr* (Agreement), is spelled out by the following rules (Halle and Marantz 1993: 126):

(41) $I =$

[+participle, +past]   ↔   /-n/   / X + _____

                                           where X = *hew, go, beat,...*

[+past]   ↔   /-Ø/   / Y + _____

                                           where Y = *beat, drive, bind,*
                                           sing,...

[+past]   ↔   /-t/   / Z + _____

                                           where Z = *dwell, buy, send,...*

[+past]   ↔   /-d/

[+participle]   ↔   /-ing/

[3sg]   ↔   /-z/

                         ↔   /Ø/

These rules are disjunctively ordered, showing again the competition between affixes for the spell-out of inflectional features. This ordering guarantees among other things that the form *drived* as a past tense form of the verb *drive* is blocked, since *drive* undergoes an earlier rule that adds a zero-affix as a spell-out of the past tense feature, thus blocking the regular or default rule that inserts -*ed*. The form *drove* only arises after the application of a second type of rule, the so-called readjustment rules. Below we give an example of such a readjustment rule that changes the vowel in the verb *to do* in different morphosyntactic environments (Halle and Marantz 1993: 128):

(42) a.   Rime   →   /i/   / Y _____   [+past, -participle]
                            |
                            x

      b.   Rime   →   /ʌ/   / Y _____   [+past, +participle]
                            | [-past, 3sg]
                            x
         where rime   Y = *do*

Rule (42a) applies in the past tense and accounts for the form *did* after the suffix -*d* has been inserted by one of the rules in (41). Rule (42b) accounts for the vowel-change in *done*, again after the insertion of the affix -*n* by the first rule of (41). It also accounts for the same vowel-change that occurs in *does*, so after the application of the final rule in (41).

    Looking over this analysis, we may now ask what decides that the affixes in (41) are the primary exponents in these examples rather than the change in stem-consonant (*life–live*) and stem vowel (*keep–kep*) that we may also observe in these forms. A first answer that one might be inclined to give is that the primary exponents correspond to affixation. However, given our autosegmental analysis above, such an answer is no longer possible; we can also analyse the change in consonant and vowel as a case of affixation.

Exactly the same question arises if we turn to the cases of blocking discussed in Section 3.3. There we saw that we can exclude a form such as *oxes by assuming that the rule attaching -en blocks the more general rule for adding -s. Assuming that the vowel-change in sing–sang is an exponent of the past tense, rather than a 'readjustment', we could block the attachment of the more general rule for the past tense suffix -ed. However, that reasoning would predict that we cannot have double markings, since the application of a more specific rule that accounts for one of the exponents would automatically block the application of another rule for the second exponent. Or, to put it the other way around, if we want to maintain the blocking explanation for the ill-formedness of oxes, then in the case of 'double markings' we need to be able to distinguish one as the primary exponent and the other as the secondary.

Noyer (1992) hypothesises that in order to separate primary exponents from readjustments, we should make a distinction between morpho-phonological changes that do not alter the structure but only add to the structure, and morpho-phonological operations that make changes to the structure rather than just add something. The idea would be that affixes are real objects that can carry information (such as the features that they discharge), whereas operations that override existing structure cannot be viewed as 'things' and therefore cannot carry information. Given this criterion, the plural -z and past tense -t are the right candidates for primary exponence in the examples above. Similarly, we can stick to the assumption that -en is a plural affix in oxen. However, we cannot maintain the idea that the change from [ɪ] to [æ] in sing–sang is a primary exponent of the past tense. If we wanted to stick to this hypothesis, we would need to assume that in those cases, there is a zero-affix that is the primary exponent of the past tense.

3.6 Morphomes

Aronoff (1994) points at an intriguing property of inflectional forms which can be easily explained on the basis of English verbal inflection. To start with, consider the following list of inflectional forms:

(43) Verb   Participle

    drive   driven
    be   been

leave	left
sing	sung
work	worked

As in the formation of the past tense, the formation of the participle varies per verb. But for each and every verb there is one and only one form of the participle. By far the most verbs choose the 'default' realisation of adding -*ed* to their base (as in *worked*), but in addition to that we see the affixation of -*en* or -*t*, vowel-changes, and combinations of the two. However, whatever the phonological form that the participle takes, it will be the same for the passive participle and the perfect participle. There are no English verbs that have a different phonological form in the syntactic context of (44a) and (44b).

(44) a. Owen's mother has been *killed.*
       b. Owen's mother has *killed* someone.

The question that Aronoff asks is why this particular state of affairs should hold. There is no obvious semantic or syntactic relation between the past (active) participle in (44b) and the passive participle in (44a). Put differently, if they had a different form it wouldn't surprise anyone and, in fact, in many other languages there is such a difference in form between these participles. Apparently, it is a morphological fact of English (and some other West Germanic languages; see also Blevins 2003) that these participles always have the same form. There exists a morphological form – call it 'participle' – that has neither meaning nor a unique morpho-phonological form (the form it takes differs per verb).

Furthermore, every verb has such a form. Aronoff calls this form a **morphome**, stressing the fact that it is neither syntactically, nor semantically, nor phonologically defined. The morphome only has status as a morphological form: it is a pure morphological form.

The picture then becomes as follows: a particular lexical verb can be combined with a morphome, such as 'participle'. This morphome is then realised through a set of realisation rules from which a choice is made dependent on the lexical verb. This new form can realise all those morphosyntactic functions that are associated with the morphome.

Exercises

1. Discuss whether you would consider comparative morphology (*green–greener*, *big–bigger*, etc.) a form of inflectional or derivational morphology.

2. a. It is often assumed that the ungrammaticality of such forms such as *singed, *hitted and *oxes is the result of a morphological blocking effect. Explain how the Elsewhere Condition is crucial for this explanation.

   b. Consider the past tense of the verb to hear. Why would an account that would not make a distinction between the exponence and readjustment run into trouble in explaining the form heared (without vowel-change)?

3. How can we see in (41) that English verbal inflection is fusional? What would we expect to find in the past tense if English verbal inflection were not fusional?

4. a. Show, using the schema in (36), how the second person past tense inflectional form of the verb to win is determined.

   b. What kind of problem arises for this morphological form when one assumes that morphosyntactic features originate in the stems and affixes, and percolate to the top node in a Lieber-style fashion?

5. Give the representation of the past tense of the verb fly in an autosegmental analysis.

6. Show how the past tense and past participle of the following verbs is derived in the system of Halle and Marantz: hit, fly, deal, leave. Try to formulate additional readjustment rules in case they are needed.

7. In German and Dutch the verbal infinitive is always identical to the 1st and 3rd person plural (German: laufen 'to walk', wir laufen 'we walk'; Dutch: lopen 'to walk', wij lopen 'we walk'). One may argue that this is a morphome in German and Dutch. Discuss whether that is also the case in English.

Further reading

Anderson, Steven R. (1992) *A-Morphous Morphology*, Cambridge: Cambridge University Press.

Harley, Heidi and Rolf Noyer (1999) 'State-of-the-Article: Distributed Morphology', *GLOT International* 4, pp. 3–9.

Stump, Gregory T. (2001) *Inflectional Morphology: A Theory of Paradigm Structure*, Cambridge Studies in Linguistics 93, Cambridge: Cambridge University Press.

4 Argument-structure: Nominalisation

4.1 Introduction

In this chapter we will introduce the notion of argument-structure, which has played an important role in the formulation of morphological theories from the beginning of the 1980s. Central to the notion of argument-structure is the idea that verbs (but not only verbs) assign thematic roles to their arguments. So, in a sentence such as (1):

(1)   John kills Mary

the verb *kill* assigns thematic roles to its object (*Mary*) and to its subject (*John*). It is more or less standardly assumed that verbs such as *kill* have a lexical semantic specification that includes the argument-structure of the verb, often assumed to be a list of thematic roles. Syntactically, any noun phrase should have one thematic role (and not more than one) and every thematic role should be discharged to some element in the structure. So the reason that

(2)   *John kills

is ungrammatical is because one of the thematic roles of *kill* cannot be discharged. Conversely, the reason that (3) is ungrammatical is because *Peter* does not get a thematic role (*kill* only has two roles to discharge).

(3)   *John kills Mary Peter

It has been argued that morphological derivation can be better understood if we acknowledge the fact that argument-structure is being manipulated by at least some derivational processes. The argument-structure of a base may change as a consequence of certain derivational operations. For example, consider the relation between the adjective *deep* in (4a), and the verb *deepen* in (4b).

(4) a. The river is deep.
   b. The dredging deepened the river.

The adjective *deep* functions as a predicate in (4a). It is assumed that its theta-role is assigned to the subject in such cases (Higginbotham 1985). In (4b) the verb *deepen* assigns a theta-role to its object, and in a sense this is the same role that *deep* assigns to its subject in (4a); so we need a theory to explain how, during the derivation, the argument-structure of the adjective becomes part of the argument-structure of the derived verb.

In this chapter we will investigate how morphological theories account for such changes of argument-structure during derivation. From a somewhat distant viewpoint we may distinguish two main lines of inquiry that we have also come across in former chapters. In the first approach, word-formation is theoretically isolated from syntax; it is assumed that syntax and morphology are two distinct modules of the grammar that both have the power to construct complex forms from more basic elements. The resulting constructions, roughly phrases and words, are of a different nature, however. Some of these approaches locate morphology in the lexicon, and assume that words have a special relation to the lexicon. Words in particular have idiosyncratic meanings, or have irregular phonology. In other approaches, but still assuming a difference between two different generating modules of the grammar, morphology is much more like syntax, in the sense that there is no special relation to the lexicon; the lexicon is the storehouse of simply everything, words and phrases, that is in some way special or irregular.

In the second approach, morphology is not a separate component of the grammar, but word-formation is considered to be just a part of syntax. Examples of this approach can be found in the works of Marantz (1997, 2001), Borer (2003, 2004, 2010), Harley (2005) and Arad (2003). One of the basic ideas of this approach to morphology is that there is just a single 'engine' (the term is from Marantz 1997) that constructs complex forms from more basic elements. Consequently, these theories predict that there are no principled differences between words and phrases.

Whether they assume word-formation to take place in the lexicon or in the syntax is just one way to classify theories of morphology. A second distinction is between theories that are 'endo-skeletal' or 'exo-skeletal' (the terms are from Borer 2003), or as Levin and Rappaport Hovav (2005) put it, between a 'projectionist' approach and a 'constructional' one. In the projectionist approach, the syntactic environment in which a particular item may be found is largely determined by the lexical semantic specifications of the item in question. Put very simply (and leaving complications aside), a particular verb comes with an object because its lexically specified argument-structure says so. In a purely constructionist approach, on the other hand, the 'construction' or syntax is responsible for the interpretation of the elements that are part of it, and there are no syntactically relevant lexical semantic specifications. In this view, a verb comes with an object because the syntactic structure of that particular sentence is such that the object forms a constituent with the verb at some point.

We thus have two dimensions along which we can distinguish theories of morphology. Theories differ in the location of word-formation: is it syntax, or is there a separate component? And theories are either endo-skeletal (the lexical item determines its environment) or exo-skeletal (the environment determines the interpretation of the lexical item). It may turn out that the sets of theories that we can distinguish by using these two criteria are extensionally equivalent in the sense that lexical theories of morphology turn out to be endo-skeletal (projectionist) and syntactic theories turn out to be exo-skeletal (constructional), but the two distinctions are at least intensionally different.

Interestingly, both endo-skeletal and exo-skeletal approaches make use of what are called thematic roles in their representations of linguistic knowledge. In a projectionist approach, these thematic roles are part of the lexical semantic specifications. For example, a verb such as *to kill* is assumed to have a thematic grid specifying that the verb projects two such thematic roles: an agent role and a theme role. Furthermore, the theory needs to specify somehow that the agent is assigned to the subject and the theme role to the object. There is a huge literature just on the question of how this mapping of lexical semantic specification onto syntactic positions is done, i.e. the 'linking problem' (see e.g. Baker 1988, 1997, Reinhart 2002).

In an exo-skeletal approach, the thematic roles do not originate in the specification of the lexical items (as theta-grids, or argument-structure), but each thematic position is licensed by a particular functional head F.

In this chapter we will first see how affixes may be seen as functors on argument-structure in derivation (Section 4.2). In Section 4.3 we will turn to compounds and discuss the relation between the head and the left-hand member of the compound in terms of argument-structure. In Section 4.4 we will look deeper into nominalisation and see that there are different types, called complex event nominals and result nominals. Very generally, we may say that result nouns have no argument-structure, whereas complex event nominals have an argument-structure just like verbs. The same distinction between nominals is also relevant in compounds. This is the topic of Section 4.5. Despite the theoretical apparatus introduced in these sections, needed to describe the empirical generalisations properly, these first four sections are mainly empirical in nature. In Section 4.6 we go deeper into the treatment of nominalisations in a syntactic exo-skeletal framework, and in Section 4.7 we will discuss the repercussions of this treatment for the analysis of synthetic compounds. In Section 4.8 we move to a lexical semantic treatment of nominalisations and synthetic compounds.

4.2 Affixes as functors on argument-structure

Let us start by looking at a particularly productive process of word-formation in English, namely the formation of so-called agentive nouns from verbs.

(5) run   runner
     kill   killer

     organise   organiser
     simplify   simplifier

The process is productive in the sense that simply any verbal stem (but see below for nuancing) in English may be picked as the basis for this word-formation process. The result is a noun of which the meaning can be informally described as 'the one who V-s', where V stands for the meaning of the verbal stem. Now, we may wonder how this meaning comes about. That is, how can this meaning be derived from the meaning of an element -*er* and the meaning of the verbal stem? In what follows we first rely on a theory developed by DiSciullo and Williams (1987).

One of the basic assumptions is that one of the lexical characteristics of a verb is an argument-structure. This argument-structure specifies what the arguments of the verb are, and whether they are internal arguments or external ones. For example, a verb such as *to run* only has one argument, which expresses the person (or thing) running. In other words, the only argument of *to run* takes up the semantic role of the **agent**. It is an **external argument**, since the argument is realised in the syntactic position of the subject. Note that not every phrase that accompanies a verb is necessarily an argument of that verb. For example, in (6) the phrase *across the street* is not an argument of *run*. It just modifies the verb; we could also add other modifiers that indicate the particular time (e.g. *yesterday*) of the running event, or the way in which the running was done (e.g. *in sneakers*). A fairly reliable test to see whether some phrase realises an argument-position or not is to see whether the argument is needed to make the sentence well-formed. Modifiers can be left out, arguments cannot. Therefore, (6a–b) are well-formed, whereas (6c) is not (cf. also example (2) above).

(6) a. John runs across the street
     b. John runs
     c. *runs across the street

A verb such as *to beat* has two arguments. It always goes (in its active use) with a subject, the external argument, that realises the one who does the beating (the agent) and an object, the internal argument, that realises the one (or the thing) beaten. This latter semantic role is often called the **theme**. We write down the argument-structure for *to run* and *to beat* as in (7). 'Ag' stands for 'agent' and 'Th' stands for 'theme'. The external argument is underlined.

(7) a. run   (<u>Ag</u>)
     b. beat   (<u>Ag</u>, Th)

DiSciullo and Williams (1987) assume that not only verbs but also nouns and adjectives have argument-structures. The argument-structure of a noun often consists of a single external argument, which is called the **reference role**. This role is assigned to the subject of a sentence in which the noun is used as a predicate. The examples in (8) illustrate the point:

(8) a. The runner didn't see the finish.
     b. John is a runner.

In (8a) the word *runner* is used to refer to a particular person. It receives a thematic role from the verb *see* (agent) of which it is the subject. In (8b), however, it is neither the subject nor the object of some verb; rather, it is used as a predicate and as such it assigns a thematic role to its subject, i.e. *John*. It is assumed that this particular role is the R-role (R for reference).

We are now in a position to be more specific about the operation performed by -*er* when attached to a verbal stem. What happens is that the external argument of -*er* itself, being an R-role, is identified with the external argument of the verb. That explains why we interpret the word *runner* as referring to the one who does the running. Thus, -*er* can be considered a functor that identifies its external role with the external role of the stem it attaches to. In (9) we have given the argument-structure of both *run* and -*er* and the argument-structure of the resulting noun (cf. DiSciullo and Williams 1987: 36):

(9) run   -er   ⇒   runner
     (Ag)   (R)   (R)
                  functor

DiSciullo and Williams (1987: 36) now formulate the following hypothesis:

(10) The argument-structure of a derived word is the argument-structure of the head and the argument-structure of the non-head if the head is a functor.

So, if we assume that -*er* is indeed a functor, then this hypothesis explains, among other things, that the expression in (11) is not ambiguous:

(11) A runner across the street

This particular noun phrase cannot mean 'the one who (always) runs across the street'. It can only refer to a runner that happens to be across the street. The reason is that, as we have seen above, the prepositional phrase *across the street* is a modifier and not an argument of *to run*. Being a modifier, it is not part of the argument-structure of *to run*, and therefore it is not part of the argument-structure of *runner*. Consequently, it cannot be part of the nominalisation in (11).

Interestingly, we now expect that in verbs with both an external and an internal argument in their argument-structure, the internal argument also becomes part of the argument-structure of the noun formed with -*er*. The theory predicts that the internal role of the verb becomes the internal role of the derived noun. The examples in (12) show that this prediction is borne out:

(12) to bake bread   a baker of bread
      to carry luggage   a carrier of luggage
      to drive trucks   a driver of trucks

The argument-structure of the base-verbs is as in (13). When -*er* attaches, the external role of the verb is identified with the external role of -*er* (13). This role becomes the external role of the derived noun. The internal role of the base-verb becomes the internal role of the noun which is satisfied by the *of*-phrases in (12):

(13) a. (Ag, Th)
      b. bake   -er   ⇒   baker
          (Ag, Th)   (R)   ((Th), R)
                        functor

If -*er* is indeed a functor that identifies its R-role with the external role of the base-verb, then we would expect that verbs without external theta-role have no -*er* derived nouns. Interestingly, it is standardly assumed that there are two classes of what are called intransitive verbs (verbs with only a single argument). One class is of of verbs like *run* that only have an external argument; these are the **unergative verbs**. Next to these, there is a class of verbs that only have an internal argument and no external one (Perlmutter 1978). These are the **unaccusative verbs**. Verbs such as *die, fall* or *arrive* are of this type. So we may represent the argument-structure of unergatives as in (14a), while that of unaccusatives is as in (14b) with no argument underlined.

(14) a. Unergatives: (<u>Ag</u>)   run, bike, walk
     b. Unaccusatives   (Th)   die, fall, arrive

In some languages the difference between these two types of verbs is reflected in the choice of auxiliary in the perfect tense. In Dutch, for example, unergatives all take *hebben* 'to have' as the auxiliary for the perfect tense, whereas unaccusatives take the verb *zijn* 'to be' (Hoekstra 1984). There are several other diagnostics that may help to distinguish unaccusative verbs from unergative ones. Given these two classes of verbs and their different argument-structures, we now expect that there are no -*er* nouns based on unaccusative verbs. The following data corroborate this prediction:

(15) a. runner, biker, walker,
     b. *dier, *faller, *arriver

We will see that the **Unaccusativity Hypothesis** – that is, the idea that there are two types of intransitive verbs, one with only an external argument and one with only an internal argument – plays an important role in the discussion about argument-structure in morphology.

Let us now turn to a second example of function composition. To see this, we take a closer look at the meaning of those words formed with the affix -*ness*. First, have a look at the examples in (16):

(16) appropriateness
      completeness
      eagerness
      redness
      willingness

If we were to give an informal characterisation of the semantics of the forms in -*ness*, we would arrive at something like 'the extent R to which something is A', where A is the meaning of the adjective. So the meaning of *redness* can be paraphrased as 'the extent to which something is red'. An adjective such as *red* has the following argument-structure:

(17) (T̲h̲)

Just as in example (8b), the external theme-role corresponds to the role that the subject receives if the adjective is used as a predicate, as in (18):

(18) The chair was red.

Note that *redness* does not refer to the thing being red. There is no way that we could refer to *the chair* in (18) by using the word *redness*. Apparently, the affix *-ness* brings in a meaning-component that corresponds to the part 'the extent R' in the informal description above. More formally, we could say that *-ness* brings in an external role R that becomes the external role of the word as a whole in accordance with the hypothesis in (10) (since *-ness* heads this word). The original external role of the adjective becomes the internal role of the derived noun. This is expressed in (19):

(19) red   ness   ⇒   redness
      (T̲h̲)   (R̲)   (Th, R̲)

Both in the case of *-er* and in the case of *-ness*, it is the external role of the head (the affix) that becomes the external role of the whole word.

After this introduction to some of the basic elements of the theory of argument-structure, we will now first in Section 4.3 take a look at what happens in compounding.

4.3 Argument-structure in compounds

In order to see what type of interactions we encounter in the argument-structure of compounds, we will first take a look at compounds of which the right-hand element, i.e. the head, is a noun that allows for two arguments. The external argument is the R-role that we encounter in all nouns. A second, internal role is the one satisfied by the argument in the *about*-phrase as in (20a).

(20) a. this is a story about trains
      b. this is a story told in the train
      c. a train story

The compound in (20c) has (at least) two interpretations. We can refer with this compound both to the story in (20a) and to the story in (20b). That is, it can be a story about a train (or trains), but it can also be a story that is told in the train (or otherwise related to trains). In the first case we could say that the non-head satisfies the internal argument of the noun *story*. In the second interpretation this is clearly not the case.

So from this we may conclude that in compounding, the non-head may, but need not, satisfy one of the arguments of the head (DiSciullo and Williams 1987: 30).

Compounding differs from affixation in that the arguments of the non-head do not play a role in the argument-structure of the compound. The examples in (21) make this point clear:

(21) a. the destruction of the city
       b. destruction story
       c. destruction story of the city

In (21a), the NP *the city* satisfies an internal argument of the (deverbal) noun *destruction* (it is the city that is being destroyed). This is a theme-argument and refers to the thing destroyed. If this internal argument were a part of the argument-structure of the compound in (21b), we would predict that in (21c) the NP *the city* could also satisfy this role. However, this is not possible in (21c). This phrase cannot have a meaning in which the story is about the destruction of a city. So we may conclude that the internal argument of *destruction* has no role to play in the argument-structure of the compound of which it is a non-head. Compare this state of affairs with the case of -*er* affixation. There we saw that (see the examples in (12)) the internal role of the base-verb becomes the internal theta-role of the noun. Compounding is clearly different in this respect.

What about the external role of the non-head? It will be clear that the external role of the compound is the external role of the head noun; so there is also no place for the R-role of the non-head in a compound.

This gives us an idea of what is going on in compounds with a nominal head. We may now turn to compounds with a verb as their head. Note that these examples are difficult to find in English: compounds with a verbal head are simply not productively formed. However, in those cases that do exist, we see that the same principles apply. The external argument of the head cannot be satisfied internally and therefore becomes the external argument of the compound as a whole. The internal argument of the head may be satisfied by the non-head (but need not be), and the argument-structure of the non-head has no role to play. (22) is an example (from DiSciullo and Williams 1987):

(22) bar   tend

The verb *tend* has an argument-structure as in (23):

(23) tend   (Ag, Th)

In these cases, as in one of the interpretations of the nominal compound *train story*, the internal argument (the thing tended) is satisfied within the compound by the non-head.

Summing up, the way that the argument-structure of complex morphological objects is determined depends on whether we are dealing with compounds or affixes. Affixes may be functors, and as such they take the argument-structure of the non-head and output a modified argument-structure in which the external role of the base becomes the internal role of the complex word. The external role of the affix (if it is the head) becomes the external role of the complex word. In compounds, however, we do not see function composition, but we see that the argument-structure of the head determines the argument-structure of the compound. The only thing that may happen is that the non-head satisfies an argument of the head.

The essential observation with respect to -*er* affixation is that the internal role of the base-verb is also part of the argument-structure of the derived noun; hence the idea that the affix is a functor operating on the argument-structure of the verb. But not all affixes work like this example. Consider the following derived nouns with the affix -*ee* (examples from Barker 1998: 708):

(24) amputee   If a doctor amputates John's leg, John is the amputee, not the leg.

twistee   how one man did brutally twist the knee of another for a good ten minutes and how the twistee groaned . . .

erase   [used in a science fiction story] An erasee [someone whose mind has been erased] was allowed six months at the institute.

These nouns in (24) do not refer to any of the arguments of the verb from which they are derived. For example, the noun *amputee* refers not to the direct object of the verb *to amputate*, but to the owner of the thing being amputated. Similarly, *twistee* and *erasee* also refer to the owners of the things twisted and erased. This possessor is not part of the verb's argument-structure and therefore an analysis in terms of a functor on the argument-structure of the verb would not make sense.

So we may ask, if -*ee* cannot be characterised as a functor on the argument-structure of the verb, then how should we characterise the relation between the derived noun and the verb? Barker (1998) proposes a semantic analysis of word-formation with the suffix -*ee*. We will come back to this in Section 4.8, where we will also discuss a more recent proposal by Lieber.

4.4 Result nouns versus complex event nominals

In the theory of DiSciullo and Williams that we have explained above, the argument-structure of a verb is a list of arguments in which one is designated as the external argument. In an influential monograph, Grimshaw (1990) put forth the idea that the argument-structure of verbs is not just a list of arguments without any particular order, but a hierarchical structure in which some arguments are more prominent than others. First of all, as we have seen above, the external argument is assumed to be the most prominent one, but in Grimshaw's theory the internal arguments also come in a particular hierarchical order. Grimshaw makes use of an earlier insight by Jackendoff (1972) that there exists a particular thematic hierarchy. She assumes that argument-structure is organised in accordance with this thematic hierarchy as given in (25) (Grimshaw 1990: 8):

(25)   (Agent (Experiencer (Goal/Source/Location (Theme))))

The idea is that this thematic hierarchy governs argument-structure. So, basically, the order of the arguments in an argument-structure representation should reflect the thematic hierarchy. For example, the argument-structure of a verb such as *give* is as follows:

(26)   *give:*   (x   (y   (z)))
                 Agent   Goal   Theme

The hierarchical nature of argument-structure is now used in an interesting way. The idea is that first the hierarchically lowest argument has to be theta-marked, after which the next highest argument can be theta-marked, working our way up the hierarchy until all theta-roles have been discharged. This makes some interesting predictions with respect to the possible thematic relations between the head and the non-head in a compound.

Consider the data in (27):

(27)   a.   chocolate-giving to children
            (z   (y   ))
       b. *child-giving of chocolate
            (y   (z   ))

The difference in grammaticality between these two verbal compounds (we will return to such compounds in Section 4.5) can be explained as follows: the lowest thematic role in the argument-structure of *give*, i.e. the theme role, can only be assigned to the compound-internal argument, whereas the higher goal-role should be discharged outside the compound. In (27) this order is reversed, necessarily leading to an ungrammatical result.

Grimshaw (1990) argues at length that there is an important difference between result nominals (not having argument-structure) and complex event nominals, which do have argument-structure. Just as in verbs in these latter cases, the argument-structure needs to be obligatorily satisfied by the arguments of the noun. Consider the following data (Grimshaw 1990: 49):

(28) a. The exam was long/in the lecture hall.
      b. The examination was long/in the lecture hall.

(29) a. *The exam of the patient took a long time
      b. The examination of the patient took a long time

The word *exam* is a **result noun**. It can be used with such predicates as *long* and *in the lecture hall.* It does not have an argument-structure and therefore it cannot be used in the context of (29), where *the patient* is construed as a theme-argument. In contrast to this, we have words such as *examination,* which are ambiguous between a result noun reading (as in (28)) and a **complex event noun** reading. Complex event nouns, according to Grimshaw, do have an argument-structure that, parallel to verbs, also needs to be satisfied by the syntactic or morphological context. According to this theory, *the patient* in (29) receives a theta-role from the noun *examination.* Since complex event nouns have an argument-structure according to the theory, this argument-structure is obligatorily satisfied. So complex event nominals should always have a complement, just as their base-verbs should. This prediction is borne out by the data in (30). (Asterisks outside brackets indicate that the sentence is ungrammatical without the material inside the brackets.)

(30) a. They fell *(the trees).
      b. The felling *(of the trees).

Many nominals are ambiguous between a complex event reading and a result reading. In some cases, it might be difficult to distinguish the result interpretation from the complex event reading. Fortunately, there are several diagnostics. For example, the adverbials *constant* and *frequent* force the complex event reading, and therefore the realisation of the arguments of the nominal is obligatory. The following examples illustrate the point:

(31) a. The expression is desirable
      b. *The frequent expression is desirable
      c. The frequent expression of one's feelings is desirable.
      d. We express *(our feelings)

As can be seen from (31d), *express* is a transitive verb. Similarly, the complex event nominal that we may derive from this verb is also necessarily 'transitive' in the sense that its complement must be realised. Since *frequent* forces the complex event reading, the non-realisation of the complement leads to an ungrammatical result (31b). Note that *expression* also has a result noun reading as can be seen from (31a). So as soon as *frequent* is added as a modifier, the complex event noun reading is forced and thus the complement needs to be realised. The same effect is visible when we use the modifier *constant*.

(32) a. The assignment is to be avoided
     b. *The constant assignment is to be avoided
     c. The constant assignment of unsolvable problems is to be avoided
     d. We constantly assign *(unsolvable problems)

A second diagnostic for the complex event reading is the subject interpretation of the possessive NP (i.e. the NP *John's* in *John's book*). If this possessive has a subject reading, the other arguments are obligatory as well:

(33) a. The examination took a long time
     b. (*)The instructor's examination took a long time
     c. The instructor's examination of the papers took a long time
     d. The instructor examined *(the papers)

The possessive NP in (33b) does not allow an interpretation in which *the instructor* is the subject (Agent) of the *examination*, i.e. she or he is the one that performed the examination. This structure is only well-formed if there is a modifier relation between *the instructor* and *the examination*. Adding an agent-oriented adverb further corroborates this observation. Such adverbs force the subject interpretation of the possessive:

(34) a. *The instructor's intentional/deliberate examination took a long time
     b. The instructor's intentional/deliberate examination of the papers took a long time

The ungrammaticality of (34a) can now be explained as follows: the adverbs *intentional* or *deliberate* force the subject interpretation of *the instructor*. This interpretation in turn forces the complex event reading of the nominal *examination*. However, this interpretation is only possible if all arguments of the nominal are realised and since the complement is not realised in (34a), the structure is ungrammatical.

A further diagnostic for complex event nominals is the occurrence of *by*-phrases that may also realise part of the argument-structure. Therefore, their presence may also force the presence of the complement (as already observed by Hornstein 1977):

(35) a. The expression *(of aggressive feelings) by the patient.
 b. The assignment *(of unsolvable problems) by the instructor
 c. The examination *(of the papers) by the instructor

However, we need to be careful in applying this diagnostics since English also allows for *by*-phrases that are only modifiers and not complements. So in some cases a result noun is modified by a *by*-phrase:

(36) a. The assignment by Fred was much too difficult.
 b. An examination by a competent instructor will reveal . . .

Furthermore, note that result nouns can easily be embedded in the phrase *this kind of* . . . . As can be seen in (37), this is not possible with complex event nominals (cf. Borer 2010: 5):

(37) a. this kind of friendship/computer/result/art/redness/beauty
 b. this kind of destruction/transformation/assignment/
 examination
 c. this kind of ??destructing of cities/??transmission of information
 d. *this kind of bullying in order to make up for low self-esteem
 e. *this kind of terrorising immature males

There are also differences between result nouns and complex event nominals with respect to the determiner system. Complex event nouns do not allow for indefinite determiners or demonstratives:

(38) a. They worked on the/an/that assignment.
 b. They worked on the/*an/*that assignment of the problem.

Finally, complex event nominals do not pluralise, whereas result nouns do.

(39) a. The assignments were difficult
 b. *The assignments of the problems were difficult

Summarising so far, we can see that there are (at least) two types of nominals in English. First, there are result nouns, which have no argument-structure and therefore do not allow for real complements. Second, there are complex event nominals, which do have argument-structure and therefore are necessarily accompanied by their complements (just as verbs are). Note, by the way, that there are also simple event nominals, which refer to events but have no argument-structure and therefore behave basically as result nominals do. An example would be the noun *event*.

Above we have somewhat loosely made a distinction between complex event nominals and result nominals in terms of argument-structure. Complex event nominals have argument-structure whereas result nouns do not. However, as the acute reader will have noticed, this cannot be the complete story, since we have already seen that result nouns also have an argument-structure: they have an external argument R. So we should be more precise in order to make a proper distinction between the two types of nominals. Note that the R-role differs in nature from the thematic roles that have a place on the thematic hierarchy. The R-role is not linked to a particular semantic role as the thematic roles are. Therefore, we may say that complex event nominals have a *thematic* argument-structure whereas result nouns do not. But there is a further distinction that becomes clear if we consider the fact that complex event nominals do not occur as predicates.

(40) a. This is an assignment.
      b. *This is an assignment of the problem.

Recall that the R-role of (result) nouns is assumed to be the role that is assigned to the subject in these predicative structures. The fact that complex event nominals do not occur as predicates may thus be an indication that they do not have an R-role. Furthermore, note that complex event nominals always refer to events and that there are no complex event nominals that refer to any of the thematic arguments of the base-verb. This leads to the assumption that complex event nominals always have an external role 'event' (Ev).

Let us summarise briefly. Result nominals have an argument-structure with an external argument, which is the R-role. Complex event nominals always have an argument-structure with an external argument, which is the Ev-role. In a nominalisation such as *examination*, the argument-structure of the verb is composed with the argument-structure of the affix *-ation*. Since *-ation* is the head, its external argument (Ev) becomes the external argument of the whole and the arguments of the verb become internal arguments of the complex event nominal.

(41) a. examine, V (x (y))
      b. -ation, N (Ev)
      c. examination, N (Ev (x (y)))

Now, note that nominals are very often ambiguous between a result reading and a complex event reading. We must therefore assume that the lexical representation of -*ation* (and other affixes of this type such as -*ment* and -*ion*) allows for this ambiguity. So the complete specification of -*ation* should be as in (42):

(42) -ation, N (Ev)/(R)

Interestingly, there is a class of deverbal nouns that does not allow for a complex event reading (and thus should be characterised as only having an R-role in the lexicon). To see this, consider the data in (43):

(43) a. John kicks Bill
     b. *John's kick of Bill
     c. John's kicking of Bill

The noun *kick* does not have a nominalising affix. Such zero-derived forms are always result nouns: they do not have an argument-structure, as follows from the ungrammaticality of (43b). So, if we assume that these cases of conversion are derived through a zero-affix, this affix only has a R-role as its argument-structure. We may wonder whether this correlation between zero-affixation and having no thematic argument-structure is coincidental. We come back to a potential answer in Section 4.6.

Nouns fall into two different categories. Complex event nominals are argument-taking nouns; they have an external Ev-role, which explains the fact that they always refer to events, and the internal arguments result from the argument-structure of the verb through function composition. Result nouns have an external R-role and have no further argument-structure.

4.5 Root compounds versus synthetic compounds

Let us now turn to cases that have played a central role in the discussion about the argument-structure of complex morphological objects: what are called verbal nexus compounds or **synthetic compounds**. These compounds have a right-hand part that is a noun or adjective derived from a verbal base. Characteristically, in these structures, the left-hand member of the compound realises an argument of this verbal base. Here are some examples:

(44) a. truck-driver
        time-saver
        cake-baker

     b. house-cleaning
        gold-mining

    c. hand-woven
       sun-baked
       life-threatening

Note that the term 'verbal compound' is a bit misleading, since the structure as a whole is a (deverbal) noun as in (44a–b), or an adjective as in (44c) and not a verb. Therefore, we will henceforth use the term 'synthetic compound'.

Simply put: a *truck-driver* is somebody who drives trucks, *life-threatening* can be said of events that threaten our lives, etc. These compounds can (and should) be distinguished from root compounds in the following way. In root compounds the relation between the two constituting elements is one of modification. Recall from Chapter 2 that basically any relation between the two elements of a nominal compound is possible. However, in synthetic compounds the left-hand member does not modify the head, but the relation is a very specific one: the left-hand member is interpreted as the argument of the base-verb.

Let us take a look at the possible relations between the derived noun or adjective and the left-hand member in a synthetic compound. Roeper and Siegel (1978), in the first paper to look into these structures, formulate the following generalisation:

(45) First Sister Principle:

    All verbal compounds are formed by incorporation of a word in first sister position of the verb. (Roeper and Siegel 1978: 208)

Roeper and Siegel's idea is that synthetic compounds are transformationally derived from underlying sentences. The first (closest to the verb) sister in the verb phrase can be incorporated into these structures, explaining the grammaticality differences between (46b) and (46c) and subsequent examples:

(46) a. She makes peace quickly
      b. peacemaker
      c. *quickly maker

(47) a. The food supports life fast
      b. life supporting
      c. *fast supporting

(48) a. This snow falls fast
      b. fast-falling snow
      c. *snow falling

The principle in (45) also covers the observation that we do not find subjects as non-heads in synthetic compounds (see (48)): subjects are not part of the verb phrase (in the syntactic theories at the time of the publication of Roeper and Siegel's paper). Consequently, they are never 'first sisters'.

The problem posed by these constructions is, in a nutshell, this: how is it possible that the argument-structure of the verb is (partly) realised in the compound structure? We can make this clearer by offering two types of structures that are possible candidates for verbal compounds:

(49)   a.

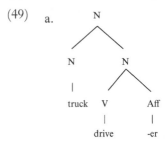

b.

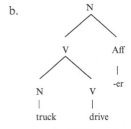

The structure in (49b) makes it easy to understand why *truck* is interpreted as an argument of *drive*. We could say that the verb discharges its theta-role in the same way as it does in syntax; since *truck* is the sister of the verb, it receives the theme-role. However, (49b) implies that the verb *truckdrive* is at least a possible verb of English, and that is simply not the case, as can be seen in the examples in (50).

(50)   a.   *Mary truckdrives all the way to Russia.
       b.   *Chris housecleans every afternoon.

Consider the following compounds in English with a verb as their right-hand member:

(51)   to breast-feed
       to pressure-clean
       to play-act
       to window-shop
       to colour-code

It turns out that we can make quite a long list of such verbal compounds (see e.g. Bauer 1983: 208), but crucially, in all of these compounds, the left-hand member is not interpreted as an argument of the right-hand member. Compounds of that type are extremely scarce. Ackema and Neeleman (2004: 55) list just two such cases: *bar-tend* and *people-watch*. One could add verbs such as *baby-sit*, *head-hunt* and *proof-read*, but as Ackema and Neeleman point out, these verbs are transitive; that is, next to the 'incorporated' argument in the compound, these verbs still have an internal argument. The left-hand member of the compound there-fore cannot be interpreted as the internal argument of the verb. The examples in (52) illustrate the transitivity of these verbs.

(52)   to baby-sit their daughter
       to proof-read the manuscript
       to head-hunt a new director

So compound verbs with a left-hand member that is interpreted as an internal argument of the verb are for some reason not possible in English. In itself it is an interesting question why this is the case, but we postpone that issue to Section 4.6. For now, it suffices to see that this conclusion makes the structure in (49b) a very unlikely candidate for the synthetic compounds.

That brings us to structure (49a) as a possible candidate. In that structure *truck* is not a sister of the verb, which makes it more dif-ficult to explain that *truck* is interpreted as the object of *drive*. In order to do so, we would have to assume that the argument-structure of the verb is somehow transferred, or 'inherited' as it is often put in the literature, by the derived noun or adjective. Let us briefly take a look at a possible execution of that idea along the lines of the theory of DiSciullo and Williams explained above. Remember that the argument-structure of a deverbal noun such as *baker* or *driver* would be as in (53):

(53)   driver   <Th, R̲>

The R-role is the external role of the noun that we see on the subject in a predicative structure, and the Th-role can be assigned to a comple-ment of *driver* as in (54):

(54)   Mary is a driver of trucks.

Now it is a small step to assume that this internal role can also be assigned inside the compound *truckdriver*. In (54), since the internal role cannot be discharged within the morphological structure *driver*, it becomes part of the argument-structure of *driver*, whereas in *truckdriver* the argument is discharged within the compound and is not a part of the argument-structure of the compound. Therefore, the sentence in (55) is ungrammatical; the NP *lorries* cannot receive a thematic role since that has been discharged to the element *truck*:

(55) *Mary is a truckdriver of lorries.

However, in order to make this work we need to assume that nouns such as *driver* have an argument-structure, which is somehow 'inherited' from their base-verb. If that were so, we might wonder why, in such cases, the arguments need not be realised obligatorily. In other words, why are the expressions in (56) with or without the argument all perfectly grammatical? If *driver* (and *baker*) have argument-structures, why is the realisation of this argument-structure optional?

(56) a. Mary is a good driver (of lorries)
      b. Claus was a lousy baker (of cookies).

The answer lies in the ambiguity of many nominals. As we have seen above, many nominals allow both a complex event reading and a result reading. So, here too, the noun *driver* may be a result noun and as such it does not have any arguments apart from its R-role. Consequently, the structures without complements are acceptable. In its complex event noun interpretation, on the other hand, the realisation of its argument-structure is obligatory, and therefore the structures with complements are also well-formed.

Looking at the difference between root compounds and synthetic compounds, it thus seems a logical step, given our discussion of the difference between result nouns and complex event nouns in Section 4.4, to identify (the right-hand members of) synthetic compounds with complex event nominals, and the right-hand members of root compounds with result nominals. This is precisely what Grimshaw (1990) proposes. This identification makes some further interesting predictions. We expect that in synthetic compounds only those relations occur that are typical of argument satisfaction, whereas in root compounds we expect other relations to occur that are excluded in argument satisfaction.

First, note that it is predicted that external arguments do not occur as the left-hand members in synthetic compounds. Recall that Grimshaw's theory predicts that the lowest arguments in the argument-structure should be discharged first. So if the base-verb is a transitive verb (having at least two arguments), then the internal argument will always be discharged before the external argument. That explains why we cannot have synthetic compounds of transitive verbs with 'subjects' as their left-hand member. However, that leaves us with the question of why, if there is no internal argument, the external argument cannot be assigned to the left-hand member of the compound. Now, consider the data in (57):

(57) a. *manwalker
     b. *man-shouting

From the examples in (57), it is clear that no subjects are allowed even if the verb is non-transitive. In our exposition above, we explained that nouns and adjectives should always have external arguments in order to function properly in syntax. In (57a), the external argument of the verb *walk* (Agent) is assigned to the left-hand member of the compound (*man*). The external R-role of -*er* is identified with that role (cf. (9)). As a consequence, the compound as a whole has no (external) role left and therefore cannot be successfully incorporated into the syntactic structure. Similarly, in the case of (57b) the adjective should have an R-role in order to act as a modifier (or as a predicate). However, the external role of *shout* is assigned to *man*, and therefore there is no role left that could be identified with the R-role.

So the theory predicts that in synthetic compounds, external arguments cannot act as left-hand members, whereas this should be possible in root compounds. This latter prediction is borne out by the data in (58). Example (58c) contrasts with the root compound in (58b), in which 'subjects' (although not as arguments) are possible:

(58) a. a dog bites
     b. a dog-bite
     c. *dog-biting (makes one afraid)

In the same way, we do not expect to find subjects of unaccusative verbs appearing in synthetic compounds where such relations are possible in root compounds:

(59) a. *rain falling, *heartaching
     b. rainfall, heartache

Recall that synthetic compounds do not allow for pluralisation. This implies that if the right-hand member of a compound is a plural noun, the compound as a whole should be a root compound. Consider the data in (60):

(60) a. Eric likes baking clams
      b. Eric likes clam baking
      c. Eric likes clam bakings

The sentence in (60b) is more or less synonymous with the sentence in (60a). The interpretation is roughly 'there is someone called Eric, and for Eric it is true that he likes [PRO baking clams]. PRO here is a silent pronoun that has the same function as *he*. The subject of the sentence (*Eric*) necessarily controls the PRO subject of the embedded clause. That is, we understand Eric to be the one who is the actor of the baking. As one can see, the interpretation of (60c) differs crucially in this respect: it does not imply that Eric is the one who does the baking. The reason for this distinction can be made to follow from the fact that the noun *baking* has an argument-structure, whereas *bakings* cannot have one. In (60a–b) the external argument of *baking* is controlled by the subject of the sentence, i.e. *Eric*. This leads to the above-mentioned interpretation. In (60c) such an interpretation is impossible, since *bakings* (being a result nominal) does not allow for arguments and therefore there can be no relation of control.

Above we have presented a view on synthetic compounds that assumes that their structure is as in (49a). Before we turn to an alternative view, we would like to point out an observation of Ackema and Neeleman (2004) that is problematic for this view. To see this, consider the data in (61) (examples from Ackema and Neeleman 2004: 56):

(61) a. John always makes trouble
          John is a troublemaker
          #John is a maker of trouble

      b. This game usually breaks the ice at parties
          This game is a real icebreaker at parties
          #This game is a real breaker of ice at parties

These data show that the idiomatic interpretation that some noun–verb combinations (*make trouble, break the ice*) may have is also present in the synthetic compounds (*troublemaker, icebreaker*). However, this idiomatic interpretation is lost (hence the hash in two of the examples in (61)) in those cases in which the deverbal noun heads an NP and the argument is syntactically realised (as part of an *of* prepositional phrase, or PP). But why would this idiomatic interpretation be lost in these constructions while it is preserved in the synthetic compounds? The theory explained above makes no relevant distinction between these two structures, and therefore we may want to look for an alternative.

4.6 A syntactic view on the derivation of nominals

We explained above that in Grimshaw's theory a synthetic compound always has a complex event nominal as its right-hand element. Since complex event nominals are argument-taking nouns, the left-hand element of a compound may be interpreted as the argument of the nominal. The argument-structure of the nominal in turn is the result of the function composition of the argument-structure of the affix (the head) and the argument-structure of the base-verb. According to Borer (2010), this view on synthetic compounds cannot be correct. It is simply not true that the right-hand members of synthetic compounds are argument-taking nouns.

Let us start by considering the following examples (Borer 2010: 16–17):

(62) a. *the transformation of the structure by the linguist
     b. *the patient's transference of his feelings
     c. the transformation of our department by the administration
     d. the transference of merit

The nominals in (62a and b) do not allow for arguments, whereas those in (62c and d) apparently do. The only difference between these nominals is that the non-argument-taking ones have an idiosyncratic interpretation, whereas the argument-taking ones are necessarily transparent. That is, *transformation* in (62a) refers to the technical linguistic term, whereas in (62c) the nominal has a fully compositional interpretation (i.e. 'the act of transforming'). The same holds with respect to the use of *transference* in (62b and d). So the question that these data pose to the analyst is why there should be a relation between idiosyncrasy of interpretation (say, listedness) and the impossibility of taking arguments. Or, to put it the other way around, why is it that the non-idiosyncratic reading of the nominals goes hand in hand with the taking of arguments?

Borer's idea is that this correlation can be explained if we assume that it is not the verb that is being nominalised in (62c), but part of the (verbal) syntactic structure. The lack of argument-structure in (62a and b) is then attributed to the fact that in these cases only the verb is being nominalised. Of course, that would not be of much help if it were the case that arguments were lexically listed with their verbs. In such a lexical scenario we would need an explanation for the fact that these arguments somehow 'disappear' under nominalisation. But in Borer's framework, argument-structure is not specified in the lexicon, but only comes about in syntax. Before we can go into some more detail on this explanation, let us first introduce Borer's syntactic approach to argument-structure and morphology in general.

The view on argument-structure explained above is mainly based on the work of DiSciullo and Williams (1987) and Grimshaw (1990). The basic idea in this approach to argument-structure (which we also encounter in e.g. Levin and Rappaport Hovav 1995 and Reinhart 2002) is that it is 'endo-skeletal'; the source of argument-structure is the lexicon. That is, an essential part of a lexical entry is formed by the representation of the argument-structure of that lexical item. This position with respect to argument-structure reflects a more general view on the nature of linguistic knowledge. As Borer puts it, linguistic theories can be positioned on a scale which ranges from pure lexical storage of information to pure rule-based computation. Recall from Chapter 2 the view that morphology is just a large set of redundancy rules which generalises over the set of stored words of a language. Such a view builds almost exclusively on the capacity of humans to store large amounts of information and hardly makes use of another human faculty: the ability to display rule-governed behaviour. At the opposite end of the scale, we find theories of morphology that only exploit this computational faculty of humans. In these approaches words are stored with as little information as possible, and all the linguistic information that is associated with these words is attributed to the (syntactic) environment in which the particular word is being inserted.

As an example, let us consider the data in (63) (the example is from Clark and Clark 1979, cited in Borer 2004):

(63) a. the factory horns sirened throughout the raid
      b. the factory horns sirened midday and everyone broke for lunch
      c. the police car sirened the Porsche to a stop
      d. the police car sirened up to the accident site
      e. the police car sirened the daylights out of me

If we were to attribute the different uses of the verb *to siren* to the lexicon, we would have to assume that there are at least five different lexical representations for this single verb. It can be used as an intransitive agentive verb as in (63a). The meaning of this intransitive verb can be paraphrased as 'to emit a siren noise'. In (63b), however, *to siren* is a transitive verb meaning 'to signal through emitting a siren noise'. Note that there are also aspectual differences between these uses of the verb *to siren*. In its intransitive use, it is an atelic verb, which means that we can easily add an adverbial modifier that expresses the duration of the activity (such as *throughout the raid*). However, in its transitive use, the verb is telic, not allowing such modifiers. In (63c–e) the verb has yet other meanings, which can respectively be paraphrased as 'to force by emitting a siren noise', 'to hurry while emitting a siren noise' and 'to frighten by emitting a siren noise'. So, we may ask, is it really the case that we are dealing with five different verbs in (63), or is another view possible which would somehow waive the requirement of setting up five different lexical items?

Such a view would start by assuming that there is just a single item *siren* which is the same in all the examples in (63) and that the differences in usage are to be attributed not to the lexical item, but to the differences in the syntactic environment in which it is inserted. Apparently, lexical items such as *siren* may display a large flexibility as to their syntactic usage. Lexical theories associate the linguistic structure (such as argument-structure and lexical category) with the lexical item. The verb *siren* alone would need at least five entries in the lexicon, each with different information as to the structure in which it can occur. Borer (2003) dubs these approaches 'endo-skeletal', since the (syntactic) skeleton in which the elements occur is determined by or built around the lexical information belonging to the element in question.

In an exo-skeletal approach, the linguistic structure is taken to be far more independent of the elements that occur in it. In such an approach, *siren* would be lexically stored with only a minimal amount of information. To begin with, *siren* would not have any categorial information, nor would its lexical entry contain any information as to its argument-structure. Such a view entails that it is the syntactic structure rather than the lexical item that somehow licenses the arguments. Basically, lexical entries such as *siren* could be inserted in just any syntactic position. The flexibility of the element *siren* as seen in (63) is then the result of this free insertion of lexical elements in any syntactic environment. In this approach we would even expect a nominal and an adjectival use of *siren*; the fact that the latter usage is apparently absent is then not a grammatical fact of English but should be explained differently.

Let us make this exo-skeletal approach more concrete. The model of the grammar that Borer proposes can be schematically presented as in (64) (redrawn from Borer 2003: 36):

(64)   ENCYCLOPEDIA   →   [$_{\text{L-D}}$ conceptual array]

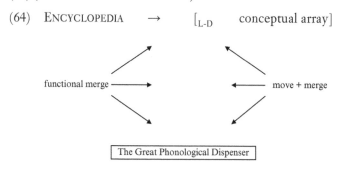

The model is explained below by going stepwise through a derivation. Borer assumes that there is a warehouse containing a set of sound–meaning pairs, called the encyclopedia. The encyclopedia houses those elements of language that are atomic, in the sense that they do not allow any further analysis. The meaning side of these 'Saussurean signs' is a meaning that is some conceptual notion, such as HOUSE, CAR, LOVE, etc., while the phonological side consists of a standard phonological representation ([haʊs],[kɑː],[lʌv]). Borer refers to these elements as encyclopedic items (EIs). These EIs are roughly equivalent to roots in distributed morphology (e.g. Marantz 1997). They do not have a lexical category, nor do they have any information as to their argument-structure. At the start of the derivation of a syntactic construct, a subset of these elements are taken from the encyclopedia and together they form the conceptual array, which is just an unordered set that is inserted in the unmarked lexical domain (the L-domain or L-D). For example, the EIs *sink, boat* and *dog* may be selected from the encyclopedia and inserted in an L-D as in (65):

(65) [$_{L-D}$ sink, boat, dog]

Apart from the encyclopedia, the grammar contains a further list of elements, called the functional lexicon, that includes functional features such as [+past], [+plural], [+def], etc., and also includes a set of grammatical formatives that are rigid designators (unlike the EIs) associated with a particular functional feature. For example, the definite article *the* is part of this functional lexicon and is associated with the feature [+def]. This can be represented as an ordered pair <[+def], *the*>.

First, consider the way Borer treats inflectional morphology (such as the formation of the past tense in English) in this model. Assume that the L-D in (65) merges with a functional head [+past] that heads a Tense-phrase, as in (66):

(66) [$_T$ [+past] [$_{L-D}$ sink, boat, dog]]

Now, any of the items in the L-D may move to the functional head and merge with it. So, for example, we may move the EI *sink* to this functional head, resulting in the structure in (67):

(67) [$_T$ sink-[+past] [$_{L-D}$ ~~sink~~, boat, dog]]

As a consequence of this movement, the element that moves to the functional head position becomes the head of the L-D, since only heads may move out of the L-D to a functional head. Furthermore, the nature of the functional head determines the category of the L-D. Since [+past] heads a Tense-projection, the L-D becomes a VP, and since *sink* is the head, *sink* will now be categorised as a verb:

(68) $[_T [sink_V]-[+past]_T [_{VP} [_V sink], boat, dog]]$

If the functional head contained a feature related to the nominal domain, such as [+def], the L-D, after movement and merger of a particular element from the L-D to this functional head, would be categorised as an NP and the head merged with this functional head D, as an N.

Now, in a later stage of the derivation, the construct [[sink]-[+past]] is phonologically realised as *sank*. So here we see, just as in the proposal of Anderson (1992) (see Chapter 3), that the morpho-phonological realisation of a form is post-syntactic.

Of course, in principle there is no objection to moving the element *boat* or *dog* to the functional head position in (66) and subsequent merger with the functional head [+past]. In a way, the fact that this is possible is the essence of the exo-skeletal approach: since *boat*, *sink* and *dog* have no category or any other grammatically relevant information, they are, as far as the grammar is concerned, fully interchangeable. This would result in verb-forms such as *dogged* and *boated*.

Apart from movement and merger of an element from the L-D with a functional head, there is a second way in which elements may be categorised. As an example, take the auxiliary *will* expressing future tense. Suppose that instead of [+past] as in (66), the feature [+fut] merges with the L-D. If we now move and merge an element from the L-D with this functional head, the structure will fail, since the construct [+fut, V] (where V stands for any possible element from the L-D) has no phonological interpretation; the phonological dispenser will not be able to provide this structure with a phonological form. Put differently, English has no synthetic future verb-form. However, apart from the feature [+fut], the functional lexicon of English also hosts the element <[+fut], *will*>. If this element merges with the same L-D that we looked at above, we get the structure in (69):

(69)   <*will*, [+fut]> $[_{L-D}$ sink, boat, dog]

In this case no element will move to the functional head. Still, categorising the L-D is possible: since *will* is a T, the L-D will be categorised as a VP. So there are two ways in which an L-D can be categorised: either through movement and merger of the head, or by way of the merger of the L-D as a whole with a rigid designator that heads a particular functional projection. The nature of this projection determines the category of the L-D.

So affixation is dealt with by assuming that the relevant inflectional feature merges with the L-D and that only after this merger is the correct phonological form provided. This theory is thus an example of a post-syntactic 'late insertion' theory of inflection. Let us now turn to the way Borer treats derivational morphology.

A basic assumption of Borer (2003) is that derivational affixes are categorial heads that, just like the elements *will* and *the*, are part of the functional lexicon. Furthermore, they not only have a category of them-selves, but they are also capable of categorising the elements with which they happen to merge. Here is an example:

(70) -ation, N, $[[_V] \underline{\hspace{1cm}}_N]$

The characterisation of the affix *-ation* in the functional lexicon stipu-lates that it is an N, and that it turns any element that it merges with into a verb. Suppose that the L-D contains an element [form]: then we may merge this element with the suffix *-ation*, giving rise to the categorisa-tion of the derivation as a noun and of the part [form] as a verb. See the derivation in (71):

(71) a. $[_{L-D} \text{ form}]$
      b. $[\text{-ation } [_{L-D} \text{ form}]]$
      c. $[[\text{form}]_V \text{ ation}]_N$

Similarly, we could derive the adjective *formal*, by merger of the same EI [form] with the suffix *-al* that derives adjectives and categorises the base as nominal.

(72) a. $[_{L-D} \text{ form}]$
      b. $[\text{-al } [_{L-D} \text{ form}]]$
      c. $[[\text{form}]_N \text{ al}]_A$

Interestingly, the same EI *form* can end up as a verb or as a noun in a morphological structure. Going back to the observation with respect to *to siren*, we see how this flexibility (in terms of its syntactic category) is dealt with in this exo-skeletal approach: it is the structure that defines the properties of the elements that become part of the structure.

The examples with *-al* and *-ation* above are examples with just a single affix interacting with an element from the L-D. Of course, the theory also needs to allow for the possibility of stacking affixes. An example would be *formalisation*, in which we first merge *form* with the affix *-al*, after which this construction as a whole is merged with the verb-forming affix *-ise*, which in turn may merge with the affix *-ation*. The derivation in (73) makes clear how these successive mergers result in the structure of the form *formalisation*. The first three steps are identical to the derivation in (72):

(73) a. $[_{L\text{-}D}$ form$]$
      b. $[$ -al $[_{L\text{-}D}$ form$]$ $]$
      c. $[$ $[$form$]_N$ al$]_A$
      d. $[$ -ise $[$ $[$form$]_N$ al$]_A]$
      e. $[$ $[$ $[$form$]_N$ al$]_A$ ise$]$ $_V$
      f. $[$-ation $[$ $[$ $[$form$]_N$ al$]_A$ ise$]$ $_V$ $]$
      g. $[$ $[$ $[$form$]_N$ al$]_A$ ise$]$ $_V$ ation$]_N$

These examples show what happens if the affixes directly interact with elements of the L-D. However, it is also possible that the affixes merge independently in the syntax, heading a particular categorial projection as in, for example, (74):

(74)

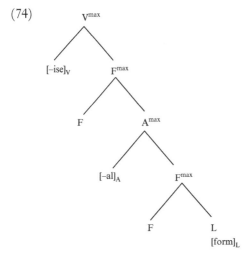

In such cases an element from the L-D will move to the different head positions, first deriving the adjective *formal*, which will categorise the original L-D as an NP. After that the complex *formal* will move to the higher verbal head -*ise*, deriving syntactically the verb *formalise*.

Let us now turn to the distinction between R-nominals and argument-structure nominals (AS-nominals). The central idea is that the difference between AS-nominals and R-nominals is that AS-nominals are derived 'in syntax', along the lines of the structure in (74), whereas R-nominals are derived 'in morphology', as in (73). The leading idea is that AS-nominals are necessarily derived in the syntax because argument-structure may only arise as the result of syntactic functional projections. EIs simply have no argument-structure properties; the only origin for argument-structure is the syntactic functional projections. Consequently, AS-nominals, hosting argument-structure, are derived in syntax.

One of the basic ideas of this theory on argument-structure is that every argument is admitted to the syntactic structure by a specific functional projection. So, rather than a list of arguments that is specified for each and every verb in the lexicon, the source of the arguments lies in the functional projections that are placed on top of the verb. For example, take a look at the structure in (75):

(75) $[_N$ N $[_{F1}$ (subj) (F1) $[_{F2}$ obj (F2) [V]]]]

Innermost in the structure we find a verb. This verb is embedded in a functional projection (F2) that introduces an object of the verb. The constituent F2 is in turn embedded in a functional projection (F1) that allows for subjects. Finally, this whole structure is embedded under a nominal head N, which turns the whole structure into a noun. The verb moves from its original position (V in structure (75)) through the several functional heads to the nominal head, as in (76):

(76) $[_N$ [$[_{F1}$ $[_{F2}$ transform]] -ation] $[_{F1}$ administration $[_{F1}$ V] $[_{F2}$ our department $[_{F2}$ V] [V]]]

The precise nature of these functional projections need not concern us here.

If we have a nominalisation of a 'bare' verb rather than a nominalisation of a part of the syntactic structure, the resulting noun simply cannot take arguments, since there are no arguments present in a 'bare' verb, the only source for the arguments being the functional projections. So the word *transformation* in its 'jargon' interpretation has a structure as in (77), which is parallel to the derivation in (71):

(77) $[_N$ $[_V$ transform] ation]

Now, we come to the question as to why the structure in (77) but not the one in (76) allows for an idiosyncratic interpretation. In other words, why is it that R-nominals, but not AS-nominals, allow for idiosyncratic interpretations? The central insight is that local structures allow for such interpretations, whereas idiosyncrasies become impossible once the different elements do not stand in a direct local relationship. Borer implements this idea in such a way that only structures not broken up by any functional boundaries allow for idiosyncratic interpretations. So in (76) we need to cross at least one functional boundary to get from *-ation* to the element *transform*. Therefore, no idiosyncratic interpretation is possible here. However, in (77) the relation between *-ation* and *transform* is strictly local, and therefore nothing prevents an idiosyncratic interpretation. So as a consequence the theory explains why AS-nominals are necessarily transparent in the sense that they do not allow for any idiosyncratic interpretation, whereas such interpretations are possible in case of R-nominals.

Borer shows that another interesting prediction follows from the theory on AS-nominals as syntactically derived and R-nominals as 'morphologically' derived. Recall from our discussion in Section 4.4 that many English nominals allow for both interpretations. However, that is not the case for so-called 'converted' nouns. The following data were given as an illustration of that fact in (43), repeated here as (78):

(78) a. John kicks Bill
      b. *John's kick of Bill
      c. John's kicking of Bill

Nominals such as *kick, hit,* etc. that have no visible affix that is responsible for the nominalisation behave differently in this respect from nominalisations in *-ation,* and similar ones that are always ambiguous. Why would that be the case? Why would there be a correlation between having an overt phonological form and being able to support argument-structure? Borer assumes that there are no zero-affixes. Therefore, such 'conversions' may only arise from the merger of a functional head that turns the L-D into an NP, and consequently, the head of that domain into an N, as in the following example:

(79) a. $<the,$ [+def]$>$ [$_L$ hit]
      b. [[$_D$$<the,$ [+def]] [$_{NP}$ [$_N$ hit]]]

However, if there is no zero-element that can be a functional head deriving nouns, then there is no way in which we could construct any AS-nominals of the type *hit* or *kick*. Therefore, conversions are necessarily R-nominals.

The theory therefore explains the fact that we find 'converted' R-nominals; they arise simply from the merger of a functional element with the L-D, which turns the L-D into an NP. These structures do not require the assumption of an empty affix that has a nominal category. Moreover, if we assumed such zero-affixes existed, we would make the wrong prediction (wrong at least for English) that we would find AS-nominals that are 'conversions'.

Above we have seen how, in a syntactic theory of morphology, the difference between R-nominals and AS-nominals may arise. R-nominals are directly formed on the basis of what we may call roots, or in Borer's terms EIs. These are elements without any further grammatical information, existing as pure form–meaning pairs. AS-nominals on the other hand are built from larger structures, involving one or more functional projections that allow for different types of arguments; these functional projections also have the effect of categorising the roots.

4.7 A syntactic view on synthetic compounds

Now what can be said from this syntactic perspective on morphology about synthetic compounds? Borer (2010) argues that it cannot be maintained that in synthetic compounds there is an argumental dependency between the non-head and the head. First of all, it simply cannot be maintained that the right-hand part of synthetic compounds is an argument-taking complex event nominal. As we have seen above, complex event nominals truly have event-structure, whereas it can be shown that synthetic compounds lack such a structure. To see this, compare the complex event nominals in (80) with the synthetic compounds in (81):

(80) a. the breaking of the door by Mary in two minutes in order to retrieve her purse
     b. the stabbing of the emperor by Brutus for ten minutes in order to kill him

(81) a. the door-breaking (*by Mary) (*in two minutes) (*in order to retrieve her purse)
     b. the emperor-stabbing (*by Brutus) (*for ten minutes) (*in order to kill him)

In addition, we can easily embed synthetic compounds in the phrase *this kind of* . . . (cf. (37)); however, this is not possible for complex event nominals, as (82) shows (from Borer 2010):

(82) a. this kind of spouse-terrorising/dog-grooming/child-parenting, etc.
     b. ??this kind of destruction of cities/*outbidding of friends/*terrorising by mature males.

We may therefore conclude that the right-hand part of a synthetic compound is not an AS-nominal, but simply an R-nominal not supporting any argument-structure.

In addition to this, recall from Section 4.4 that, as Ackema and Neeleman (2004) observe, synthetic compounds allow for idiomatic interpretations. Consider the data (from Ackema and Neeleman 2004: 56) in (83):

(83) a. John is a real trouble-maker

    b. The company didn't know who the whistle-blower was

    c. This game is a great ice-breaker at parties

In Borer's theory, such interpretations are incompatible with the idea that the right-hand elements of these synthetic compounds are AS-nominals. AS-nominals include functional projections (that allow for the argument-structure), and therefore are necessarily transparent. We would have to cross functional boundaries in order to get the interpretation, thus barring any idiosyncrasies. Consequently, the possible idiomatic interpretation of synthetic compounds supports the conclusion that the right-hand element of these constructions is not an AS-nominal.

But how then do we account for the difference between root compounds and synthetic compounds? In essence, Borer argues that synthetic compounds are just root compounds. The only difference between the two is that the specific properties of synthetic compounds must be attributed to the properties of the affixes *-ing* and *-er*. More specifically, *-ing* forces an interpretation of the derivative as a simple event noun with a so-called originator (a thematic role that is more or less identical to Agent). Now consider the following examples:

(84) a. *chef stewing (of the dish) (in the reading that the chef is the agent/originator)

      b. chef stewing (of the dish) (in a manner reading; the way it was prepared)

The ungrammaticality of (84a) is explained as follows. Since the affix *-ing* brings with it the interpretation of an originator, there is no room in the same domain for a second originator. Of course, this explains the observation expressed by the First Sister Principle of Roeper and Siegel that subjects are not possible as non-heads within synthetic compounds. Interestingly, the same left-hand part is licit when interpreted as a modifier. So only the interpretation that the stewing is done in the way chefs do it is possible.

It would go beyond the limits of this chapter to go into the technical details of Borer's proposed explanation and its further consequences. However, there is one more point we need to address with respect to the analysis of synthetic compounds. The basic idea of the analysis is that the synthetic compounds have the structure $[\, [a \, b]_v \, \text{-er/-ing}]_N$. That brings us to the question of why the verbs of the type $[a \, b]$ are lacking.

Recall from our discussion in Section 4.4 that Ackema and Neeleman (2004) observe that verbal compounds are only possible when the left-hand member of such a compound is not interpreted as the object of the verb. So the verbs in (85a) are all perfect verbs of English, whereas those in (85b) are impossible:

(85) a. to breast-feed   b. *to milk-drink   c. milk-drink-ing/er
          to chain-smoke   *to cigarette-smoke   cigarette-smok-ing/er

          to play-act   *to ball-kick   ball-kick-ing/er
          to window-shop   *to book-read   book-read-ing/er

However, as soon as the verbal compounds are embedded in a larger structure, suddenly they become well-formed. The words in (85c) are all possible in English. Marchand (1969) assumes that compounds with a verb as their right-hand member are in fact impossible in English. The existence of the compounds in (85c) is then the result of backformation. **Backformation** is a process in which a word is reconstructed from a more complex form by dropping the affix. From *air-conditioner* through backformation we may derive the verb *to air-condition*, from *chain-smoker* we derive to *chain-smoke*, etc. However, many morphologists have argued against backformation as a possible synchronic morphological process. The essential point is that in order to be able to drop the affix, the base would have to be reanalysed as a compound verb. But if compound verbs are impossible in the language, what could make such a reconstruction possible?

Ackema and Neeleman explain this state of affairs as follows. They assume, following Williams (2007) and DiSciullo and Williams (1987) in this respect, that the grammar has two distinct components: a morphological component building words, and a syntactic component that builds phrases. The general idea is (leaving out technical details for the moment) that if the same structure may arise in the syntax and in the morphology, resulting in the encoding of the same semantic relation between a head and a complement, then the syntactic structure prevails. Put differently, their idea is that under certain conditions words are blocked by phrases. If we apply this reasoning to the data in (85), we can see that the verbs have an identical semantic relation between the head (i.e. the verb) and the object (the left-hand part of the compound) to that of the verb phrases in (86):

(86) to drink milk
      to smoke a cigarette
      to kick a ball
      to read a book

Since syntax 'goes before' morphology, the verbal compounds in (85b) are blocked, and hence their impossibility. According to Ackema and Neeleman (2004: 50), the structures compared are the ones in (87):

(87)   a.   b.

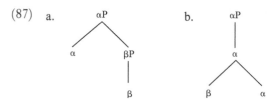

If structures of this type encode the same semantic relation between α and β, the structure in (87a) blocks the one in (87b).

Now, what can we say about the verb compounds in (85) which are existing verbs of English? In those cases the syntactic structure differs from the one in (87a). In all of these cases a preposition is needed in syntax to express the relationship between the head and the complement. That makes the structure of the syntactic counterparts of these verbs more complex, and therefore they do not block the morphological structures. Also, the morphological structures in (85a) do not have syntactic counterparts with a comparable structure, and therefore they are possible words of English.

Borer cannot pursue such a blocking explanation since in her syntactic theory of morphology, there is only a single grammatical component that is responsible for the formation of both words and of phrases. Borer (2010) therefore simply stipulates that NV-compounds cannot exist without further morphological derivation. Such a stipulation makes the verbs in (85a) rather problematic, but there is an interesting difference between these verbs and the impossible ones in (85b). The former all have an idiomatic interpretation. Therefore, they must result from a single inspection of the encyclopedia. Put differently, these verbs are almost indistinguishable from un-derived verbs, and therefore they do not fall under whatever stipulation one may formulate as to the non-existence of compound verbs. They are essentially simplex verbs.

4.8 A lexical semantic approach

As will be clear from the above discussion, one of the central questions concerning the role of argument-structure in the derivation of words is how we may characterise the meaning of the derived words in relation to the meaning of their bases. We have looked at a lexical view in which affixes were considered to be functors on argument-structure, and we have discussed a purely syntactic approach. In this final section we will introduce a third approach to these questions. This approach, put forth by Lieber (2004), is also lexical in the sense that the word-formation operations are assumed to take place in a separate domain of the grammar that is clearly different from syntax. Moreover, as in DiSciullo and Williams' approach, the operations of word-formation make use of lexical representations. In Borer's terminology, Lieber's lexical semantic theory would qualify as an endo-skeletal approach, since the syntactic distribution of lexical items is, at least partly, a function of their lexical specification.

Lieber makes a distinction between two different kinds of knowledge that native speakers have of the meaning of a word. The first kind, referred to as the 'skeleton', is the same for every speaker and isolates that part of the meaning of the word that is relevant to the syntax. The second kind, referred to as the 'body', is more variant across speakers and involves what we have so far called encyclopedic knowledge. The skeletal meaning of a word is not only stable and the same for each speaker within the language community, but is also that part which is formal and determined by grammatical principles. The body is largely determined by the speaker's experiences, individual knowledge, etc. and has no bearing on the grammar.

In order to characterise the skeletal meaning of words, Lieber makes use of three features: [± material], [± dynamic] and [± IEPS]. We will refrain from discussing the [±IEPS] feature here (see Chapter 5 for further discussion) since it is not immediately relevant to the empirical issues we would like to address in the remainder of this chapter. The feature [material] is used to separate concrete nouns from abstract nouns, the former having a feature [+material] and the latter being [−material]. The same feature is irrelevant for verbs and adjectives, and therefore absent from their lexical specifications. The feature [dynamic] is used to separate stative verbs and adjectives on the one hand (specified as [−dynamic]) from eventive verbs ([+dynamic]). These features (and maybe one or two more) form the set of primitives from which the skeletal meaning of words is constructed. Following Williams (1981) and Higginbotham (1985), Lieber further assumes that words from all major lexical categories take arguments. It is the features that are responsible for this argument-taking property: they are the argument-taking functions. Furthermore, the arguments of these features may in turn be argument-taking functions themselves. This property will be necessary to deal with affixation; in those cases the argument of the affix is the skeleton of the base.

Consider first some simple examples of the skeletal meaning of words. These are taken from Lieber (2004: 25):

(88) chair   [+material ([ ])]   leg   [+material ([ ], [ ])]
      happy   [−dynamic ([ ])]   fond   [−dynamic ([ ], [ ])]
      snore   [+dynamic ([ ])]   kiss   [+dynamic ([ ], [ ])]

The word *chair* has as its external function the feature [+material]. This feature takes a single argument, which we can identify with Williams' R-role. The adjective *happy* also takes a single argument but here it is the argument of the feature [−dynamic], expressing the fact that this adjective refers to a state. The verb *snore* has the same structure; in this case the feature [+dynamic] expresses the eventive character of this verb. Note that the same functions are present in the words *leg, fond* and *kiss* respectively, but these words are 'transitive', i.e. they take two arguments: an external one which is identical to the ones present in the items with a single argument and an additional internal one. The adjective *fond* has an internal argument as can be seen in *John is fond of Mary*. Lieber assumes that in *the leg of the table, the table* also receives a role from *leg*.

So far, verbs and adjectives have different featural semantics from that of nouns. However, in principle the features cross such categorial boundaries. Lieber shows that the feature [± dynamic] also plays a role in nouns. She notes that nouns such as *parent, author, chef* and *war* all imply a specific type of event, and therefore she assumes that the lexical semantic specification of these nouns includes the feature [dynamic]. This feature is used here in a privative way: it can only be present or absent in nouns; there does not seem to be a meaningful interpretation of [−dynamic] in a nominal context. This leads to the following classification of nouns (from Lieber 2004: 27):

(89)

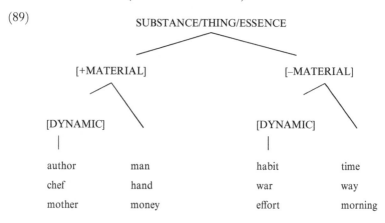

Lieber further proposes that affixes can have the same type of skeletons that specify their lexical semantics as can the lexical items in e.g. (88) and (89). Consider the affix -*er*. Words formed with this affix are concrete dynamic nouns. Lieber therefore proposes that the lexical semantic skeleton of this affix is [+material, dynamic ([ ], <base>)].

In order to make this theory actually 'do' something in the case of word-formation, we need a bit more theory that tells us how the inter-action of the skeleton of the base and the skeleton of the affix proceeds during derivation in such a way that the empirical facts with respect to affixation and compounding follow. To do this, Lieber proposes the following principle (Lieber 2004: 61):

(90) Principle of Coindexation:
In a configuration in which semantic skeletons are composed, coindex the highest nonhead argument with the highest (preferably unindexed) head argument. Indexing must be consistent with semantic conditions on the head argument, if any.

The principle predicts that in compounding, the reference of the left-hand member and that of the right-hand member are identified with one another. Take as an example the compound *clergyman-poet*. Their skeletons are given in

(91) clergyman   [+material, dynamic ([ ])
     poet   [+material, dynamic ([ ])

Following the Principle of Coindexation, we expect that in the compound *clergyman-poet* the two arguments of these nouns are being coindexed, and thus we predict that their reference is the same:

(92) [+material, dynamic ([ ]$_i$)] [+material, dynamic ([ ]$_i$)]

This works nicely for such copulative compounds as *clergyman-poet*, *producer-director*, *writer-editor*, etc. However, it is far from being the case that all compounds allow this copulative interpretation. In standard compounding, the right-hand element is the head and the left-hand member is interpreted as a modifier. In order to get this result from the assumptions made thus far, Lieber reasons as follows. In the copulative compounds not only are the skeletons identical but also the semantic bodies largely overlap. A clergyman is a human being as is a poet; they are both male, learned people; etc. This makes identification of the references with one another easy. However, if the semantic bodies of the two elements of a compound are not overlapping to a certain extent, then the identification of the references with one another is no longer possible and the best option left is for an interpretation as modification. If the identification with one another of references between head and non-head is not possible because the semantic bodies of the two elements contain conflicting information, the second-best possible interpretation is the one in which the non-head modifies the head.

We are now in a position to take a look at synthetic compounds from this perspective. In (93) we have listed the lexical semantic skeletons of the elements involved in our favourite and prototypical synthetic compound: *truckdriver*.

(93)   *-er*   [+material, dynamic ([ ], <base>)
       truck   [+material ([ ])]
       drive   [+dynamic ([ ], [ ])

If we first derive the word *driver*, according to the principle of coindexation, we get the following indexed structure:

(94) [+material, dynamic ([ ]$_i$, [+dynamic ([ ]$_i$, [ ])])]
       -er   *drive*

The principle in (90) forces an interpretation in which the highest argument of the verb *drive* is coindexed with the argument of *-er*. (Note that this works in much the same way as DiSciullo and Williams' proposal discussed above.) The next step is that the structure in (94) as a whole is compounded with the noun *truck*. The principle forces coindexation of the internal argument of *drive* with the external argument of *truck* (its R-role), since the highest argument of *drive* is already 'occupied' by being coindexed with the external argument of *-er*. So the result is the structure in (95):

(95) [+material ([ ]$_j$)] [+material, dynamic ([ ]$_i$, [+dynamic ([ ]$_i$, [ ]$_j$)])]
      truck   *driver*

Let us now briefly turn to Lieber's treatment of the affix *-ee*. Since words formed with this affix also denote concrete dynamic nouns, this affix has the same lexical semantic skeleton as the affix *-er*. Basing herself mainly on the work of Barker (1998), Lieber notes that this affix can only be coindexed with arguments that are 'sentient' and 'non-volitional'. So the subcategorisation frame of *-ee* looks as follows (Lieber 1998: 62):

(96) *-ee*:
      Syntactic subcategorisation: attaches to V, N
      Skeleton: [+material, dynamic ([$_{sentient, nonvolitional}$], <base>)]

As can be seen in (96), this additional semantic requirement of *-ee* is part of its skeleton. The Principle of Coindexation is formulated in such a way that it checks whether such additional semantic conditions are met. In such a way, the difference between the distribution and meaning of *-er* and *-ee* is accounted for.

Above we have briefly sketched how, in Lieber's lexical semantic approach, an account of synthetic compounds can be given. We will come back to her theory of morphology in Chapter 5, where we will be discussing the formation of verbs.

Exercises

1. Give the argument-structure of the following nouns first in the theory of DiSciullo and Williams and second in the lexical semantic theory of Lieber. How are (e) and (f) ruled out by these theories (if that is so)?

   a. killer   c. biographee   e. *faller
   b. controller d. escapee   f. *walkee

2. Which of the following verbs are unergative and which are unaccusative? Provide arguments for your position.

   a. to part   b. to jump   c. to go   d. to leave

3. Decide, using a range of different criteria, whether the following nouns are complex event nominal or result nouns:

   a. surprise b. discussion c. pollution d. argument

4. How does Borer explain the ungrammaticality of the following expressions?

   a. *the hit of Bill was really mean   [in the reading that Bill is the one who is hit]
   b. *the kill of the mouse took the cat less than a second

5. Explain for each verb in (85a) why it is an existing verb of English according to Ackema and Neeleman's view. Try to think of two or three compound verbs that Ackema and Neeleman would predict are grammatical.

6. Give the lexical semantic skeleton of the following words, illustrating the Principle of Coindexation:

   a. singer-songwriter
   b. escapee

Further reading

Alexiadou, Artemis (2001) *Functional Structure in Nominals: Nominalization and Ergativitiy*, Amsterdam and Philadelphia: John Benjamins.

Borer, Hagit (2005) *Structuring Sense. Vol. I: In Name Only*, Oxford: Oxford University Press.

Harley, Heidi (2009) 'The Morphology of Nominalization and the Syntax of vP', in Giannakidou, Artemis and Monika Rathert (eds.), *Quantification, Definiteness and Nominalization*, Oxford: Oxford University Press, pp. 321–43.

5 Argument-structure: Derived verbs

5.1 Introduction

In Chapter 4, we saw that argument-structure plays an important role in the derivation of nouns from verbs. In this chapter, we will see how argument-structure also plays a role in the derivation of verbs from nouns and adjectives. It is very easy to coin a new verb on the basis of a noun or an adjective in English. To begin with, verb-forming conversion is extremely productive: nouns verb easily. Clark and Clark (1979) give numerous examples of this process, which is characterised by a lack of visible affixation. Among the verb-forming morphological processes, conversion is by far the most productive. However, it is not the only derivational means by which verbs can be formed. There are also a series of verbal affixes that can be used to derive verbs. Below we list some examples:

(1) a. paint   to paint   cool   to cool
         cover   to cover   dry   to dry
         saddle   to saddle
         shelf   to shelve

     b. apology   to apologise   eternal   to eternalise
         carbon   to carbonise   minimal   to minimalise
         cannibal to cannibalise general   to generalise
         civilian to civilianise
         hospital to hospitalise

     c. glory   glorify   humid   humidify
         pure   purify
         solid   solidify

     d. deep   deepen
         red   redden
         soft   soften

The data in (1) show that both adjectives and nouns can be verbalised by suffixes such as -*ise*, -*ify* and -*en* and by zero-derivation (or conversion). Moreover, verbs can also be derived from nominal and adjectival bases by prefixation:

(2)   a.   bark   to embark
           body   to embody
           gender   to engender
           compass   to encompass

        b.   large   to enlarge
           noble   to ennoble
           rich   to enrich

Questions arise at the moment we realise that the meaning of these denominal and deadjectival verbs is to a certain extent predictable given the meaning of the base-noun or base-adjective. For example, a verb such as *to deepen* may have precisely two separate meanings: it can either mean 'to cause to become deep', which for obvious reasons is called the **causative** reading, or simply 'to become deep', which is – less perspicuously – called the **inchoative** reading. It is impossible for this verb to mean something like 'to recover from the depth', or 'to stow away in a deep hole'. We therefore need a theory that explains why the first two readings are possible where other interpretations are excluded.

Such a theory of lexical knowledge will include a theory of word-formation that tries to break up these lexical items into smaller constituting elements. The aim is then to derive restrictions on the possible meanings of these complex verbs from a (hopefully rather small) set of elements and the way these elements can be combined into larger constructs. Different types of theories have been proposed. Some theories claim that the same principles that guide the formation of phrases in syntax are also applicable in this lexical domain (e.g. Hale and Keyser 1993, 1998, 2002, Harley 1999, 2005). Others, basing themselves on the foundational work of Jackendoff (1990), have developed theories of lexical semantics using what is called lexical conceptual structure in order to express the relation between the meaning of the derived verb and the base-noun or base-adjective (e.g. Levin and Rappaport Hovav 1995, 2005, Plag 1999, Booij and Lieber 2004, Lieber 1998, 2004).

Before we get to a discussion of these approaches it is important to realise that it is not just grammatical knowledge that determines the interpretation of these complex words. First of all, pragmatic context provides many clues to the language user as to the correct interpretation of a newly coined word. Clark and Clark (1979: 784) provide the following example:

(3)   My sister Houdini'd her way out of the locked closet.

They ask how the proper noun *Houdini* can be successfully turned into a verb, especially since it is generally assumed that proper nouns have no real meaning. Proper nouns or names just refer to a particular individual. Apparently, in this example, it is mainly encyclopedic knowledge – that is, the fact that Houdini is a famous magician, well known for his disappearance tricks – in combination with the context that enables the hearer to get at the intended interpretation. In order to use a verb like this successfully, speaker and hearer need to co-operate closely in the sense that both at least have to share this piece of knowledge. More specifically, the speaker needs to ascertain that the listener shares this particular piece of knowledge. In general, according to Clark and Clark (1979: 787), speakers follow the innovative denominal verb convention:

(4)   The Innovative Denominal Verb Convention:
      In using an innovative denominal sincerely, the speaker means to denote:
      a. the kind of situation
      b. that he has good reason to believe
      c. that on this occasion the listener can readily compute
      d. uniquely
      e. on the basis of their mutual knowledge
      f. in such a way that the parent noun denotes one role in the situation, and the remaining surface arguments of the denominal verb denote other roles in the situation.

This convention is formulated as a purely pragmatic one. The question that morphologists have addressed is whether linguistic knowledge is also involved in determining the lexical semantics of the derived verb. That is, are there any restrictions (morphological or otherwise) on the potential role that the noun (or adjective) that forms the base of the denominal verb plays in the semantics of the derived verb? We will see below that morphologists have tried to answer this question in different ways. At the same time it is clear that context plays an important role in the determination of the semantics of the derived verbs, particularly if the verb is derived from a noun or an adjective through conversion.

  Aronoff (1980) proposes that the importance of context in getting the correct interpretation of denominal verbs derives from the fact that the WFR responsible for conversion simply does not give any semantic information. In his words: '[t]he fact that there is such a wide variety of meanings follows directly from the fact that the meaning of the verb is limited only to an activity which has some connection to the noun' (1980: 747).

We will see in the course of this chapter that different authors have tried to explain the wide variety of possible meanings associated with converted verbs in different ways, but these more recent explanations in general follow the views expressed by Clark and Clark and by Aronoff in the sense that they all stress the importance of contextual interpretation and the relative openness of the semantics of the converted verbs.

Apart from the contribution of encyclopedic knowledge that is certainly required during interpretation, the speaker/hearer also has knowledge of such words that is not encyclopedic in nature, but conceptual. Kiparsky (1997) cites the following example that illustrates the point. Consider the verb *to paint*. We may have learned from exposure to this verb that it means something like *to cover with paint*. Kiparsky notes that speakers wouldn't hesitate to use this verb for the same process if the painting was done not with an ordinary brush particularly intended for that task but with a less prototypical instrument that may function as a brush. However, he also points out that when, for example, a vat of paint explodes in a paint factory, we couldn't describe this situation with sentence (5a), nor could we describe a situation in which Velázquez dips his brush in paint with sentence (5b) (examples from Kiparsky 1997: 473):

(5) a. The explosion painted the workers red.
     b. Velázquez painted his brush.

A proper theory of verb-formation, therefore, should account for such conceptual knowledge and should be able to explain why it is that we 'know' such things about the semantics of these words on the basis of the limited experience that we get during acquisition. Kiparsky suggests that *painting*, being a denominal causative verb, implies that there is an intentional activity. For this reason (5a) is at least odd, since explosions do not have intentions. This is corroborated by the following observation. One could imagine a situation in which the explosion is intended to have the effect of making the workers red. In such a situation it wouldn't be so odd to use (5a). Similarly (5b) is only odd if the dipping of the brush into the paint is not done with the intention of 'painting' the brush.

It is characteristic of the study of verb-formation that researchers try to answer the question as to what type of relations are possible between the meaning of the derived verb and the meaning of the base-noun or base-adjective. With a look at the wealth of data from Clark and Clark's contribution, and Aronoff's claim that conversions allow for any interpretation as long as there is any connection between the meaning of the base-noun and the activity expressed by the verb, it is tempting to say: anything goes. Clark and Clark classify derived verbs in terms of the relations between the meaning of the base-noun and the meaning of the derived verb. They distinguish the following classes: locatum verbs (*to blanket the bed*), location verbs (*to kennel the dog*), duration verbs (*to summer in France*), agent verbs (*to butcher the cow*), experiencer verbs (*to witness the evidence*), goal verbs (*to cripple the man*), source verbs (*to word the sentence*), instrument verbs (*to hammer the nail*) and a 'miscellaneous' class including such verbs as *to lunch* and *to rain*. As an example, let us take a closer look at two of their classes (which make up a large part of their total) in (6):

(6)   a.   to blanket (the bed)   b.   to kennel (the dog)
           to linoleum (the floor)   to beach (the boats)
           to camouflage (the tent)   to spit (the chicken)
           to paint (the wall)   to list (the verbs)
           to wallpaper (the room)   to book (the flight)
           to roof (the house)   to front-page (the news)
           to plaster (the wall)   to hive (the bees)

The verbs in (6a) are dubbed **locatum verbs** by Clark and Clark since the base-noun of these verbs is the thing that is somehow placed on, in, along, etc. the verb's object (examples of these objects are given in brackets). The ones in (6b) are called **location verbs** since in these cases it is the object of the verb that is somehow placed on, in, along, etc. the base-noun of the verb. So we can paraphrase the meaning of the locatum verbs roughly as follows: 'to put the <name of the verb> on/in/along the <object of the verb>', while the meaning of the location verbs is roughly: 'to put the <object of the verb> on/in/along the <name of the verb>'.

The main challenge thus posed by these data for morphological theory is how to account for the lexical meaning of the derived verbs in terms of the meaning of the base-noun or base-adjective. If really any relation between base and derived verb is possible, there is not much ground to build a theory on, but as it turns out, it is simply not the case that 'anything goes'. At least, there seem to be preferred relations between base and derived verbs, and it is claimed that some relations are simply impossible. In other words, apart from the conceptual and pragmatic constraints on the interpretation of derived verbs, there may also be grammatical (morphological) restrictions.

Furthermore, the **zero-derived** forms pose an additional question. These derived forms are characterised by the fact that there is no (overt) affix that marks the derivational process. For some researchers (Allen 1978, Kiparsky 1982) this is a reason to believe that there is a zero-affix present in these cases; others have proposed 'headless rules' that simply change the category of the base (Williams 1981, Strauss 1982). Yet others (Lieber 2004) have proposed that conversion is a case of relisting. We will come back to these proposals in Section 5.5.

Also, since there is no affixation or any other phonological marking involved in such cases, we may ask which direction the process of derivation takes in these examples. It seems 'natural' to assume for the data in (6) that the verbs are derived from the nouns (as depicted in (7a)). However, it may also be the case that the verbs are simply based on the same root as the noun. Under such an analysis there is no direction from noun or adjective to verb, but both the noun and the verb are derived from the same underlying root (7b).

(7) a. N → V   b. √ → N

                             √ → V

Some theorists (Hale and Keyser 1993, 2002) explain the role played by the base-noun or base-adjective in the formation of the derived verbs in terms of their syntactic structure. To these authors, the derived verbs are the result of a syntactic process called incorporation that 'conflates' the base-noun, a complement of the underlying verbal head, with that same head. Others (e.g. Harley 2004, 2005, Borer 2005a, 2005b) have further developed these ideas into a theory that does not make a distinction between morphology and syntax. For them verb-formation (like any word-formation process) is simply a part of syntax. We will discuss these proposals in Section 5.2.

Others (e.g. Lieber 1998, Plag 1999) explain these relations in terms of a theory of lexical semantics, first proposed by Jackendoff (1990). In such theories every lexical item has what is called a lexical conceptual structure (LCS) that represents the lexical meaning of that particular item. LCSs are built from a limited set of predicates, such as GO, CAUSE, TO and INCH (inchoative), which take arguments that come in different types such as events, paths, things and so on. Verb-formation in these theories is now seen as an operation on these LCSs such that the LCS of the affix determines the LCS of the derived verb, and the base-noun takes one of the argument positions in this new LCS. These theories are the topic of Section 5.3. More recently, Lieber (2004) makes a proposal inspired by these theories but in terms of semantic features. This will be the topic of Section 5.4.

5.2 A syntactic approach: Denominal verbs as incorporation

Before turning to a somewhat more detailed discussion of the approach to verb-formation as a syntactic process of incorporation, we will first try to make the intuition behind this approach clear. Walinska de

Hackbeil (1986) proposed such a syntactic approach towards denominal and deadjectival verbs. Consider the verbs in (8):

(8)   to laugh
       to embark
       to saddle
       to shelve

The meaning of these verbs can be roughly paraphrased as 'to do a laugh', 'to cause someone to go into a bark', 'to put a saddle on something' and 'to put something on a shelf'. The idea of the lexico-syntactic approach to these derivations is that there is a syntactic structure underlying these derived verbs that closely mirrors these paraphrases. The semantics of these verbs can be directly read off this syntactic structure. That is, this level of representation encodes the semantic relation between base-noun and derived verb, and any restrictions on the possible interpretation of the derived verb should in this theory follow from the way these representations are derived. The crucial operation that derives the complex verb from the underlying structure is syntactic movement. So any known restrictions on syntactic movement should explain the range of possible denominal complex verbs.

The central idea of the analysis is that there is an empty verbal position heading the underlying verb phrase. These syntactic empty verbal positions semantically correspond to elements such as 'do', 'cause', 'go' and 'put' in the paraphrases above. The base-noun or base-adjective originates in the underlying syntactic structure in the complement position of these empty verbs, and moves, either directly or through other head positions, to this verbal head in the process of verb-formation. The structure in (9) illustrates this idea for a simple case, here *to laugh* (cf. Hale and Keyser 1993: 54–5):

(9)

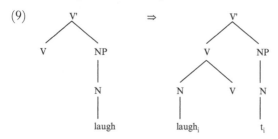

The noun *laugh* in (9) moves from the head position in the object NP (as a complement of the empty verb) to the verbal head. As a result, a verbal complex is formed and the head position of the NP becomes empty (leaving behind a trace *t*).

This idea of movement of a syntactic complement into the head position comes from the work of Baker (1988) on **incorporation**. This phenomenon, well known from what are called polysynthetic languages, involves the formation of a compound verb in which the non-head originates as a complement of that verb or as an adverbial modifier, while the verb itself retains its original syntactic function. Below we give a simple example from Chukchee (from Spencer 1991: 15), a Paleo-Siberian language spoken in Siberia. In (10a) the verb *pelarken* 'leave' takes the object *qorane* 'reindeer'. In (10b) this object is incorporated into the verb, thus deriving a verbal compound.

(10) a. tə -pelarkən   qoraŋə   'I am leaving the reindeer'
          I   -leave   reindeer

      b. tə -qora-pelarkən   'I am leaving the reindeer'
          I   -reindeer-leave

Hale and Keyser propose in a series of articles (including Hale and Keyser 1993, 1998, 1999) culminating in a book (Hale and Keyser 2002) that the formation of denominal verbs in English is in fact also a type of incorporation. Intransitive verbs such as *laugh, sneeze, drool, dance,* etc. are all formed by incorporation on the basis of the identical nouns as in (9).

A somewhat more complicated case is a locatum verb as in (6a). The example discussed by Hale and Keyser (1993) concerns the verb *to shelve*, which can be paraphrased as 'to put something on a shelf'. Before we turn to the derived verb *to shelve*, we will first take a look at the assumed syntactic structure of the verb *to put* (from Hale and Keyser 1993: 56):

(11)

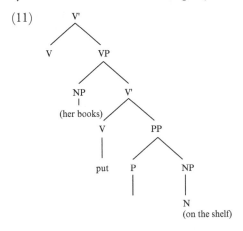

This syntactic structure is argued for by Larson (1988) for 'double-object' constructions that have both a direct and indirect object, such as *to give,*

and for verbs such as *to put* that take a PP-complement (*on the shelf*) in addition to a direct object (*her books*). It is important to see that the structure involves two verbal nodes: one higher up, taking the direct object (*her books*) as its complement, and a second one lower in the structure that takes a PP-complement (*on the shelf*). The arguments that Larson put forth to motivate this particular structure need not concern us here; we simply assume this structure in our discussion of Hale and Keyser's proposal.

Given the structure in (11) for the verb *to put*, we can now see how the verb *to shelve* is derived by incorporation of the PP-complement into the higher empty verbal node. Hale and Keyser propose the following underlying structure for this verb (1993: 57):

(12)

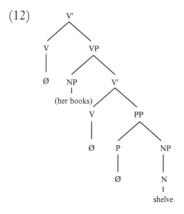

First, the noun *shelf* moves from its original position in (12) to the (empty) prepositional head, and then further on to the immediately dominating verbal head. From there, it further moves to the higher verbal head, deriving the structure in (13):

(13)

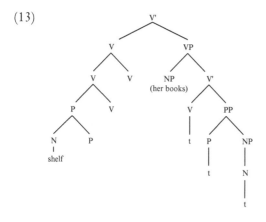

Not only does this 'syntactic movement' approach work in the case of conversion, but verbal suffixes may also receive the same treatment. In such cases it is the affix that originates in the verbal head position to which the noun or adjective moves.

An important argument for this syntactic approach to the formation of denominal verbs is the non-existence of certain types of denominal verbs that we might expect to find. Their ungrammaticality can be explained by the same principles that govern the syntactic incorporation structures. For example, Baker (1988) shows that incorporation is not possible in the case of subjects. So in languages such as Chukchee we will not find examples of the following type:

(14) a. reindeer   walk   across the plane
      b. *it   reindeer-walks   across the plane

Baker (1988) attributes this fact to general syntactic restrictions on movement (in particular, the Empty Category Principle) that forbid such movement from subject position to a lower position in the syntactic structure. From the impossibility of subjects incorporating, Hale and Keyser derive the fact that certain types of transitive verbs do not exist, despite the general productivity of the verb-forming process, as observed and documented by Clark and Clark (1979). To see this point more clearly, consider the data in (15) (from Hale and Keyser 1993: 60):

(15) a. *it cowed a calf
         (cf. A cow had a calf. A cow calved.)
      b. *it mared a foal
         (cf. A mare had a foal. A mare foaled.)
      c. *it dusted the horses blind
         (cf. The dust made the horses blind. The dust blinded the horses.)
      d. *it machined the wine into bottles
         (cf. A machine got the wine into bottles. The machine bottled
         the wine.)

The structure that is required in order to derive the impossible denominal verb *to cow* (*a calf*), meaning that the cow is the one that had a calf, would be as in (16):

(16)

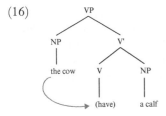

In order to derive the verbs in (15), the subject needs to be incorporated into the verb. However, as we can see in (16) this requires movement of the subject to the verbal head position, which is an illicit syntactic operation according to well-established syntactic restrictions on movement. In such a way the theory accounts for the impossibility of such verbs as those in (15).

Similarly, the theory may also account for the fact that recipients do not make proper bases for verb conversion. To see this, consider the data in (17):

(17) a. he gave money to the church
     b. *he churched the money
     c. he received money from his friend
     d. *he friended the money

The incorporation of the indirect object (*church* and *friend* respectively) would also involve an illicit movement, and thus the ungrammaticality of (17b and d) is taken as support for the syntactic approach of Hale and Keyser.

This approach is further elaborated upon in work by Harley (2004, 2005). Harley (2005) derives some aspectual properties of denominal verbs from properties of the underlying noun. First, take a look at the data in (18), which illustrate a basic aspectual difference between **telic verbs**, which have a natural end-point, and **atelic**, or **durative verbs**, which lack such an end-point. A diagnostic between these two classes is whether the verbs can be modified by adverbials expressing a duration, such as *for hours*, or by adverbials that imply an end-point, such as *in an hour*. The sentences marked with the symbol # are not necessarily ungrammatical but ask for a non-standard interpretation.

(18) a. Mary drank/wrote for hours
     b. #Mary drank/wrote in 5 minutes
     c. #Mary left/arrived for hours
     d. Mary left/arrived in 5 minutes

Since (18a) is fine and (18b) is odd, we can conclude that the verbs *drink* and *write*, at least in their intransitive use (without an object), are clearly durative, whereas the verbs in (18c) and (18d) show the opposite judgements and therefore must be considered telic verbs. Interestingly, telicity is not a property of verbs alone but can be influenced by the object of the verb. The atelic verbs *drink* and *write* become telic as soon as they are combined with a particular object. However, apparently not just any object can perform this change.

(19) a. Mary ate a sandwich in an hour/#for hours
    b. Mary ate sandwiches #in an hour/for hours
    c. Mary wrote a letter in an hour/#for hours
    d. Mary wrote letters #in an hour/for hours

If *ate* takes a bounded object (*sandwich*), the VP becomes telic; however, that effect disappears if we combine the same verb *eat* with an unbounded object (the plural of *sandwich*). Sentence (19b) shows *eat sandwiches* as atelic. The same shift in telicity happens to the verb *write* in combination with a bounded object such as *letter*, as in (19c), and in the case of an unbounded object (*letters*) as in (19d).

Harley now reasons thus: following the observations above, the aspectual properties of a verb are apparently dependent upon the properties of its object. If the object is bounded, the verb (or the verb phrase) has a telic aspect; if the object is unbounded, the verb phrase will be atelic.

Now we make the step towards the denominal verbs and see how the above observations with respect to telicity may support the incorporation analysis. If the incorporation analysis of denominal verbs is on the right track, one would expect that the aspectual properties of these denominal (intransitive) verbs are dependent upon the boundedness of the noun that forms the basis of these verbs. Since in the incorporation analysis these nouns start out as objects in the underlying syntactic structure, they should have the same effect as the objects in (19). The following examples can be given as an illustration of the correctness of this prediction (examples from Harley 2005):

(20) a. The mare foaled in 2 hours/#for 2 hours
    b. The cow calved in 2 hours/#for 2 hours
    c. The baby drooled #in 2 hours/for 2 hours
    d. The athlete sweated #in 2 hours/for 2 hours

The nouns (or roots) *foal* and *calve* are bounded objects and therefore it is expected that their corresponding verbs will be telic. The nouns *drool* and *sweat*, on the other hand, are unbounded and therefore their corresponding verbs are expected to be atelic. This is in accordance with the judgements given in (20).

Interestingly, if we take the structure that Hale and Keyser propose for locatum verbs in (12) and (13), we expect that the boundedness properties of the noun that is in the PP would determine the aspectual properties of the denominal verb. Again, this seems to be the correct prediction, as may be concluded from the following data (Harley 2005: 59–60):

(21) a. John saddled the horse # for 5 minutes/in 5 minutes.

    b. Sue boxed the computer #for 5 minutes/in 5 minutes.
    c. Mom blindfolded her child #for a minute/in a minute.

(22) a. Susan watered the garden for an hour/in an hour.
      b. Bill greased the chain for 5 minutes/in 5 minutes.
      c. Jill painted the wall for an hour/in an hour.

Harley claims that the possibility of an atelic reading of the verbs in (22) derives from the unboundedness of the incorporated noun (*water, grease, paint*), whereas the impossibility of such an atelic reading in (21) is due to the boundedness of the incorporated nouns (*saddle, box, blindfold*).

As we have already pointed out in the introduction to this chapter, the incorporation proposal has been criticised for the fact that it does not take into account any conceptual knowledge. Furthermore, Kiparsky (1997) observes that the system of Hale and Keyser over-generates to a large extent. Take again, for example, the location and locatum verbs. One may wonder why a location verb such as *to shelve* exists, while there is no locatum verb *to shelve* meaning 'to put shelves onto something' (**John shelved the wall*). Or why there is a location verb *to paint* (meaning 'to put paint onto something'), but no locatum verb *to paint* with the meaning 'to put something into paint'. (Note that if such a verb existed, the sentence in (5b) would be fine under the intended reading.) Kiparsky (1997: 482) proposes (following earlier propos-als by Bierwisch and Schreuder 1992 and Wunderlich 1997a) that a general conceptual principle applies that governs the interpretations of denominal verbs:

(23) If an action is named after a thing, it involves a canonical use of
      the thing.

Such a principle explains why we do not have a locatum verb *to paint*, since it is not a canonical use of paint to dip something in it. Similarly, it is not a canonical use of shelves to hang them on a wall, and thus a locational reading of this verb is impossible.

This shows at least that it is not the lexico-syntactic representation alone that determines the set of possible denominal and deadjectival verbs, but there is also a crucial role to play for conceptual knowledge. Now one may go a step further and ask whether we actually need the syntactic principles of Hale and Keyser and Harley, or whether the conceptual principles on their own would suffice to explain the range of possible meanings of denominal verbs. Farrell (1998) suggests that we may understand the restrictions on verb-forming conversion solely by making use of such conceptual principles. He proposes the following constraints on noun-to-verb conversion (Farrell 1998: 47):

(24) A verb of the form [v [N]] is appropriately named if
  a. a characteristic behavior of the thing designated by N is the
      type of behavior the verb designates, or
  b. a central property of the thing designated by N is involvement
      in the type of event that the verb designates.

Note that the constraint in (24a) is in intention almost identical to
the one proposed by Kiparsky. Farrell argues that these conditions on
noun-to-verb conversion may also explain the ungrammaticality of the
data in (17b and d), since 'giving to' is not a characteristic behaviour of
a church, nor is 'getting from' a characteristic of friends. Furthermore,
given (24b) we can also understand why the subject incorporation interpretation does not exist in the cases of *to cow* and *to dust* in (15).

   Summarising, the approach put forth by Hale and Keyser makes use
of syntactic means (head movement, the Empty Category Principle)
to explain the relation between the base-noun and the derived verb.
The semantic relation between the two is expressed by means of a
lexico-syntactic structure. However, several researchers have pointed
out that conceptual knowledge plays a crucial role in the interpretation
of denominal verbs. It turns out that the prototypicality or canonicity of
the activity in relation to the noun is crucial for our understanding of
the interpretation of denominal verbs.

5.3 Lexical semantic approaches

Next to the syntactic theories proposed to account for the relation
between the meaning of the base-noun or base-adjective and the meaning
of the derived verb, theories have also been proposed that account for the
verb meanings in terms of lexical semantic representations in which the
base-noun or base-adjective somehow plays a role. Jackendoff (1990)
proposes that lexical semantic representations take the form of LCSs.
As mentioned in Section 5.1, these LCSs are built from a limited set of
predicates, such as GO, TO, BE, INCH, CAUSE, etc., taking arguments
of different types such as paths, things, places or events. LCSs are predicate argument-structures. Each predicate takes one or more argument
of a specific type. Furthermore, predicates can also take predicates as
their arguments, thus allowing hierarchical structures in which we may
find different layers of predication. The central idea of this approach to
verb-formation is that during this process the LCS of an affix (the morphological head) determines the LCS of the derived verb in such a way
that the base takes one of the argument positions in the LCS of the affix.
Below we give an example (from Lieber 1998) for the verb *civilianise* (25):

(25) $[_{\text{Event}}$ ACT $([_{\text{Thing}}], [_{\text{Event}}$ INCH $[_{\text{State}}$ BE $([_{\text{Thing}}], [_{\text{Place}}$ AT

$([_{\text{Thing}}$ civilian$])])])]$

The LCS of the verb *civilianise* is a predicate named ACT. This is a predicate of the event type and it takes two arguments (both given between round brackets, separated by a comma): the first argument is of the thing type and stands for the thing or person acting (informally: 'somebody acts on something'); the second is again a predicate of the event type and stands for what might be called the result of the ACT predicate ('somebody acts on something so that it becomes'). This event is an INCHOATIVE (INCH) predicate, roughly to be paraphrased as 'to become'. Again this predicate takes a predicate as its first (and only) argument. This is the stative two-place predicate BE. This BE-predicate takes two arguments: a thing (that what is being civilianised) and a predicate AT of the place type. This predicate finally takes the base-noun as its argument. So *civilianise* in this analysis can be informally paraphrased as 'to act on something so that it becomes at civilian'.

Investigating a large set of verbs all formed with the affix *-ise*, Lieber (1998) concludes that we need four different LCSs for *-ise* in order to characterise its behaviour in verb-formation. We have listed these four different LCSs in (26):

(26)   a. $[_{\text{Event}}$ $\underline{\text{ACT} ([_{\text{Thing}}}$ $], [_{\text{Event}}$ INCH $[_{\text{State}}$ BE $([_{\text{Thing}}],$

$[_{\text{Place}}$ AT $([_{\text{Thing, Property}}$ base$])])])])]$

   b. $[_{\text{Event}}$ $\underline{\text{ACT} ([_{\text{Thing}}}$ $], [_{\text{Event}}$ GO $([_{\text{Thing}}$ base$],$

$[_{\text{Path}}$ TO/ON/IN $([_{\text{Thing}}])])])]$

   c. $[_{\text{Event}}$ ACT $([_{\text{Thing}}$ $], [_{\text{Event}}$ GO $([_{\text{Thing}}], [_{\text{Path}}$ TO

$([_{\text{Thing}}$ base$])])])]$

   d. $[_{\text{Event}}$ ACT $([_{\text{Thing}}$ $], [_{\text{Manner}}$ LIKE $([_{\text{Thing, Property}}$ base$])])]$

The LCS in (26a) characterises the lexical semantics of verbs such as *civilianise, unionise, velarise*, etc. (in the way sketched above). Note that *civilian* in the structure of (25) has been replaced by a variable 'base' that stands for any particular base expressing a property. This base of these verbs is a property or thing argument of a place predicate. For a verb such as *to velarise*, this lexical conceptual semantic structure may be paraphrased as 'to act on something so that it becomes at a <base = velar> place'. The underlining of the first predicate and argument in this LCS expresses that this part of the structure is optional. So *to velar-*

ise may also be paraphrased as 'something becomes at a <base = velar> position', thus accounting for the inchoative reading.

This optionality expresses what is known as the causative–inchoative alternation. This alternation can be illustrated with the following examples (from Levin and Rappaport Hovav 1995: 85):

(27) a. Antonia broke the vase
      b. The vase broke
      c. Jean opened the window
      d. The window opened.
      e. The wind cleared the sky.
      f. The sky cleared.

Many (but not all) verbs with a causative reading also allow for a so-called inchoative reading. In (27a and b) this is illustrated for an un-derived verb; the verbs in (27c–f) are probably derived from under-lying adjectives and show the same alternation. The alternation simply involves the presence or absence of a causative predicate as part of the verb, and with this predicate an extra argument that takes the role as the causer. In Lieber's analysis this is expressed by the optionality of the predicate 'CAUSE' and its concomitant argument.

The LCS in (26b) characterises verbs such as *carbonise, oxidise, apolo-gise*, etc. Again, an informal paraphrase of their LCS would be 'to do something so that <base> goes to something'. The only difference between the LCSs in (26b) and (26c) is the position of the base. In a verb such as *to hospitalise* it is the object of the verb that goes to the hospital, whereas in the verbs characterised by (26b) it is the base of the verb that goes onto the object of the verb. Here we recognise the pattern that we discussed in Section 5.1 in talking about the difference between the locatum and locational verbs. The same LCSs that are proposed here for verbs derived with *-ise* are also applicable to some converted verbs. The LCS in (26c) nicely covers the lexical meaning of a verb such as *to shelve*. In a way, the syntactic analysis by Hale and Keyser is largely mirrored in this lexical semantic analysis by Lieber (or vice versa). The syntactic heads in Hale and Keyser's structure correspond to the predi-cates in Lieber's LCS. Finally, the LCS in (26d) differs somewhat from the others because another predicate is involved. The predicate LIKE is used to express the fact that in, for example, the verb *to hooliganise*, the lexical meaning could be paraphrased as 'to act in the way of a hooligan'.

Lieber (1998) stresses the fact that these four different LCSs have the first predicate and argument in common. This correspondence in the LCSs is enough for her to claim that the affix *-ise* is polyfunctional rather than that we are dealing with four different homophonous affixes.

Plag (1999) criticises Lieber's proposal and modifies it accordingly. One of the points of critique is that the four different LCSs proposed by Lieber do not account for the polyfunctionality of the affix. Plag for this reason aims at a single LCS to characterise the affix. If that is possible, we have a more principled account of polyfunctionality: polyfunctionality then only arises from the fact that bases may take different positions in the LCS of the affix. Plag proposes the following LCS to account for all derivations in -*ise*:

(28)   <u>CAUSE ([ ]_i</u>, [GO ([_{PROPERTY, THING}] _{THEME/BASE}, [TO [_{PROPERTY,THING}]

_{BASE/THEME}])])

As before, the underlining of the first predicate and argument indicates optionality. These verbs can be either causative or inchoative. Furthermore, as in Lieber's analysis, verbs such as *hospitalise* and *carbonise* only differ from each other in the position of the base in the LCS. In the former the base is an argument of the TO function, while in the latter it is an argument of the GO function.

The LCS in (28) differs from the four offered by Lieber in the choice of the function GO. For Plag this function covers both verbs such as *carbonise* and *apologise*, which are analysed with the predicates GO and TO by Lieber (1998) (see (26c)), and verbs such as *civilianise* and *velarise*, which are analysed with the predicates INCH and BE by Lieber (see (26a)). So GO becomes a somewhat more abstract function that may express both a change of position and a change of state of a particular property. In doing this, Plag is able to give a more principled account of polyfunctionality: affixes are polyfunctional if they have one and the same LCS and the bases of the complex forms may occupy different argument positions in this structure.

At this point, let us briefly compare the lexico-syntactic approach of Hale and Keyser with the lexical-semantic approach of Lieber and Plag. One might wish to say that Hale and Keyser have a strong point in comparison with these lexical semantic analyses in the fact that they have a more principled account of the non-existence of certain types of verbs. For example, the ban on subject incorporation in their theory follows from a principle that is independently motivated in syntax. It would be difficult to explain in Lieber's framework why a particular LCS is not possible. However, this is largely balanced by the observation that there are some serious problems with Hale and Keyser's syntactic analysis. Kiparsky (1997), for example, points out that we never find any 'stranding' in the case of incorporation. If indeed verb-formation is an instantiation of incorporation, then we would expect that modifiers of such an incorporated element could be left behind, i.e. could 'strand', to use the common syntactic terminology, as in (29a) (from Kiparsky 1997: 481).

(29) a. *We saddled her horse Western
     b. We saddled her horse with a Western saddle

Or, the other way around, how could we derive (29b) from an underlying structure in which the incorporated element *saddle* has the same thematic role as is expressed by the instrumental PP *with a Western saddle*?

Summarising, the lexico-semantic approach of Lieber (and Plag) makes an explicit and precise account of the way that the meaning of the base becomes part of the meaning of the derived verb. It resembles the syntactic approach of Hale and Keyser but avoids the syntactic problems that this approach seems to encounter.

5.4 Semantic features

The proposals in terms of LCSs get a follow-up in the work of Lieber (2004, 2009a). She proposes a theory of lexical semantics in which similar structures play a crucial role, but in this theory feature bundles replace the Jackendovian predicates such as GO, INCH, CAUSE, TO and others. One of the reasons for Lieber to propose a different set of predicates as part of the LCSs is that she searches for a cross-categorial characterisation of lexical semantics. The same features that are helpful in characterising the lexical semantics of verbs should also help us characterise the lexical semantics of nouns, adjectives and prepositions.

At the heart of Lieber's theory lies the difference between the semantic skeleton and the semantic body. The semantic skeleton is a function argument-structure that is more or less familiar from our discussion in Section 5.2, the only difference being that the predicates in these structures have been replaced by features that characterise argument-taking functions, to which we will turn shortly. The skeleton is that part of the lexical semantics of a word that is relevant to the syntactic structure and that, for derived words, is predictable from the skeletons of the composing elements. Put differently, it is that part of the representation that characterises our grammatical knowledge. The semantic body is a far less formal structure. It represents that part of the lexical semantics that is encyclopedic and may differ from person to person. Lieber represents this information as a list of 'bits and pieces in no particular order' (Lieber 2004: 35). As an example, consider the compound *clergyman-poet* (also briefly discussed in Chapter 4). Lieber (2004: 51) gives the following representation of this word, which makes clear the distinction between the skeleton and the body:

(30) skeleton   [+material, dynamic ([$_i$])] [+material, dynamic ([$_i$])]
                   clergyman   *poet*
      body   <natural>   <natural>
                   <human>   <human>
                   <male>   <writes poetry>
                   <cleric>

The body is represented as a list of things that are associated with these words. As we have said, this list can be different from person to person, and will be longer for those that are specialists on the topic in question, etc. (Recall our discussion of encyclopedic knowledge in Chapter 1.) Also, note that the skeletons of these nouns are function argument-structures using the same features that characterise the lexical semantic predicates of verbs, adjectives and prepositions.

The features that the functions are composed of are [±material], [± dynamic] and [±IEPS]. In Chapter 4 (Section 4.8) we have already seen how the first two features may be used to define a nominal taxonomy. Here we will see how these same features also define a verbal taxonomy. The feature [+IEPS] stands for 'inferable eventual position or state', and is used to make a distinction between verbs such as *walk* that have no particular end-state and verbs such as *descend* that project a particular path. The examples below illustrate the difference between these two classes of verbs (Lieber 2004: 31):

(31) a. ? After having descended the ladder, Morgan found himself to
          be in exactly the same place he had started from.
      b. After having walked for five hours, Daisy found herself to be
          in exactly the same place she had started from.

Sentence (31a) is at least odd, since the verb *descend* projects a particular path in which the end-point does not coincide with the initial point. This path is in contradiction of the rest of the sentence. However, the verb *walk* does not project such a path, and therefore (31b) is fully acceptable. Verbs such as *descend* are partly characterised by the feature [+IEPS]. Since (31b) is acceptable, *walk* belongs to the class of verbs characterised by the feature [−IEPS].

Given the features [±dynamic] and [±IEPS], Lieber gives the following taxonomy of verbs (Lieber 2004: 30):

(32)

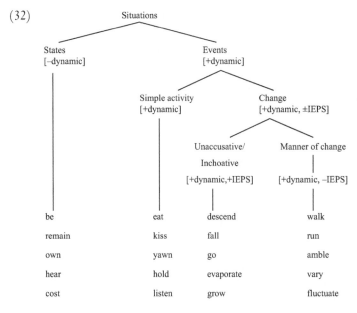

We can now see how the predicates in the LCSs of Jackendoff have been replaced by these featural representations. Interestingly, Lieber's proposal is that affixes are just like other lexical items, in the sense that these same semantic features also characterised the affixes. So, given the featural matrices discussed so far, and limiting ourselves to verb-formation, in principle we may expect to find affixes that add functions such as [+dynamic] (forming activities) and [−dynamic] (forming statives), and also affixes that add more complex functions such as [+dynamic, +IEPS] (forming unaccusatives/inchoatives) or [+dynamic, −IEPS] (forming 'manner' verbs). However, English does not have that many verb-forming affixes, and it seems to be the case that most verb-formation is done through conversion. Nonetheless, there are two verb-forming affixes, -*ise* and -*ify*, that may lend themselves to an analysis in terms of the addition of a function to the skeleton of the base.

Lieber (2004: 82) proposes the following lexical semantic representation for the affixes -*ise* and -*ify*:

(33) [+ dynamic ([$_{volitional-i}$], [$_j$])]; [+dynamic ([i], [+dynamic, + IEPS

([$_j$], [+Loc ([ ])])]),]

We can distinguish two different parts in this representation, separated by the semi-colon. The first part may be paraphrased as 'x does something (on purpose) to y', and the second part by 'x causes y to become z go to z'. Let us compare this representation to the one proposed by Plag in (28). The Jackendovian predicates GO, expressing change of location, and INCH, expressing change of state, are brought together under the predicate [+dynamic, + IEPS (), ()] (as has already been seen in the schema in (32)). In this way, Lieber is able to have a single lexical semantic representation for verbs that express a change of location and verbs that express a change of state.

The skeleton in (33) expresses a causative reading. But, as we have seen above, most English causative verbs also have an inchoative reading. Consider now how this lexical semantic skeleton of the affix composes with the lexical semantic skeleton of a particular base. During this process of composition the Principle of Coindexation (see Chapter 4) applies. We repeat it below:

(34) Principle of Coindexation (Lieber 2004: 61):
In a configuration in which semantic skeletons are composed, coindex the highest nonhead argument with the highest (preferably unindexed) head argument. Indexing must be consistent with semantic conditions on the head argument, if any.

The skeleton for bases such as *standard* or *pure*, which both represent states, is assumed to be a simple non-dynamic predicate taking a single argument: [−dynamic ()]. The argument of this predicate is to be identified with the referential R-role (Higginbotham 1985), introduced in Chapter 4, that we see in adjectives and nouns. So the analysis for nouns and adjectives is in fact identical to that of Williams, who proposes an argument-structure with a single external argument for these cases. The skeleton for these bases takes the appropriate place in the skeleton of the affix. The skeleton of the verbs *standardise* and *purify* thus composed then look as follows:

(35) $[+ \text{dynamic} ([_{\text{volitional}-i}], [_j])]$; $[+\text{dynamic} ([_i], [+\text{dynamic}, + \text{IEPS}$

$$([_j], [+\text{Loc} ([_k])])]), [-\text{dynamic} ([_k])]]$$

The argument of the base (the deepest embedded part [−dynamic ([ ]) is coindexed with the locative argument of the affixal skeleton (the index k in (35)). The reason for this coindexing is that the other argument positions in the skeleton of the affix already have an index, and according to the principle of coindexation, preference is given to the non-indexed argument. Therefore, the bases *standard* and *pure* are interpreted as the end-state (the relevant event is of the type [+IEPS] projecting such a state) of the process that may or may not have a causative reading. A verb such as *hospitalise* can be treated in the same way, the only difference being that the skeleton of its base is not a state (characterised by [−dynamic]) but a thing, characterised by the feature [+material].

The formulation of the principle of coindexation leaves room for some bases to be coindexed with an already indexed argument. The principle gives preference to unindexed arguments, but does not exclude the possibility of indexing with other indexed arguments. Lieber uses this possibility to give an account for verbs such as *glorify* and *apologise* in which *glory* and *apology* act as the themes that are transferred from one place to the other, rather than as the end-states of that transfer. *Apologise* does not mean that something becomes in an apology state, but rather that an apology moves from one place (the apologiser) to another (the one who is apologised to).

This possibility of coindexation with an already coindexed argument allows Lieber to have a single semantic skeleton for both -*ify* and -*ise* to characterise all the different classes of derived verbs. The polyfunction-ality of the affixes is expressed by the fact that different bases can be of different types (states or things, i.e. elements being characterised by the features [−dynamic] and [+material] respectively), or by the fact that different bases can take different argument-positions in the skeleton of the affix.

However, there is one class of verbs that still cannot be captured given this limited flexibility. Intransitive verbs such as *hooliganise* or *philosophise*, dubbed 'performatives' by Plag (1999), cannot be properly treated by the skeleton in (33). These verbs allow for a far simpler paraphrase than the skeleton for -*ise* suggests. *Hooliganise*, for example, does not mean that somebody does something in such a way that some-thing becomes hooligan, but simply means 'to act as a hooligan'. Lieber proposes that these interpretations do not arise from the core skeleton for -*ise* but result from a serious modification of this skeleton, which is due to what she calls the 'pragmatic' pressure that arises from the need for words with a specific semantic interpretation. English lacks a mor-phological process that produces verbs with the interpretation 'to act like . . . '. Nevertheless, speakers may feel the need to use such verbs. This pragmatic pressure, according to Lieber, is enough to modify the skeleton of the affix closest in meaning to the speaker's needs. In this way, the skeleton of -*ise* may be extended so that it can yield performa-tive verbs. The extended version of the skeleton is given below (Lieber 2004: 87):

(36)   [+ dynamic ([$_{volitional-i}$], [$_j$])]; [+dynamic ([$_i$], [+dynamic, + IEPS ([$_i$],

$$[+Loc ([\ ])])])]$$

↓

Ø

Summarising, in Lieber's (2004) approach to derived verbs, verbal affixes are given a lexical semantic specification that is built up from the same type of elements that other lexical items are constructed from. Given these feature structures, the Principle of Coindexation tells us what possible interpretations are possible once the feature structures of the base and the affix are composed. In analysing verb-formation in this way, Lieber is able to come up with a single lexical specification of verbal affixes and still account for the different types of readings that we find. However, there is a single class of performative verbs that seem to behave differently. These verbs are treated by assuming that 'pragmatic pressure' may sometimes lead to a modification of the computed lexical skeletons.

5.5 Conversion

Composition of skeletons and the Principle of Coindexation are the means by which Lieber accounts for affixation. However, she treats conversion in a somewhat different manner. In the literature there are several different proposals that have been made to account for conversion. Allen (1978) and Kiparsky (1982) assume that conversion should be analysed as a regular form of derivation, the only difference being that conversion involves a zero-affix. Such an affix has similar semantic and morphosyntactic properties to those of other affixes; it only differs in its phonology by being zero. In Chapter 2 we have seen how Kiparsky deals with noun-to-verb conversion (and verb-to-noun conversion) in a level-ordered morphology. Williams (1981) proposes a 'headless' rule that simply changes the category of a certain lexical item without any form of affixation. More recently, morphologists from different theoretical persuasions have proposed that lexical items may be category-neutral (e.g. Marantz 1997, Giegerich 1999, Farrell 2001, Borer 2003) and that the category is determined by the syntax (or by inflectional morphology as in the case of Myers 1984), rather than by the lexical item itself. Under such a view it is not the case that, given a conversion pair, one of the lexical items is derived from the other, but there is in fact only a single lexical item that can be used in nominal and verbal environments. We have already seen examples of these approaches in Chapters 2 and 4.

Here we would like to focus on a particular property of English verb-forming conversion that motivates Lieber to treat it in a radically different way from affixation. Lieber observes, following earlier observations from Clark and Clark (1979), Bauer (1983) and Plag (1999), that verb-forming conversion is extremely productive and seems to allow all kinds of interpretations, such that one would be hard pressed to come up with a single skeleton to express all possible interpretations.

As we have already noted in the introduction to this chapter, and as has been documented very extensively by Clark and Clark (1979), verb-forming conversion is indeed an extremely productive process in English. We have seen that Hale and Keyser treat the phenomenon on a par with other verb-forming affixations. However, for Lieber there is a fundamental difference between affixation and conversion, not as a matter of principle, but just because of the productivity and, even more importantly, the rich variety of possible interpretations that converted verbs allow for in comparison to the fairly limited interpretations that affixed verbs do. Plag (1999: 220), basing himself on different studies into verb-forming conversion (Kulak 1964, Marchand 1964, 1969, Rose 1973, Karius 1985), lists the following semantic categories and examples of each of these categories:

(37) | Locative | 'put into X' | jail |
Ornative	'provide with X'	staff
Causative	'make (more) X'	yellow
Resultative	'make into X'	bundle
Inchoative	'become X'	cool
Performative	'perform X'	counterattack
Similative	'act like X'	chauffeur, pelican
Instrumental	'use X'	hammer
Privative	'remove X'	bark
Stative	'be X'	hostess

Plag (1999: 220) observes that there is 'growing consensus in the linguistic literature that the variety of meanings that can be expressed by zero-affixation is so large that there should be no specific meaning attached to the process of zero-derivation at all.' For Lieber, this is a reason for a treatment of conversion that somehow explains this wide variety of meanings, which crucially differs from what we observe in regular verb-forming affixation. It is simply not possible to describe in a single lexical-semantic skeleton the wide range of meanings that result from verb-forming conversion. Lieber notes that verb-forming conversion yields even more semantic categories than listed by Plag, to such an extent that she concludes: 'conversion verbs cover much the same semantic range as simplex verbs do' (Lieber 2004: 93). Therefore, Lieber proposes that conversion should be analysed as **relisting**. Relisting is a mechanism of coinage, the same process that is responsible for the formation of new un-derived lexemes such as *twitter*. So it is not a grammatical process but rather a metalinguistic act during which a noun (or an adjective) re-enters the lexicon as a verb. The possible interpretation of the relisted items is then determined by the same possibilities that determine the interpretation of any un-derived lexical item. Lieber suggests that the interpretation is further determined by the Innovative Denominal Verb Convention (given in (4) above) proposed by Clark and Clark (1979).

Exercises

1. Consider the following sentences:
   (i)   John breaks a glass
   (ii) The glass is broken by John
   (iii) The glass breaks (*by John)
   These sentences show that *break* has both a causative and an inchoative reading. Try to explain why the *by*-phrase is allowed in (ii) but not in (iii).

2. For each of the following verbs, decide whether it belongs to the class of locatum or locational verbs, or to neither of them:

to cork	to redden
to bottle	to film
to tape	to jump
to encircle	to carpet

3. As we have seen, we may fruitfully distinguish between locatum and location verbs. In the main text a lexico-syntactic structure is given of the location verb *to shelve*. However, no lexico-syntactic structure is given for a locatum verb. Draw the lexico-syntactic structure that Hale and Keyser would assign to a locatum verb (such as *to saddle* (*the horse*)).

4. Explain why you would expect the following sentences to be grammatical if English denominal verbs were derived through incorporation:
   (i) *The policeman kenneled the Dalmatian big
   (ii) *The linguist never stopped listing verbs long

5. Give the LCS of the verb *to saddle*. (Compare it to the lexico-syntactic structure that you have given in answer to question 3 and try to formulate a correspondence relation between the two structures.)

6. Give the featural lexical semantic structure of the verb *to saddle*.

Further reading

Borer, Hagit (2005) *Structuring Sense. Vol. II: The Normal Course of Events*, Oxford: Oxford University Press.

Fu, J., T. Roeper and H. Borer (2001) 'The VP within Process Nominals: Evidence from Adverbs and the VP Anaphor *Do-So*', *Natural Language & Linguistic Theory*, 19 (3), pp. 549–82.

Levin, Beth and Malka Rappaport Hovav (2013) 'Lexicalized Meaning and Manner/Result Complementarity', in Arsenijević, Boban, Berit Gehrke and Rafael Marín (eds.), *Studies in the Composition and Decomposition of Event Predicates*, Dordrecht: Springer, pp. 49–70.

Rappaport Hovav, Malka and Beth Levin (1998) 'Building Verb Meanings', in Butt, Miriam and Wilhelm Geuder (eds.), *The Projection of Arguments*, Stanford, CA: CSLI, pp. 97–134.

6 Analogy, storage and rules

6.1 Introduction

Linguistics is not an isolated discipline. More and more it is seen as part of a much broader enterprise that seeks to understand the cognitive capacities of humans; linguistics has become part of cognitive science (see Jackendoff 2002 for an introduction to linguistics as a cognitive science). Perhaps of all the major contributions of Noam Chomsky to the study of language, the most important one is the insight that language is a cognitive capacity and that linguistic structures are representations of a mental reality that is part of each and every human being. If a morphologist claims that the structure of the word *studied* is as in (1):

(1) $[[_V \text{ study}]_{PAST} \text{ ed}]$

there are two possible 'cognitive' interpretations of this claim. The strong interpretation would be that upon processing the word *studied*, a speaker/hearer of English constructs a representation 'online' (that is, while speaking/listening) in his or her mind that to all intents and purposes is identical to the structure in (1). A weaker interpretation would be that the form in (1) is stored in memory as a whole; that is, the structure as such is present in the mind/brain but the language user has 'precompiled' the structure, which makes it available without the need for online parsing or production.

Of course, there is also a third interpretation possible that is also defended in the literature. In this interpretation the structure in (1), or any morphological structure in general, has no bearing on the psychological processes that take place in relation to the interpretation and production of language either online or offline. In this view the structure in (1) is merely an invention of the linguist to allow an economical description of the language. We will come back to this theoretical position in due course.

Linguistics proper concerns itself with the question of whether (1) is indeed the correct representation given a theory of morphology that is motivated by other data of English or data from other languages. For example, as we have seen in Chapter 5, we might wonder whether a lexical item such as *study* comes with a categorial label or is a category-neutral element that only gets categorised when inserted into a particular context. The different positions are defended by giving arguments based on linguistic data (e.g. the observation that *study* can also be used as a noun) and theoretical considerations (e.g. the consideration that we do not need separate rules for conversion). However, if the structure in (1) is also intended to represent a particular claim about the cognitive reality of the mind/brain of the speaker/hearer at some point, evidence other than the purely linguistic may and should play a role in determining the correctness of (1).

Somewhat surprisingly the morphology of English, and in particular the morphology of the English past tense, has become the topic of an extensive debate in which psycholinguists, psychologists, cognitive scientists and linguists all are involved. The central question of this discussion is whether the English past tense is indeed represented in the mind/brain of the speaker/hearer as in (1), or in some variant of that structure, or whether a different representation is called for. The starting point of this discussion is a publication by Rumelhart et al. (1986) in which they present a purely analogical model of the language learner that learns to produce the correct forms of the English past tense of both regular and irregular verbs. In such an analogical model there is no place or need for representations such as (1). The model has no knowledge of any linguistic structure, but 'learns' purely on the basis of analogy with examples that it has previously 'seen' and somehow stored in memory. The reasoning is that if such models can indeed be shown to be effective learners of morphology, this would obviate the need for linguistic rules and linguistic structures; at least it would cast serious doubt on the psychological (cognitive) reality of such structures.

It is small wonder that this model received extensive criticism (e.g. Pinker and Prince 1988, 1994) from a linguistic perspective. This was the start of a long, ongoing debate that has triggered new research and new models of representing morphological knowledge. In this chapter we will try to summarise this debate and to sketch the most important arguments from both sides. In doing so, we will see that the discussion is not limited to morphology proper, but we will also come across arguments from language change and language acquisition.

This chapter is structured as follows. In Section 6.2, the central issue concerning the rules versus analogy debate is introduced in more detail. In Section 6.3, the discussion focuses on how earlier models of generative phonology and morphology approached the formation of the English past tense, and more specifically the way irregular forms are generated in these models. In Section 6.4, we turn to the proposals that only use storage, for both irregular and regular past tense formation. The discussion of the rule-based and storage-based accounts brings us in Section 6.5 to dual-mechanism models that employ both storage and computation. Finally, we turn to more recent versions of the computation-only approach in Section 6.6.

6.2 Storage and computation

Many questions concerning the processing of English morphology centre on the issue of storage versus computation. Are complex words stored as unanalysable entities in the mind of the speaker/hearer, or are they computed online? That is, in recognition, does one need to undo the morphology of a word and recognise the base before being able to recognise the complex word? In other words, do speakers entertain a **parsing** strategy? Or does one just retrieve the complex form as such from memory through **rote processing**? And, in production, do speakers build up words by adding affixes or do they just pick the ready-made complex forms and insert them into the appropriate syntactic context?

A famous experiment by Berko (1958) shows that young children are able to produce new, morphologically complex forms online. In what is called a 'wug' test, children are presented with a picture of an object or an animal they haven't seen before. The experimenter, pointing at a picture of the unknown object or animal, says: 'This is a wug.' Next the experimenter shows a second picture in which we see two (or more) instances of the same object or animal. The experimenter asks: 'Now, you see two of them, these are two . . . ' Thus prompted, the children can successfully complete the sentence with a newly produced form *wugs*. The children have never heard this plural form before, so apparently they have some means to produce such inflected forms online. Of course, that is not to say that all complex morphological forms are produced online. It may well be the case that at least some of the complex linguistic forms, for example those that are most frequently used, are stored in memory.

A plausible hypothesis is that irregular forms are stored whereas regular forms are computed (Pinker 1999, Clahsen 1999). The logic behind this idea is straightforward: a regular form behaves according to a rule that predicts its formal and semantic properties, whereas an irregular form does not behave according to rule and thus needs to be memorised for some reason, whether because it has a deviant form, a non-compositional semantics or both.

A second hypothesis that one often encounters among psycholinguists and linguists alike is that it is not necessary for each complex form to be analysed into its constituting parts, even when regular (see e.g. Bybee and Slobin 1982, 1985, Schreuder et al. 1999, Baayen 2007). Not only simplex forms but also complex forms may be stored as wholes in memory, provided that the complex form is frequent enough in language use to warrant such storage. The idea is that in learning and use there is a certain threshold for complex forms to be stored in memory. If the frequency of the complex form is above this threshold, the form will be stored; if not, it needs to be computed online. The reasoning behind this idea is that computation of a form takes some effort every time it has to be produced or recognised. This effort is smaller if the form can be retrieved from memory *in toto*. However, if a specific form is used very little, the price for its storage does not outweigh the summed costs of online production. So in theory there is a break-even point where the frequency of usage is just enough to make long-term storage profitable. Below that point, forms are produced online; above that point, forms are stored.

Combined, these two hypotheses give the following picture: irregular forms will be stored in the lexicon but only if their usage is above a certain frequency threshold. What if, for whatever reason, the use of a particular irregular form drops to a level below the threshold? According to the combined hypotheses, since it can no longer be stored, the form will lose its irregular character; in other words, the form will regularise. There is a lot of empirical evidence that supports these hypotheses. For example, the most frequent verbs of English are all irregular verbs (Francis and Kučera 1982), whereas verbs with lower frequencies are all regular. Further empirical evidence comes from diachronic change: irregular verbs that, in the course of history, for whatever reason become less frequent get regular inflection. Pinker (1999: 69) mentions several examples, such as *to chide, to glide* and *to gripe*, which have become regular during the course of history.

These hypotheses lead Pinker to propose what is known as the dual-mechanism model. This model employs two mechanisms: storage and computation. Irregular forms are stored while regular forms are computed by rule. Before we discuss this dual-mechanism model any further, we will first look at two radically different alternatives that both employ a single mechanism. First, in Section 6.3 we take a closer look at a rules-only theory (Chomsky and Halle 1968, Halle and Mohanan

1985). Then in Section 6.4 we turn to models that only use storage, turning to the dual-mechanism model in Section 6.5.

6.3 Rules-only

Claiming that something is irregular implies that no rule or pattern can be found. In this respect the notion 'irregular verbs' is not really apt, since there is a lot of regularity to be found in the set of irregular verbs. Rather than a random set of roughly 180 verbs that all have their own forms for the past tense and the past participle – a situation that would be really irregular – the set of irregular verbs is organised into several more or less well-behaved classes. Bloch (1947) identifies twenty such classes. By looking at the patterns of changes we find between the infinitive and the past tense form, we may quickly identify a few such classes. A first class of irregular verbs can be defined by the fact that the past tense is identical to the (stem of the) present tense. This class includes such verbs as *to cost, to hit, to knit, to put, to quit*, etc. Note that in these verbs stems are all *t*-final, an observation to which we will return below. A second class is defined by a change in the stem vowel from [ɪ] to [æ], as in *to begin (began), to sing (sang), to sink (sank), to sit (sat)*, etc. Another vowel-change is present in the class hosting verbs such as *to cling (clung), to dig (dug), to shine (shone)*, etc. In some cases a change of vowel is paired with the addition of the suffix -*t* or -*d*, as in *to feel (felt), to keep (kept), to leave (left)* and *to sleep (slept)*. So, from this quick glance, we can already conclude that irregular verbs fall into different classes; class members form their past tenses and past participles in the same way, and the different classes are identified by the changes that are made to the stem in order to derive the past tense and participle. Note that these changes in themselves may be shared by more than one class of verbs.

Given this regularity, it is not surprising that linguists have tried to find rules behind the formation of the past tense (and participles) in the different classes of irregular verbs. Halle and Mohanan (1985) (following Chomsky and Halle 1968) propose that the form of the past tense and past participles of irregular verbs in English is derived by rule. Consider, for example, verbs such as *sit, begin, drink, sing, spit, ring, spring*, and a few more. These verbs have past tenses in which the stem vowel is [æ]. Since the verbs all have an [ɪ] in the present tense, Halle and Mohanan propose the following rule that changes this [ɪ] to [æ] (Halle and Mohanan 1985: 107):

(2) Lowering:

V → [+low, −high]

The idea is that this rule is triggered in a specific class of verbs by the past tense feature. Verbs that undergo this rule are lexically specified as such (e.g. by a feature [+Lowering]). The application of the rule is further restricted by the requirement that the verb in question be specified for past tense (or past participle). In Halle and Mohanan's theory this latter marking is due to syntax. It is not the case that the rule in (2) itself adds a past tense feature to the verb. The rule in (2) is therefore, strictly speaking not even a morphological rule; the only thing it does is change the phonological form of the verb if it is marked for past tense. In the terminology of Halle and Mohanan, it is a **readjustment rule** (see also Chapter 3).

In this way, Halle and Mohanan are able to derive the different classes of irregular verbs with a minimum number of rules. The ingenuity of their rule system comes from the idea that different classes of irregular verbs result from different combinations of the same readjustment rules. They are thus able to derive particular irregular patterns by different combinations chosen from the same limited set of rules. Moreover, many of the details of these patterns result from more general rules that were already part of the system developed by Chomsky and Halle (1968). These rules are not specifically developed to account for the irregular patterns, but are independently motivated on the basis of more general sound patterns in the language. For example, a verb such as *eat–ate* is also subject to the rule in (2). The fact that it is not the vowel [æ] that surfaces here, but [e], is a consequence of the application of a further rule (Vowel Shift) that changes the [æ] to [e] in this context. This latter rule is independently motivated by other sound patterns in English.

Furthermore, for some classes of verbs, such as *bring–brought, seek–sought*, etc., the proposed rules are highly abstract in the sense that they set up underlying structures that never surface as such. The underlying structure is only needed to trigger specific rules, and after having fulfilled this task, the structure is wiped out by further rules. For example, in the alternation *bring–brought* it is assumed at some stage in the derivation that there is an underlying [x] which is deleted before [t]. However, there is no single form in the English language in which this velar fricative surfaces.

A detailed discussion of the analysis of Halle and Mohanan would take us too far away from the central morphological issues. However, before turning to other models, we would like to point out a few objections or problems that the rule-based approach faces.

First, some would argue that the rule-based analysis leads to rules that apply only in a very limited number of cases. That may cast doubt on the notion 'rule'. Put differently, viewed from the perspective of the language learner, how can such rules ever be acquired if the evidence for the rule only comes from a few cases? And would it not be more economical for the language learner simply to store this limited number of forms rather than setting up a complex rule system for them? These questions will be addressed in the following sections.

Second, as we indicated above, the analyses of Chomsky, Halle and Mohanan are sometimes highly abstract. Again, the issue arises of how a child can learn such abstract representations if there is no evidence for them. (For extensive discussion see Kiparsky 1968, 1982, Dresher 1981 and others.) For example, the velar fricative proposed in some forms does not surface in any English word, so how would a language learner ever be capable of setting up such a consonant?

Third, it turns out not only that the classes of irregular verbs are defined by the patterns of irregularity in the realisation of the past tense, but that the stems displaying the same pattern of irregularity also share certain phonological characteristics. For example, the pattern that we see in *cling–clung* is shared by many verbs ending in the phonological string *-ing* [ɪŋ] (e.g. *fling, sting, swing, spring, wring,* etc.). Moreover, it seems that most of these verbs start with a consonant cluster containing [s]. This pattern is productive to a certain extent, in the sense that speakers of English are able to come up with such 'irregular' forms in a wug test (Bybee and Moder 1983, Prasada and Pinker 1993). In these tests, subjects make irregular past tenses (e.g. *spling–splung*), provided that these verbs show substantial overlap with the form of existing irregular verbs. An obvious and direct way to account for this productive aspect of the irregular patterns in a rule-based account would be to assume that there is a rule such as (3):

(3)   ɪ   →   ʌ   /___ ŋ]$_{+PAST}$

However, Pinker (1999) points out that such a rule would be too general, since it does not apply in words such as *bring, sing,* etc. Moreover, the rule would also under-generalise in the sense that verbs such as *stick–stuck* and *spin–spun* follow the same pattern, but fail to meet the structural description of the rule. Pinker concludes that the set of verbs displaying this particular pattern in the past tense formation form a 'family' that has more central (prototypical) and less central members. The prototypical members of the family display all or most of the phonological characteristics that define the class, while the less prototypical members only share one or two such characteristics. The verbs *stick* and *spin* are less prototypical members, whereas *spring* and *swing* are in the heart of the family. Apparently, the family is partly defined by the fact that the stem-final consonant is a velar nasal. The verb *stick* therefore is not expected to be a member; however, *stick* may qualify as a less central member of the family since it has a final velar sound, even though it is not a nasal. Similarly, the verb *to spin* also partly fulfils the requirements of being a family member: it has a final nasal. Such family resemblances are not suited to a rule-based treatment, according to Pinker, and therefore a rule-base treatment of the irregular verbs is on the wrong track. We will come back to this point in section Sections 6.4 and 6.5.

It thus seems that there is no direct and obvious way in which the rule-based approach has an answer as to why certain patterns of past tense formation are identical in a family of verbs. These 'families' consist of some core members, defined by several phonological characteristics, that share some of these characteristics with less central members of the family. In the rule-based system, the only thing these verbs have in common is a feature saying that rule (2) should be applied in the past tense. But there is no reason whatsoever why this feature mostly shows up in stems that end in *-ing*. So there is no beginning of an answer to the question of why verbs with the same phonological make-up cluster together in groups that show the same patterns of irregularity. It thus seems that storage-based analogical approaches are in a better position to answer such questions.

6.4 Storage-only

In a way, Rumelhart et al. (1986) approach the formation of the past tense in English from a perspective that is radically opposite to the Chomsky–Halle–Mohanan approach. Rumelhart et al. build a model without any rule; that is, even the 'regular' forms are fully stored. Their goal is to model the language-learning child who learns the past tense forms of the English verbs without any previous knowledge but is purely 'data-driven', that is, learns exclusively on the basis of the ambient language. The analogical network model they propose is first trained on the basis of a (large) set of pairs of input verbs and their corresponding past tenses. The associative network 'stores' the information in the form of connections between the nodes of the network and by adjusting the 'weights' on these connections. The network consists of three layers: an input layer, an output layer and a hidden layer in between these two. An incoming stem is represented in the input layer by turning on those nodes that correspond to features of the stem input. These turned-on input nodes send signals via the hidden layer to the output layer, triggering those nodes that correspond to features of the past tense form. During the learning stage these correspondences are supervised, and, if necessary, corrected by adjusting the weights on the connections in such a way that the difference between the computed output and the correct output is minimal. In a second stage, new forms that were not part of the training-set are given a past tense form based on analogies with the information present in the network. We will refrain from further technical explanation of the workings of the network model. The interested reader is referred to an explanation of it in Pinker (1999). The model is perfectly suited to dealing with the family resemblances that are claimed to be so characteristic of the classes of irregular verbs. The network can store the information that verbs ending in -*ing* have a good chance of having their past tense in -*ung*, but not if the verb begins with *s*, for example.

In an extensive criticism of Rumelhart et al.'s model, Pinker and Prince (1988) show that it suffers from a series of serious problems. One of the most important seems to be that the model can just learn any rule or pattern of language, even those patterns or rules that we do not find in any natural language. For example, the model would quickly learn a pattern in which every verb starting with [p], [l] or [s] would have a past tense that has a long version of the vowel that is in the first syllable of the verb stem and all other verbs would form their past tense by reversing the order of the phonemes. If Rumelhart et al.'s model can learn such patterns, then it cannot be taken as a model of language.

A second problem is that the model relies only on the phonological properties of the stem in order to compute the past tense form. However, there are some important morphological properties that should also be taken into account. For example, the verb *to ring* in the sense of 'chime' is an irregular verb, whereas the verb that sounds the same and means 'to put a ring on' (of birds, for example) is a regular verb (see Chapter 2). The reason for this difference is well understood morphologically. Whereas the former verb is un-derived, the latter is derived from the noun *ring* (through zero-derivation or conversion). Such derivations always have regular inflection. Furthermore, a verb such as *withdraw* is irregular because *draw* is irregular. Since *draw* is the head of this complex verb (see Chapter 2), this is a predictable property of the complex verb that one would like to derive from this linguistic analysis. However, since Rumelhart et al.'s model does not take morphological analysis into consideration, it is in principle unable to deal with such cases.

Another storage-only model is proposed by Bybee and Slobin (1982). Mainly on the basis of acquisitional data, they conclude that irregular past tense forms take the form of what are called schemas. They propose that children do not acquire rules that change a particular feature of a stem to derive the past tense form (as the rule in (2)), but acquire schemas instead that tell them which forms the past tense may take. For example, Bybee and Slobin propose the following two schemas (1982: 269, 279) (see also Bybee 2006):

(4)   a.   . . .t/d]$_{\text{VERB PAST}}$
      b.   . . .æŋ (k)]$_{\text{VERB PAST}}$

These schemas should be interpreted as follows: a form ending in [d] or [t] may be interpreted as the past tense of a verb, as in (4a). Or, similarly, a form ending in the sequence [æŋ] or [æŋk] can be a past tense form of a verb, as in (4b). In the view of Bybee and Slobin the different schemas define the different classes of irregular verbs. Note that the schema in (4a) may explain why so many forms having identical present and past tense stems end in [t] or [d]. The idea is that such forms may already be interpreted as the past tense according to this schema, and therefore no further modification is needed.

Bybee (1995) argues that complex morphological words are fully stored in the lexicon. Furthermore, they enter the lexicon with a certain 'lexical strength' which is determined by their token frequency. Once stored, they form networks in which identical forms and identical meanings are connected. For example, a word such as *cats* is part of a network as in Figure 6.1.

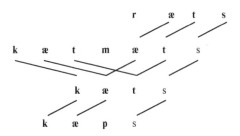

Figure 6.1 Lexical connections in plural nouns, redrawn after Bybee (1995: 429)

The phonemes that make up the word *cat* are all connected to the same individual phonemes of the word *cats*, apart from the final *s*. However, this phoneme in final position is present in a lot of other plural forms, and therefore connections are made between all these occurrences of -*s*. In this way, these connections between morphologically complex words lead to the emergence of affixes. The more plural lexical items ending in -*s* enter the lexicon, the stronger the schema will be that says that a word ending in -*s* is a potential plural. In other words, the type frequency of the plural -*s* – that is, the total number of different lexical items that share the plural -*s* – determines the strength of the morphological schema in (5):

(5) s] $_{\text{N-PLURAL}}$

This model allows for what Bybee calls 'product-oriented' generalisations. That is, in the model of Chomsky, Halle and Mohanan explained above, the rules that define the past tense form of a given verb are input-based: a class of verbs is lexically specified for a particular feature which triggers the application of a rule that determines the past tense form specific to that irregular verb class. In Bybee's model it is also possible to state a generalisation over the past tense forms as such. Since the assumption is that all words, complex or not, are stored in the lexicon, there may be lexical connections between different past tense forms that are not necessarily restricted to the past tense affix. Figure 6.2 illustrates how the class including verbs such as *cling, sting* and *sing* may be lexically connected.

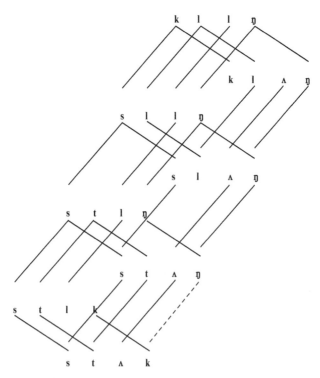

Figure 6.2 Lexical connections between irregular verbs, redrawn after Bybee (1995: 431)

From these lexical connections, the following product-oriented schema may be derived (Bybee 1995: 431):

(6) $[C (C) (C) \wedge \{\text{velar, nasal}\}]_{\text{PAST}}$

These schemas provide a possible explanation for the fact that verbs with a present tense form ending in a velar nasal may become irregular. Once such schema has been established, there is no reason to think that it only holds for a particular class of (irregular) verbs. The schema simply states that the past tense form may have this particular form. Therefore, regular verbs that satisfy the requirements of this schema may be 'attracted' by it and become irregular. This may also explain the fact that in experimental conditions subjects are to some extent willing to produce irregular past tenses for nonce verbs.

Similarly, given this model we might expect that irregular verbs once they become less frequent tend to regularise. Becoming less frequent will immediately weaken the strength of their lexical representations. At some point this strength will no longer be sufficient to uphold a similar schema to the one in (6).

In this model, as in Rumelhart et al.'s, there is no strict dichotomy between regular verbs and irregular verbs. There is only lexical storage that is sensitive to the token frequency of the lexical item. Consequently, the past tense affix -ed is also a schema on a par with the one in (6). This schema for -ed will be particularly strong since a lot of different verbs take -ed as their past tense affix. So the fact that this is the regular or 'default' affix is the result not so much of a different treatment or status of this affix as of the combined frequencies of all the different past tenses that contribute to this same schema. Moreover, since so many different types contribute to it, the schema itself will be very general. The following may make this somewhat clearer. Verbs with very different phonological make-ups, whether ending in vowels or consonants, whether multisyllabic or monosyllabic, whether stress-initial or stress-final, will all have particular verbs that form their past tenses with the affix -ed. Therefore, the schema of this affix will ultimately be simple: it only requires a phonologically well-formed string to which -ed can be attached:

(7) $[X\text{ -}ed]_{\text{PAST}}$

Put differently, there are no phonological features specific to the class of verbs that forms the past tense with the affix -ed. Consequently, the resulting schema puts no particular constraints on the form of these verbs.

Summarising so far, Bybee's model accounts for the fact that there is quite considerable regularity in the set of verbs that we call 'irregular'.

We have seen that verbs sharing certain stem features (having -*ing* rhymes, for example) also tend to share their past tense forms. If we try to make this somewhat more precise, we see that this statement in fact encompasses two types of regularity. First, the set of stems that show a particular past tense form have some phonological characteristics in common. Second, the past tenses of such verbs are all formed in the same way. It will be clear from our exposition above how these properties are accounted for in Bybee's model.

But there is even more regularity in the irregular verbs that we should also take into account. Note that irregular verbs have past tenses that do not deviate wildly (apart from a very few exceptional cases) from the stem form. The patterns go *cling–clung, sing–sang, hit–hit*, and not *cling–kluf, sing–trand, hit–pick*. That is, the stem form is adjusted in one or two features in the past tense, but overall there is a lot of similarity between the past tense forms and the present tenses of the corresponding verbs (with *to go* and *to be* as the obvious exceptions). This implies that we cannot simply say that irregular past tenses are stored and leave it at that. Bybee's model accounts for this similarity between stems and their past tenses, since a form that deviated radically from this would be completely isolated, as there are no connections between identical phonemes. Therefore such a form is doomed unless its frequency (its lexical strength) is such that it is able to survive without any connection to its stem. This is only the case in a few very high-frequency verbs, such as *to go* and *to be*, that have suppletive forms as their past tenses (*went* and *was/were*).

6.5 Dual-mechanism models

Pinker (1999) and Clahsen (1999) propose a different model from the ones discussed above. According to their **dual-mechanism model**, both storage and computation play a role in the formation of words. In their view there is a dichotomy between regular inflection and irregular inflection. Irregulars should be treated through storage; that is, for the formation of irregular verbs Pinker accepts the solution that the forms are stored in the lexicon and that there should be some mechanism along the lines of Rumelhart et al. or Bybee. Such mechanisms are ideally suited to accounting for the 'family resemblance' effects that we see in the formation of irregulars. Such models also explain the willingness of speakers to produce new irregular forms if such verbs show a sufficient amount of overlap with the patterns stored in memory. However, the proponents of the dual-mechanism model claim that regular past tense formation is different in principle and should be treated by rule.

This regular case is called the **default** case. This notion stresses the fact that this option only applies if all of the other options fail. The regular case in the formation of the English past tense is, according to the dual-mechanism model, not one of a set of possibilities as in the storage-based models, but a separate case that functions as a 'last resort'. It is important to see that this notion of 'default' is not identical to 'being the most frequent'. In the case of English past tenses, it is empirically true that the default case is also the form that has the highest token frequency (the total number of occurrences of the regular verbs will be higher than the number of occurrences of any irregular pattern in a given corpus), but this is not a theoretical necessity. It may very well be that the different stored forms are more frequent than the default case. Marcus et al. (1995) show that in German, the nominal plural -*s* is the default case; it is only used when no other plural formation rule applies; for example, in such cases as the plural of family names, abbreviations, acronyms, etc. However, it is certainly not the case that this -*s* in German is the most frequent nominal plural form.

One of the main reasons for Pinker to believe that regular inflection is different in principle from irregular inflection is based on the observation that language users freely add the past tense suffix to simply any sound-form. There is no 'family relation' or 'phonological overlap' between the verbs that share the regular past tense suffix. If, however, the attachment of this suffix were the result of associations with existing forms, we would expect such family relations to occur. In other words, we would expect that the set of verbs sharing the -*ed* suffixation would also share some set of phonological properties that triggers this suffixation rule (rather than a vowel-change or any other pattern). In this line of thinking, it is important that the rule attaching -*ed* to the stem of a verb is unconditional: it applies to just any form. Moreover, even in the case of unfamiliar phonological strings such as *ploamph* or *anastomose*, Pinker expects that language users will readily use the 'default' rule. They do not need a family resemblance to other verbs to be able to use the -*ed* attaching rule; there is no specific trigger for the attachment of -*ed*. Note, by the way, that the stored past tenses should have some kind of priority over this rule in order to avoid the irregular verbs also becoming subject to the regular rule. This is a standard case of blocking (see Chapter 3).

Prasada and Pinker (1993) tested these claims and found that native speakers' well-formedness judgements of the past tense forms of pseudo-irregular verbs depend on the similarity of the nonce verbs to the set of existing irregulars. This does not come as a surprise. However, they also found that the regular past tense forms of nonce verbs are judged better if the past tense forms are more similar to existing regular verbs. In a way this is surprising, since in a dual-mechanism model the

-*ed* rule is completely unconditional. However, as Prasada and Pinker stress, the experiment is confounded by the fact that in order to create nonce verbs that are dissimilar from existing regular verbs, one is forced to construct nonce verbs that (almost) violate phonological or phonotactic well-formedness conditions. This may have influenced the judgements of the subjects considerably, even though they were instructed to judge the past tense form as a past tense form of the nonce stem. In order to control for this confounding factor, Prasada and Pinker ran a second experiment in which the nonce stems and the past tense forms used in the first experiment were judged. It turned out that the goodness of the regular cases is not dependent on the distance from the existing regular forms but only depends on the naturalness of the stem.

What other evidence could support the dual-mechanism account as opposed to the storage-based account discussed above? Prasada and Pinker (1993) showed that a storage-based model has in fact more difficulty in deriving regular forms from bases that have phonological forms that are quite dissimilar from the existing regulars. The reason is simple: in the storage-based account there is no principled difference between the regular and irregular patterns, and in Rumelhart et al.'s model they are both the result of comparisons to stored cases. If there are no 'comparable' cases, the storage-only model is doomed to make errors. So in this respect the rule-based account seems to fare better.

However, note that Bybee's model differs in the treatment of the regular inflection from the analogical network model. As we have seen above, just because so many different verbs all use the -*ed* suffix to form their past tenses, the emerging pattern from the stored forms is the one given in (7) above. This pattern is essentially identical to the unconditional 'default' rule in a dual-mechanism account. Therefore, this model predicts that native speakers won't have any problems in adding the -*ed* suffix to any verb, whether it looks like any existing regulars or not. So the argument that Prasada and Pinker raise against the Rumelhart et al. model does not seem to hold against Bybee's model.

6.6 Rules-only again

In reaction to the dual-mechanism architecture, Albright and Hayes (2003) propose a model that is purely rule-based. In a way this model returns to the Chomsky and Halle approach, but with a crucial difference. In Albright and Hayes' model, the rules that form the core of the model are stochastic in nature. That is, these rules come with information about the chance of their applicability in a particular environment. We will first explain the model, roughly following the exposition of

Albright and Hayes (2003), and then compare it to the ones previously discussed.

The model is computationally implemented, which guarantees that it is fully explicit and its predictions can be checked against any experimental results. In the first phase, the algorithm is trained on a set of existing verbs. The present and past tenses of these verbs are given and the model extracts rules on the basis of this information. So, given a pair *shine–shined*, the model will set up the rule in (8):

(8) $\emptyset \rightarrow$ d / [ʃaɪn ____]$_{[+\text{PAST}]}$

This rule inserts the phoneme [d] after the form *shine*. Later the algorithm may encounter the pair *consign–consigned*. On the basis of this pair it sets up the rule in (9):

(9) $\emptyset \rightarrow$ d / [kənsaɪn ____]$_{[+\text{PAST}]}$

Given these rules that have identical structural changes (they both insert a [d]), the algorithm will combine the two and set up a single rule by generalising over the contexts. The algorithm finds the maximal context that is shared by the two rules and sets up a third:

(10) $\emptyset \rightarrow$ d / X [+strident] aɪn ____]$_{[+\text{PAST}]}$
[+contin]
[−voice]

We can now see how this procedure finds the 'correct' context for the rule that adds the suffix [-ɪd], that is, only if the stem-final consonant is a [d] or [t]. Given the pairs *vote–voted* and *need–needed*, two rules will be set up:

(11) $\emptyset \rightarrow$ ɪd / [vot ____]$_{[+\text{PAST}]}$
$\emptyset \rightarrow$ ɪd / [need ____]$_{[+\text{PAST}]}$

Again, since the structural descriptions of these rules are identical, the procedure of minimal generalisation applies and will find the shared feature-set of the stem-final [t] and [d] and construct the following rule:

(12) $\emptyset \rightarrow$ əd / [X [+coronal] ____]$_{[+\text{PAST}]}$
[+anterior]
[−nasal]
[−continuant]

By reiterating the process of setting up rules on the basis of stem–past tense pairs, and combining these rules where possible through minimal generalisation, increasingly general rules are constructed. In the end, three rules come out of the process, one for each past tense allomorph (Albright and Hayes 2003: 124):

(13)   a.   Ø   →   d/[X [+voice] ___]$_{[+PAST]}$
        b.   Ø   →   t/[X [−voice] ___]$_{[+PAST]}$
        c.   (= (12))

Before the algorithm arrives at these very general rules, far more rules have been set up, such as the ones in (8)–(11). Crucially, the model does not simply dispense with these rules, but keeps them. All rules will be evaluated for accuracy, and the most accurate ones play an important role in determining the output of new forms, as we will see below. For each rule, the accuracy value is determined. This is a value between 0 and 1, calculated by dividing the number of contexts in which the rule successfully applies by the total number of contexts that meets its structural description. This value is adjusted by a parameter of the model (which can be determined by the modellers) taking the total number of hits of the particular rule (i.e. its 'trustworthiness') into account. A rule that is accurate but only works in a limited number of cases is far less trustworthy than a rule based on a large number of hits.

Interestingly, the model yields a set of 'islands of reliability'. These are phonologically defined subdomains in which a particular rule is more reliable than the general rules in (13). For example, it turns out that the rule adding *-ed* after a voiceless fricative is completely without exceptions in all of the 352 verbs that meet this phonological condition. Therefore, this particular rule is assigned a very high confidence value, higher in fact than the more general rule in (13). The claim of Albright and Hayes is that these islands of reliability are recognised by language users and are needed to explain their behaviour. Similar islands also exist for irregular forms. For example, the rule that changes [ɪ] to [ʌ] between a voiced dental consonant and a voiced velar consonant (as in *cling* and *dig*) turns out to be a highly reliable rule. As such it may determine the output in nonce forms such as *clig* or *tig*.

Before we turn to some experimental results, let us first see how the model yields outputs given a set of rules and a set of adjusted accuracy values for each of the rules in the set. Suppose we feed the model the input nonce word *gleed*; the output generated is *gleeded*. First, all rules apply of which the structural descriptions are met. This results in a set of candidate outputs consisting of the forms *gleeded* (as a result of the rule that adds [ɪd], as in *wanted* and *needed*), *gled* (as a result of the rule that changes [i] to [e] after [r] or [l] and before a [d], as in *bleed* and *read*), *glode* (as a result of the rule that changes [i] to [əʊ] between two consonants, as in *speak* and *weave*), and finally *gleed* (as a result of the rule that does not change the stem if the stem ends in [d] or [t], as in *spread* and *hit*). The confidence values from each rule are compared and the rule with the highest score is allowed to yield the actual output. In the example at hand, the rule adding the suffix *-ed* is chosen, since all other rules have lower confidence values.

The question is whether native speakers, in determining the past tense form of nonce verbs, rely on phonological closeness to the stored forms only if the form is irregular or also in the case of regular forms. In a dual-mechanism account we would expect the first part of that question to be answered positively but the second negatively. However, Albright and Hayes' model expects native speakers to rely on phonological forms in both cases: both irregular and regular forms are predicted to be sensitive to 'islands of reliability'.

Albright and Hayes tested this prediction and were able to show that islands of reliability indeed play a role in determining not only irregular past tenses (as is also predicted by a dual-mechanism model) but also regular past tenses (*contra* the dual-mechanism model). Also, in comparing their rule-based model to an analogical model, Albright and Hayes conclude that their model fares better: the rule-based model better predicted the outcome of an experiment in which subjects were asked to produce past tense forms of nonce verbs than did an analogical model. The analogical model makes too global comparisons between forms and cannot make use of more specific information that is available in the rules of Albright and Hayes' model. The lesson here seems to be that the fine-grained, detailed, local information of the rules is necessary to predict subjects' behaviour in production of past tenses from nonce verbs.

Yang (2002) also proposes a learning algorithm that will learn the different forms of the past tense in English verbs. Before going into any detail on his rule-and-competition model, it is important to note that this model has a far more general use in natural language learning. The model can learn syntactic rules as well as phonological or morphological ones. Yang (2002) also applies his model to the learning of the English past tense, comparing the prediction of his formalised model with the outcomes of the empirical study by Marcus et al. (1992). Yang's model is a direct continuation of the rule-based tradition in generative grammar, in particular the rule-based approach put forward in generative phonology starting with Chomsky and Halle (1968) and continuing in Halle and Mohanan (1985) and Halle and Marantz (1993) (see also Chapter 2).

Yang assumes, following the words-and-rules model of Pinker (1999), that there is a 'default' rule for the formation of the English past tense that adds -*d* to the verbal stem. However, in contrast to Pinker's model, Yang also assumes that all the irregular verbs form their past tenses by rule, rather than that these forms are all retrieved from 'memory'. It goes without saying that the irregular verbs somehow need to be memorised (they are irregulars, after all), but the way the memorisation is done in Yang's model crucially differs from the word-and-rules model. In Yang's rule-and-competition model (R&C) the language user sets up rules for different classes of irregular verbs. For example, if the child encounters the forms *sing–sang* and *ring–rang* it will set up a rule 'In case of /X*ing*/ change to /X*ang*/.' Now, the child at some point will become aware of the fact that this particular rule meets some counterevidence. Forms such as *bring–brought*, *swing–swung* and *wing–winged* make it clear that the rule is limited in scope. Therefore, the child will retain the rule but store it with the additional information that it only applies in a particular set of verbs that will be stored with the rule. Yang dubs this type of rule (following an original proposal by Anderson 1974) a **morpholexical rule**. A morpholexical rule is a rule with limited productivity such that it only applies in a subset of the forms that one would expect given its structural description. In Anderson's (1992) approach, we may view these morpholexical rules as being ordered before the 'default' rule or general rule that comes last. That is, the Elsewhere Condition will order the morpholexical rules in such a way that the productive rule 'add -*ed*' comes last.

What needs to be memorised in Yang's model is not every individual past tense form, but only the class (and hence the particular rule) that is associated with each irregular verb. Rules are associated with a set of verbs as visualised in (14) (from Yang 2002: 64):

(14)   {feed, shoot, . . .}   → $R_{\text{Vowel Shortening}}$
       {bring, think, . . .}   → $R_{\text{-t suffixation \& Rime} \rightarrow a}$

The language user memorises the fact that verbs belonging to the class of *feed*, *shoot*, etc. form their past tenses through vowel shortening; verbs belonging to the class of *bring* form their past tenses by means of -*t* suffixation and a change in the stem vowel to [ɔ]. In this way all irregular verbs are attributed to a particular class. Finally, as a default, if a verb does not belong to either of these classes, it will form its past tense by the default rule.

Yang assumes that the language-learning child is well capable of picking up the particular phonological changes that constitute the possible markings of the past tense in irregular verbs. To corroborate this claim Yang points to the fact that young children hardly make any mistakes in the formation of the past tense (90 per cent correct, according to Marcus et al. 1992), and that the mistakes that they do make are in over-generalising the default rule and not in the phonological changes. Second, there is ample cross-linguistic evidence that children are very good at getting their inflection right from a very young age (basically as soon as they start producing it). Apparently, they are particularly good at parsing inflectional elements from the stem. Any errors that are made are largely over-application of the default form.

Thus, assuming that young children are able to deduce what the relevant phonological changes are that can be made to a stem in order to mark the past tense, the question is how they learn when to apply which changes.

A crucial property of the R&C model is that the language learner entertains more than one rule/grammar at the same time. The rules are not absolute in the sense that they always apply when their structural description is met, but they are in competition with one another and stochastic in nature. This means that every rule comes with a particular probability P. Since the errors that children make in this domain are almost exclusively over-generalising the default form, Yang concludes that children are quite conservative in applying the irregular rules. Put differently, children need quite considerable evidence before they decide that an irregular rule is applicable in a particular form. This can be described in the model as follows. Consider the form *singed*. The rule responsible for the form *sang* comes with a certain probability (lower than 1). Therefore, the child does not always apply this rule, and where he or she doesn't the default rule steps in, yielding *singed*. So this looks a lot like the Elsewhere Condition (see Chapter 2), but with a crucial difference: the blocking of the default form is not absolute but is dependent upon the probability value of the 'special rule' that comes first. During acquisition, the frequency of the special forms will determine the probability of the special rules in the following way. Each time that a special rule is successfully applied, it will receive a 'reward' by having its probability raised. So a higher frequency of special forms in the input will lead to quicker raising of the probability of the relevant rule and more effective blocking. What we see here is that the Elsewhere Condition is not a principle of grammar but is derived as a result of the learning mechanism (if successful).

To see this more clearly, consider the following. Let us assume that the learner starts out with two rules: R_{-ed} and $R_{0+ablaut}$. The latter rule will derive the form *sang* as the past tense of *sing*. Since the language learner has no further knowledge about when to apply these rules, the probabilities of both rules will be equal, that is, 0.5 for both R_{-ed} and $R_{0+ablaut}$ for the verb *sing* at the start of learning. Only when $R_{0+ablaut}$ is selected will a match result in the case of *sing*, so gradually, and depending upon the frequency of occurrence of the form *sang*, the rule $R_{0+ablaut}$ will increase its P-value for *sing* and the P-value of the default rule will decrease, since it is punished by having its P-value decreased for every 'wrong' application. At some point the P-value for $R_{0+ablaut}$ will reach 1 for the verb *sing*: no more over-generalisations with -*ed* are made in this form.

The schema in Figure 6.3 from Yang (2002: 71) may be helpful in understanding how the model works and what predictions it makes. When presented with a past tense form, the child will first reconstruct the root (giving X in Figure 6.3). The child will then have to choose to which class of verbs X belongs and thus which rules apply to form the past tense. This choice is determined by the value P(X ε S); that is, the chance that the child assigns the verb X to class S. If the child decides that X does not belong to any irregular class S, he or she will form the past tense with the default rule. The child will then check whether there is a match with the input X_{past}. If there is a match, the value P(X ε S)

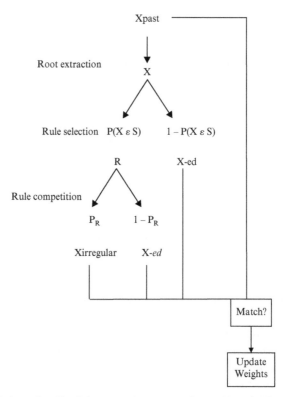

Figure 6.3 Learning English past tenses according to Yang, redrawn after Yang (2002: 71)

will be lowered. If the child, however, decides that X does belong to S, he or she will be prompted with a second choice, namely whether to apply rule R or not. This choice is determined by the probability value P_R, that is, the chance that the child applies R to X. Again, if the child decides not to apply R, then he or she will revert to the default option of adding the suffix -*ed* to X. If that form matches the input, the value P_R will be lowered. If the child decides to apply rule R, then the resulting form will either match the input (which will lead to increasing the values $P(X \varepsilon S)$ and $P_{R)}$ or not match, again leading to a decrease of P_R.

Assuming that the model is used in both comprehension and production (which is arguably the null hypothesis), the model makes precise predictions of the acquisition of the irregular forms and the role of frequency in the input. Given this model, it is easy to see that the percentage of correct usage of a particular verb X, Correct(X), is determined by the product of the probabilities that the child assigns the verb to the correct verb class and the chance that the child applies the matching irregular rule; that is, Correct(X) = $P(X S) P_R$. It is easy to see that $P(X \varepsilon S)$ increases upon any encounter with the past tense of X. Interestingly, however, P_R is increased with every occurrence in the input of a verb from class S.

This leads to the following predictions. First, within the same class, verbs with higher frequency will be learned more quickly (less prone to over-generalisation) than verbs with lower frequency. Second, for two verbs with the same frequency but from different classes, the verb that belongs to a class with higher frequency will be learned more quickly than the verb that comes from a class with lower frequency.

Yang shows that these predictions are correct. He computed the value Correct(X) by dividing the total number of correct past tenses of X by the total number of past tenses of X in the corpus from Marcus et al. (1992) for each irregular verb. It turns out that in general children are extremely good at acquiring the past tenses. The average correct use over the four children in the corpus was 89.9 per cent. Furthermore, it turns out that within each verb class the higher-frequency verbs (determined by counting the verbs in the input to the children) are indeed less prone to over-generalisation than the lower-frequency verbs. For example, if we consider the verb class characterised by no suffix and no change [Ø + no change], we see the following results (Yang 2002: 79):

(15)

Verb	Correct use in corpus	Verb frequency in corpus
put	239/251 = 95.2)	2,248
hit	79/87 = 90.8%	66
hurt	58/67 = 86.6%	25
cut	32/45 = 71.1%	21

As can be seen from these figures, the predicted correlation between the input frequency and the correct use of the irregular past tense is indeed found, and, as Yang shows, the same holds for the other verb classes. Turning now to the second prediction, it is expected that for verbs with the same frequency but from classes that differ in frequency, the frequency of the class will determine correct usage. To see this, let us compare the verbs *hurt* and *cut* with the verbs *know* and *throw* from the class that forms the past tense without an affix but with a change of vowel. Their frequencies and error rates are in (17) (Yang 2002: 81):

(16) Verb class

	Verb frequency in corpus	Correct use in corpus
[-Ø & No Change]	*hurt* (25), *cut* (21)	80.4%
[-Ø & Rime u]	*know* (58), *throw* (31)	49.1%

Despite the fact that the frequencies of *know* and *throw* are considerably higher than the verbs *hurt* and *cut*, the latter two are far less prone to over-generalisation. This is a completely unexpected result for the word-and-rules model. In such a model, the frequencies of the irregular verbs are simply predicted to correlate with the amount of over-generalisation. However, in the R&C model this result is predicted. The verb class to which *hurt* and *cut* belong also includes very high-frequency verbs such as *hit*, *let*, *set* and *put*. This implies that the value of P_R for this class will be very high and consequently, $P(X \varepsilon S) P_R$ is also relatively high for verbs belonging to this class despite their own relatively low frequencies. Because of this bandwagon effect, the verbs *hurt* and *cut* are less prone to over-generalisation.

Of course, any model we have discussed so far will be able to account for the first empirical result; the fact that the frequency in the input of a particular irregular past tense correlates with the number of errors that is made in these verbs is not at all surprising. However, none of the other models seems to be able to account for the second result, that is, that verbs belonging to a more frequent class may benefit from a bandwagon effect, even when their own frequency is not that high.

Both rule models presented above show in different ways that analogy fails. The 'family resemblance' of irregular verbs stressed in those models that store the irregular forms is a historical remnant. At some point in time there was a reason why verbs with similar stem forms formed their past tenses in the same way. These were simply the productive rules of a far earlier stage of the language; however, in modern English these patterns have no role to play. That is not to say that there are no patterns in irregular verbs; the patterns that we see, however, have no meaning to the language user.

Exercises

1. What do you think that language users would do if they were asked to give the present tense of nonce past tense irregular forms? Would they be able to construct the infinitive (or present tense) of such nonce forms? And if so, how does that bear on the psychological reality of a rule to derive irregular past tense forms?

2. What does it tell us about analogy that verbs converted from nouns are not irregularly inflected? Or more generally, that the morphological structure may preclude a verb-form from becoming irregular?

3. Explain why frequency effects (e.g. the idea that reaction times in lexical decision are shorter when a word is more frequent) may be used as a litmus test for storage.

4. a. Try to find at least one other 'family' of irregular verbs in English.
   b. What criticism does Yang formulate of the notion of 'family' of irregular verbs?
   c. Show how this criticism is also applicable to your 'family' of irregular verbs.

5. In the case of English nominal plural forms, would you also propose one or more morpholexical rules? Why, or why not?

6. Yang's model, just like Chomsky and Halle's (and Mohanan's) model, only uses rules to account for the irregular patterns. What is the crucial difference between Yang's rules and those of Chomsky and Halle (1968)?

Further reading

Clahsen, H. (1986) 'Verbal Inflections in German Child Language: Acquisition of Agreement Markers and the Functions they Encode', *Linguistics* 24, pp. 79–121.

Clahsen, H. and K. Neubauer (2010) 'Morphology, Frequency, and the Processing of Derived Words in Native and Non-Native Speakers', *Lingua* 120, pp. 2627–37.

Marcus, Gary F., Ursula Brinkmann, Harald Clahsen, Richard Wiese and Steven Pinker (1995) 'German Inflection: The Exception that Proves the Rule', *Cognitive Psychology* 29, pp. 189–256.

Pinker, Steven (1999) *Words and Rules: The Ingredients of Language*, New York: HarperCollins.

Bibliography

Ackema, Peter (1995) *Syntax below Zero*, Utrecht: Led.

Ackema, Peter and Ad Neeleman (2004) *Beyond Morphology*, Oxford: Oxford University Press.

Ackema, Peter and Ad Neeleman (2007) 'Morphology ≠ Syntax', in Ramchand, Gillian and Charles Reiss (eds.), *The Oxford Handbook of Linguistic Interfaces*, Oxford: Oxford University Press, pp. 325–52.

Acquaviva, Paolo (2004) 'Constraining Inherent Inflection: Number and Nominal Aspect', *Folia Linguistica* 38 (3–4), pp. 333–54.

Acquaviva, Paolo (2008) *Lexical Plurals: A Morphosemantic Approach*, Oxford: Oxford University Press.

Albright, Adam and Bruce Hayes (2003) 'Rules vs. Analogy in English Past Tenses: A Computational/Experimental Study', *Cognition* 90, pp. 119–61.

Alexiadou, Artemis (2001) *Functional Structure in Nominals: Nominalization and Ergativitiy*, Amsterdam and Philadelphia: John Benjamins.

Allen, Margaret (1978) *Morphological Investigations*, PhD dissertation, University of Connecticut.

Anderson, Stephen R. (1974) 'On the Typology of Phonological Rules', in Bruck, Anthony, Robert A. Fox and Michael W. La Galy (eds.), *Papers from the Parasession on Natural Phonology*, Chicago: University of Chicago Department of Linguistics, pp. 1–12.

Anderson, Steven R. (1982) 'Where's Morphology?', *Linguistic Inquiry* 13, pp. 571–612.

Anderson, Steven R. (1992) *A-Morphous Morphology*, Cambridge: Cambridge University Press.

Arad, Maya (2003) 'Locality Constraints on the Interpretation of Roots: The Case of Hebrew Denominal Verbs', *Natural Language & Linguistic Theory* 21, pp. 737–78.

Aronoff, Mark (1976) *Morphology in Generative Grammar*, Cambridge, MA: MIT Press.

Aronoff, Mark (1980) 'Contextuals', *Language* 56 (4), pp. 744–58.

Aronoff, Mark (1994) *Morphology by Itself*, Cambridge: Cambridge University Press.

Aronoff, Mark (2008) 'In the Beginning Was the Word', *Language* 83 (4), pp. 803–30.

Aronoff, Mark and S. N. Sridhar (1983) 'Morphological Levels in English and Kannada', in Richardson, John F., Mitchell Marks and Amy Chukerman (eds.), *Papers from the Parasession on the Interplay of Phonology, Morphology and Syntax*, Chicago: CLS.

Aronoff, Mark and S.N. Shridhar (1988) 'Prefixation in Kannada', in Hammond, Michael and Mark Noonan (eds.), *Theoretical Morphology*, San Diego and London: Academic Press, pp. 179–91.

Baayen, R. Harald (2007) 'Storage and Computation in the Mental Lexicon', in Jarema, Gonia and Gary Libben (eds.), *The Mental Lexicon: Core Perspectives*, Amsterdam: Elsevier, pp. 81–104.

Baayen, R. Harald (2009) 'Corpus Linguistics in Morphology: Morphological Productivity', in Luedeling, Anke. and Merja Kyto (eds.), *Corpus Linguistics: An International Handbook*, Berlin: Mouton de Gruyter, pp. 900–19.

Baker, Mark (1988) *Incorporation: A Theory of Grammatical Function Changing*, Chicago: University of Chicago Press.

Baker, Mark (1997) 'Thematic Roles and Syntactic Structures', in Haegeman, Lilian (ed.), *Elements of Grammar: Handbook of Generative Grammar*, Dordrecht: Kluwer, pp. 73–137.

Barker, Chris (1998) 'Episodic *-ee* in English: A Thematic Role Constraint on New Word Formation', *Language* 74 (4), pp. 695–727.

Bauer, Laurie (1983) *English Word Formation*, Cambridge: Cambridge University Press.

Bauer, Laurie (1990) 'Be-Heading the Word', *Journal of Linguistics* 26 (1), pp. 1–31.

Bauer, Laurie (2001) *Morphological Productivity*, Cambridge: Cambridge University Press.

Bauer, Laurie (2006) 'Compound', in Brown, Keith (ed.), *Encyclopedia of Language and Linguistics*, Amsterdam: Elsevier, pp. 719–26.

Beard, Robert (1990) 'The Nature and Origins of Derivational Polysemy', *Lingua* 81, pp. 101–40.

Beard, Robert (1995) *Lexeme-Morpheme Base Morphology*, Albany, NY: SUNY Press.

Belder, Marijke de (2011) *Roots and Affixes: Eliminating Lexical Categories from Syntax*, Utrecht: LOT Dissertations.

Berko, Jean (1958) 'The Child's Learning of English Morphology', *Word* 14, pp. 150–77.

Bermúdez-Otero, Ricardo (2012) 'The Architecture of Grammar and the Division of Labor in Exponence', in Trommer, Jochen (ed.), *The Morphology and Phonology of Exponence*, Oxford Studies in Theoretical Linguistics 41, Oxford: Oxford University Press, pp. 8–83.

Bierwisch, Manfred and Robert Schreuder (1992) 'From Concepts to Lexical Items', *Cognition* 42, pp. 23–60.

Blevins, James P. (2003) 'Stems and Paradigms', *Language* 79 (4), pp. 737–67.

Bloch, Bernard (1947) 'English Verb Inflection', *Language* 23, pp. 399–418.

Bloomfield, Leonard (1933) *Linguistics*, London: George Allen & Unwin.

Bochner, Harry (1993) *Simplicity in Generative Morphology*, Berlin: Mouton de Gruyter.

Booij, Geert (1996a) 'Autonomous Morphology and Paradigmatic Relations', in Booij, Geert and Jaap van Marle (eds.), *Yearbook of Morphology 1996*, Dordrecht: Kluwer, pp. 35–53.

Booij, Geert (1996b) 'Inherent versus Contextual Inflection and the Split Morphology Hypothesis', in Booij, Geert and Jaap van Marle (eds.), *Yearbook of Morphology 1995*, Dordrecht: Kluwer, pp. 1–16.

Booij, Geert (1997) 'Allomorphy and the Autonomy of Morphology', *Folia Linguistica* 31 (1–2), pp. 25–56.

Booij, Geert (2010) *Construction Morphology*, Oxford: Oxford University Press.

Booij, Geert and Rochelle Lieber (2004) 'On the Paradigmatic Nature of Affixal Semantics in English and Dutch', *Linguistics* 42, pp. 327–57.

Borer, Hagit (1991) 'The Causative–Inchoative Alternation: A Case Study in Parallel Morphology', *Linguistic Review* 8, pp. 119–58.

Borer, Hagit (2003) 'Exo-Skeletal vs. Endo-Skeletal Explanations: Syntactic Projections and the lexicon', in Moore, John and Maria Polinsky (eds.), *The Nature of Explanation in Linguistic Theory*, Stanford, CA: CSLI, pp. 31–67.

Borer, Hagit (2004) 'The Grammar Machine', in Alexiadou, Artemis, Elena Anagnostopoulou and Martin Everaert (eds.), *The Unaccusativity Puzzle: Explorations of the Syntax–Lexicon Interface*, Oxford: Oxford University Press, pp. 288–331.

Borer, Hagit (2005a) *Structuring Sense. Vol. I: In Name Only*, Oxford: Oxford University Press.

Borer, Hagit (2005b) *Structuring Sense. Vol. II: The Normal Course of Events*, Oxford: Oxford University Press.

Borer, Hagit (2010) 'In the Event of a Nominal', in Everaert, Martin, Mariana Marelj and Tal Siloni (eds.), *The Theta System: Argument Structure at the Interface*, Oxford: Oxford University Press, pp. 103–49.

Bybee, Joan (1985) *Morphology: A Study of the Relation between Meaning and Form*, Amsterdam and Philadelphia: John Benjamins.

Bybee, Joan (1988) 'Morphology as Lexical Organization', in Hammond, Michael and Michael Noonan (eds.), *Theoretical Morphology*, San Diego: Academic Press.

Bybee, Joan (1995) 'Regular Morphology and the Lexicon', *Language and Cognitive Processes* 10 (5), pp. 425–55.

Bybee, Joan (2006) 'From Usage to Grammar: The Mind's Response to Repetition', *Language* 82 (4), pp. 711–33.

Bybee, Joan and C. L. Moder (1983) 'Morphological Classes as Natural Categories', *Language* 59, pp. 251–70.

Bybee, Joan and Dan Slobin (1982) 'Rules and Schemes in the Development and Use of the English Past Tense', *Language* 58, pp. 265–89.

Carden, Guy (1983) 'The Non-Finite-State-Ness of Morphology', *Linguistic Inquiry* 14 (3), pp. 537–41.

Chomsky, Noam (1965) *Aspects of the Theory of Syntax*, Cambridge, MA: MIT Press.

Chomsky, Noam (1972) 'Remarks on Nominalization', in Chomsky, Noam, *Studies on Semantics in Generative Grammar*, The Hague: Mouton, pp. 11–61.

Chomsky, Noam and Morris Halle (1968) *The Sound Pattern of English*, New York: Harper and Row.

Clahsen, Harald (1986) 'Verbal Inflections in German Child Language: Acquisition of Agreement Markers and the Functions they Encode', *Linguistics* 24, pp. 79–121.

Clahsen, Harald (1999) 'Lexical Entries and Rules of Language: A Multidisciplinary Study in German Inflection', *Behavioral and Brain Sciences* 22, pp. 991–1060.

Clahsen, Harald and Kathleen Neubauer (2010) 'Morphology, Frequency, and the Processing of Derived Words in Native and Non-Native Speakers', *Lingua* 120, pp. 2627–37.

Clark, Eve and Herbert Clark (1979) 'When Nouns Surface as Verbs', *Language* 55, pp. 767–811.

Di Sciullo, Anna-Maria and Edwin Williams (1987) *On the Definition of Word*, Cambridge, MA: MIT Press.

Dresher, Elan B. (1981) 'Abstractness and Explanation in Phonology', in Hornstein, Norbert and David Lightfoot (eds.), *Explanation in Linguistics: The Logical Problem of Language Acquisition*, London and New York: Longman, pp. 76–115.

Fabb, Nigel (1988) 'English Suffixation Is Constrained Only by Selectional Restrictions', *Natural Language & Linguistic Theory* 6, pp. 527–39.

Farrell, Patrick (1998) 'Comments on the Paper by Lieber', in Lapointe, Steven G., Diane K. Brentari and Patrick M. Farrell (eds.), *Morphology and its Relation to Phonology and Syntax*, Stanford, CA: CSLI, pp. 12–34.

Farrell, Patrick (2001) 'Functional Shift as Category Underspecification', *English Language and Linguistics* 5 (1), pp. 109–30.

Folli, Rafaella and Heidi Harley (2007) 'Causation, Obligation, and Argument Structure: On the Nature of Little v', *Linguistic Inquiry* 38 (2), pp. 197–238.

Francis, W. Nelson and Henry Kučera (1982) *Frequency Analysis of English Usage: Lexicon and Grammar*, Boston: Houghton Mifflin.

Fu, Jingqi., Tom Roeper and Hagit Borer (2001) 'The VP within Process Nominals: Evidence from Adverbs and the VP Anaphor *Do-So*', *Natural Language & Linguistic Theory*, 19 (3), pp. 549–82.

Giegerich, Heinz (1999) *Lexical Strata in English: Morphological Causes, Phonological Effects*, Cambridge: Cambridge University Press.

Grimshaw, Jane (1990) *Argument Structure*, Cambridge, MA: MIT Press.

Gussmann, Edmund (1988) 'Review of Mohanan (1986)', *Journal of Linguistics* 24, pp. 232–9.

Hacken, Pius ten (2009) 'Early Generative Theories', in Lieber, Rochelle and Pavol Štekauer (eds.), *The Oxford Handbook of Compounding*, Oxford: Oxford University Press, pp. 54–77.

Hale, Kenneth and Samuel Jay Keyser (1993) 'Argument Structure', in Hale,

Kenneth and Samuel Jay Keyser, *The View from Building 20: Essays in Linguistics in Honor of Sylvain Bromberger*, Cambridge, MA: MIT Press, pp. 53–109.

Hale, Kenneth and Samuel Jay Keyser (1998) 'The Basic Elements of Argument Structure', in Harley, Heidi (ed.), *Papers from the Upenn/MIT Roundtable on Argument Structure and Aspect*, MIT Working Papers in Linguistics 32, Cambridge, MA: MIT Dept of Linguistics and Philosophy, pp. 73–118.

Hale, Kenneth and Samuel Jay Keyser (1999) 'Bound Features, Merge and Transitivity Alternations', in Pylkkänen, Liina, Angeliek van Hout and Heidi Harley (eds.), *Papers from the UPenn/MIT Roundtable on the Lexicon*, MIT Working Papers in Linguistics 35, Cambridge, MA: MIT Dept of Linguistics and Philosophy, pp. 49–72.

Hale, Kenneth and Samuel Jay Keyser (2002) *Prolegomenon to a Theory of Argument Structure*, Cambridge, MA: MIT Press.

Halle, Morris (1973) 'Prolegomena to a Theory of Word Formation', *Linguistic Inquiry* 4 (1), pp. 3–16.

Halle, Morris (1997) 'Distributed Morphology: Impoverishment and Fission', in Bruening, Benjamin, Yoonjung Kang and Martha McGinnis (eds.), *Papers at the Interface*, MIT Working Papers in Linguistics 30, Cambridge, MA: MIT Dept of Linguistics and Philosophy, pp. 425–49.

Halle, Morris and Alec Marantz (1993) 'Distributed Morphology and the Pieces of Inflection', in Hale, Kenneth and Samual Jay Keyser (eds.), *The View from Building 20: Essays in Linguistics in Honor of Sylvain Bromberger*, Cambridge, MA: MIT Press, pp. 111–76.

Halle, Morris and Alec Marantz (1994) 'Some Key Features of Distributed Morphology', in Carnie, Andrew and Heidi Harley (eds.), *Papers on Phonology and Morphology*, MIT Working Papers in Linguistics 21, Cambridge, MA: MIT Dept of Linguistics and Philosophy, pp. 275–88.

Halle, Morris and K. P. Mohanan (1985) 'Segmental Phonology of Modern English', *Linguistic Inquiry* 16, pp. 57–116.

Hankamer, Jorge (1989) 'Morphological Parsing and the Lexicon', in Marslen-Wilson, William (ed.), *Lexical Representation and Process*, Cambridge, MA: MIT Press, pp. 392–408.

Harley, Heidi (1999) 'Denominal Verbs and *Aktionsart*', in Pylkkänen, Liina, Angeliek van Hout and Heidi Harley (eds.), *Papers from the UPenn/MIT Roundtable on the Lexicon*, MIT Working Papers in Linguistics 35, Cambridge, MA: MIT Dept of Linguistics and Philosophy, pp. 73–85.

Harley, Heidi (2004) 'Merge, Conflation and Head Movement: The First Sister Principle Revisited', in Moulton, Keir and Matthew Wolf (eds.), *Proceedings of NELS 34*, Amherst: UMass, GSLA, pp. 239–54.

Harley, Heidi (2005) 'How Do Verbs Get their Names? Denominal Verbs, Manner Incorporation and the Ontology of Verb Roots in English' in Erteschik-Shir, Nomi and Tova Rapoport (eds.), *The Syntax of Aspect*, Oxford: Oxford University Press, pp. 42–64.

Harley, Heidi (2009) 'The Morphology of Nominalization and the Syntax of vP', in Giannakidou, Artemis and Monika Rathert (eds.), *Quantification, Definiteness and Nominalization*, Oxford: Oxford University Press, pp. 321–43.

Harley, Heidi (2010) 'Thematic Roles', in Hogan, Patrick (ed.), *The Cambridge Encyclopedia of the Language Sciences*, Cambridge: Cambridge University Press, pp. 861–2.

Harley, Heidi and Rolf Noyer (1999) 'State-of-the-Article: Distributed Morphology', *GLOT International* 4, pp. 3–9.

Hay, Jennifer and Ingo Plag (2004) 'What Constrains Possible Suffix Combinations? On the Interaction of Grammatical and Processing Restrictions in Derivational Morphology', *Natural Language & Linguistic Theory* 22, pp. 565–96.

Higginbotham, James (1985) 'On Semantics', *Linguistic Inquiry* 16 (4), pp. 547–93. Reprinted in LePore, Ernest (ed.), *New Directions in Semantics*, London: Academic Press, 1987, pp. 1–54.

Hoekstra, Teun (1984) *Transitivity: Grammatical Relations in Government-Binding Theory*, Dordrecht: Foris.

Hogg, Richard (ed.) (1992) *The Cambridge History of the English Language. Vol. I: The Beginnings to 1066*, Cambridge: Cambridge University Press.

Hornstein, Norbert (1977) 'S and X' Convention', *Linguistic Analysis* 3, pp. 137–76.

Jackendoff, Ray (1972) *Semantic Interpretation in Generative Grammar*, Cambridge, MA: MIT Press.

Jackendoff, Ray (1975) 'Morphological and Semantic Regularities in the Lexicon', *Language* 51(3), pp. 639–71.

Jackendoff, Ray (1990) *Semantic Structures*, Cambridge, MA: MIT Press.

Jackendoff, Ray (2002) *Foundations of Language: Brain, Meaning, Grammar, Evolution*, Oxford: Oxford University Press.

Jensen, John T. and Margaret Strong-Jensen (1984) 'Morphology Is in the Lexicon!', *Linguistic Inquiry* 15, pp. 474–98.

Karius, Ilse (1985) *Die Ableitung der denominalen Verben mit Nullsuffigierung im Englischen*, Tübingen: Niemeyer.

Katamba, Francis X. (2002) 'Review of H. J. Giegerich (1999) *Lexical Strata in English: Morphological Causes, Phonological Effects*', *English Language and Linguistics* 6 (2), pp. 379–416.

Kiparsky, Paul (1968) *How Abstract Is Phonology?*, Bloomington: IULC.

Kiparsky, Paul (1973) 'Elsewhere in Phonology', in Anderson, Steven R. and Paul Kiparsky (eds.), *Festschrift for Morris Halle*, New York: Holt, Rinehart and Winston. pp. 93–106.

Kiparsky, Paul (1982) 'From Cyclic to Lexical Phonology', in Smith, Norval and Harry van der Hulst (eds.), *The Structure of Phonological Representation. Vol. 1*, Dordrecht: Foris, pp. 131–75.

Kiparsky, Paul (1985) 'Some Consequences of Lexical Phonology', *Phonology Yearbook* 2, pp. 85–138.

Kiparsky, Paul (1997) 'Remarks on Denominal Verbs', in Alsina, Alex., Joan Bresnan and Peter Sells (eds.), *Complex Predicates*, Palo Alto, CA: CSLI, pp. 473–99.

Kulak, Manfred (1964) *Die semantische Kategorien der mit Nullmorphem abgeleiteten desubstantievischen Verben des heutigen Englischen und Deutschen*, Unveröffentliche Dissertation, Universität Tübingen.

Langendoen, Terence D. (1981) 'The Generative Capacity of Word-Formation Components', *Linguistic Inquiry* 12 (2), pp. 320–2.

Larson, Richard (1988) 'On the Double Object Construction', *Linguistic Inquiry* 19, pp. 335–91.

Lees, Robert, B. (1960) *The Grammar of English Nominalizations*, Bloomington: Indiana University Press/The Hague: Mouton.

Levin, Beth and Malka Rappaport Hovav (1995) *Unaccusativity at the Syntax–Lexical Semantics Interface*, Cambridge, MA: MIT Press.

Levin, Beth and Malka Rappaport Hovav (2005) *Argument Realization*, Cambridge: Cambridge University Press.

Levin, Beth and Malka Rappaport Hovav (2013) 'Lexicalized Meaning and Manner/Result Complementarity', in Arsenijevi', Boban, Berit Gehrke and Rafael Marín (eds.), *Studies in the Composition and Decomposition of Event Predicates*, Dordrecht: Springer, pp. 49–70.

Lieber, Rochelle (1980) *On the Organization of the Lexicon*, PhD dissertation, MIT (distributed by IULC, 1981).

Lieber, Rochelle (1998) 'The Suffix *-ize* in English: Implications for Morphology', in Lapointe, Steven G., Diane K. Brentari and Patrick M. Farrell (eds.), *Morphology and its Relation to Phonology and Syntax*, Stanford, CA: CSLI, pp. 12–34.

Lieber, Rochelle (2004) *Morphology and Lexical Semantics*, Cambridge: Cambridge University Press.

Lieber, Rochelle (2005) 'English Word-Formation Processes', in Štekauer, Pavol and Rochelle Lieber (eds.), *Handbook of Word-Formation*, Dordrecht: Springer, pp. 375–422.

Lieber, Rochelle (2009a) 'A Lexical Semantic Approach to Compounding', in Lieber, Rochelle and Pavol Štekauer (eds.), *The Oxford Handbook of Compounding*, Oxford: Oxford University Press, pp. 78–105.

Lieber, Rochelle (2009b) 'IE, Germanic: English', in Lieber, Rochelle and Pavol Štekauer (eds.), *The Oxford Handbook of Compounding*, Oxford: Oxford University Press, pp. 357–69.

Lieber, Rochelle and Pavol Štekauer (2009) 'Introduction: Status and Definition of Compounding', in Lieber, Rochelle and Pavol Štekauer (eds.), *The Oxford Handbook of Compounding*, Oxford: Oxford University Press, pp. 3–18.

Marantz, Alec (1997) 'No Escape from Syntax: Don't Try Morphological Analysis in the Privacy of Your Own Lexicon', in Dimitriadis, Alexis, Laura Siegel, Clarissa Surek-Clark and Alexander Williams (eds.), *Proceedings of the 21st Annual Penn Linguistics Colloquium*, Penn Working Papers in Linguistics 4, Philadelphia: University of Pennsylvania, Dept of Linguistics, pp. 201–25.

Marantz, Alec (2001) 'Words', paper presented at West Coast Conference of Formal Linguistics, UCLA.

Marchand, Hans (1964) 'Die Ableitung desubstantivischer Verben mit

Nullmorphem im Englischen, Französischen, und Deutschen', *Die Neueren Sprachen* 63, pp. 105–18.

Marchand, Hans (1969) *The Categories and Types of Present-Day English Word Formation: A Synchronic-Diachronic Approach*, 2nd edn, Munich: Beck.

Marcus, Gary F., Steven Pinker, Michael Ullman, Michelle Hollander, T. John Rosen, Fei Xu and Harald Clahsen (1992) *Overregularization in Language Acquisition*, Monographs of the Society for Research in Child Development, 57 (4), Stanford, CA: Society for Research in Child Development.

Marcus, Gary F., Ursula Brinkmann, Harald Clahsen, Richard Wiese and Steven Pinker (1995) 'German Inflection: The Exception that Proves the Rule', *Cognitive Psychology* 29, pp. 189–256.

Matthews, Peter (1974) *Morphology: An Introduction to the Theory of Word-Structure*, Cambridge: Cambridge University Press.

McCarthy, John (1981) 'A Prosodic Theory of Nonconcatenative Morphology', *Linguistic Inquiry* 12 (3), pp. 373–418.

Mohanan, K. P. (1982) *Lexical Phonology*, Bloomington: IULC.

Myers, Scott (1984) 'Zero-Derivation and Inflection', in Speas, Margareth and Richard Sproat (eds.), *Papers from the January 1984 MIT Workshop in Morphology*, MIT Working Papers in Linguistics 7, Cambridge, MA: MIT Dept of Linguistics and Philosophy, pp. 53–69.

Noyer, Rolf (1992) *Features, Positions and Affixes in Autonomous Morphological Structure*, PhD dissertation, MIT (distributed by MIT Working Papers in Linguistics).

Noyer, Rolf (1998) 'Impoverishment Theory and Morphosyntactic Markedness', in Lapointe, Steven G., Diane K. Brentari and Patrick M. Farrell (eds.), *Morphology and its Relation to Phonology and Syntax*, Stanford, CA: CSLI, pp. 264–85.

Perlmutter, David (1978) 'Impersonal Passives and the Unaccusativity Hypothesis', *Proceedings of the Fourth Annual Meeting of the Berkeley Linguistics Society*, pp. 157–89.

Pinker, Steven (1999) *Words and Rules: The Ingredients of Language*, New York: HarperCollins.

Pinker, Steven and Alan Prince (1988) 'On Language and Connectionism: Analysis of a Parallel Distributed Processing Model of Language Acquisition', *Cognition* 28, pp. 73–193.

Pinker, Steven and Alan Prince (1994) 'Regular and Irregular Morphology and the Psychological Status of Rules of Grammar', in Lima, Susan, Roberta Corrigan and Gregory Iverson (eds.), *The Reality of Linguistic Rules*, Amsterdam and Philadelphia: John Benjamins, pp. 321–51.

Plag, Ingo (1999) *Morphological Productivity: Structural Constraints in English Derivation*, Berlin and New York: Mouton de Gruyter.

Plag, Ingo and R. Harald Baayen (2009) 'Suffix Ordering and Morphological Processing', *Language* 85, pp. 106–49.

Prasada, Sandeep and Steven Pinker (1993) 'Generalization of Regular and Irregular Morphological Patterns', *Language and Cognitive Processes* 8, pp. 1–56.

Rappaport Hovav, Malka and Beth Levin (1998) 'Building Verb Meanings', in Butt, Miriam and Wilhelm Geuder (eds.), *The Projection of Arguments*, Stanford, CA: CSLI, pp. 97–134.

Reinhart, Tanya (2002) 'The Theta System: An Overview', *Theoretical Linguistics* 28(3), pp. 229–90.

Roeper, Thomas and Muffy E. A. Siegel (1978) 'A Lexical Transformation for Verbal Compounds', *Linguistic Inquiry* 9 (2), pp. 199–260.

Rose, James (1973) 'Principled Limitations on Productivity in Denominal Verbs', *Foundations of Language* 10, pp. 509–26.

Rumelhart, David E., James L. McClelland and the PDP Research Group (1986) *Parallel Distributed Processing: Explorations in the Microstructure of Cognition. Vols. I and II.* Cambridge, MA: MIT Press.

Scalise, Sergio and Emiliano Guevara (2005) 'The Lexicalist Approach to Word-Formation and the Notion of the Lexicon', in Lieber, Rochelle and Pavol Štekauer (eds.), *Handbook of Word-Formation*, Dordrecht: Springer, pp. 147–87.

Schreuder, Rob, Nivja de Jong, Andrea Krott and R. Harald Baayen (1999) 'Rules and Rote: Beyond the Linguistic *Either-Or* Fallacy', *Behavioral and Brain Sciences* 22, pp. 1038–9.

Selkirk, Elisabeth O. (1982) *The Syntax of Words*, Cambridge, MA: MIT Press.

Siegel, Dorothy (1974) *Topics in English Morphology*, PhD dissertation, MIT.

Spencer, Andrew (1991) *Morphological Theory: An Introduction to Word Structure in Generative Grammar*, Oxford: Blackwell.

Strauss, Steven (1982) *Lexicalist Phonology of English and German*, Dordrecht: Foris.

Stump, Gregory T. (2001) *Inflectional Morphology: A Theory of Paradigm Structure*, Cambridge Studies in Linguistics 93, Cambridge: Cambridge University Press.

Szpyra, Jolanta (1989) *The Morphology–Phonology Interface: Cycles, Levels and Words*, London and New York: Routledge.

Taft, Marcus (1979) 'Recognition of Affixed Words and the Word Frequency Effect', *Memory and Cognition* 7, pp. 263–72.

Vaan, L., Rob Schreuder and R. Harald Baayen (2007) 'Regular Morphologically Complex Neologisms Leave Detectable Traces in the Mental Lexicon', *Mental Lexicon* 2, pp. 1–23.

Walinska de Hackbeil, Hannah (1986) *The Roots of Phrase Structure: The Syntactic Basis of English Morphology*, PhD dissertation, University of Washington, Seattle.

Williams, Edwin (1981) 'Argument Structure and Morphology', *Linguistic Review* 1, pp. 81–114.

Williams, Edwin (1994) 'Remarks on Lexical Knowledge', *Lingua* 92, pp. 7–34.

Williams, Edwin (2007) 'Dumping Lexicalism', in Ramchand, Gillian and Charles Reiss (eds.), *The Oxford Handbook of Linguistic Interfaces*, Oxford: Oxford University Press, pp. 353–81.

Wunderlich, Dieter (1996) 'Minimalist Morphology: The Role of Paradigms', in Booij, Geert and Jaap van Marle (eds.), *Yearbook of Morphology 1995*, Amsterdam: Kluwer, pp. 93–114.

Wunderlich, Dieter (1997a) 'Cause and the Structure of Verbs', *Linguistic Inquiry* 28, pp. 27–68.

Wunderlich, Dieter (1997b) 'A Minimalist Model of Inflectional Morphology', in Wilder, Chris, Hans-Martin Gärtner and Manfred Bierwisch, *The Role of Economy Principles in Linguistic Theory*, Berlin: Akademie.

Wunderlich, Dieter and Ray Fabri (1995) 'Minimalist Morphology: An Approach to Inflection', *Zeitschrift für Sprachwissenschaft* 14, pp. 236–94.

Yang, Charles (2002) *Knowledge and Learning in Natural Language*, Oxford: Oxford University Press.

Yang, Charles (2005) 'On Productivity', *Linguistic Variation Yearbook* 5, pp. 265–302.

Index